A Descriptive Checklist
of Book Catalogues
Separately Printed
in America
1693–1800

A Descriptive Checklist
of Book Catalogues

Separately Printed
in America
1693–1800

by

ROBERT B. WINANS

WORCESTER

AMERICAN ANTIQUARIAN SOCIETY

1981

TABLE OF CONTENTS

567118

INTRODUCTION

Scope

THIS checklist describes printed catalogues of books separately issued in America prior to 1801 by booksellers, publishers, book auctioneers, circulating libraries, social libraries, college libraries, and private libraries. It is the first of three parts of a project to list and describe all American eighteenth-century book catalogues. The three segments will list printed catalogues issued as separate entities; printed catalogues issued as part of a larger unit, such as those appearing as a section of a book or of a newspaper or periodical; and manuscript catalogues. This division is made to render the project more manageable and because the methods for finding and describing these three types of catalogues differ. The distinction between the first and second categories, however, is not always clear. Some catalogues printed as back matter of a book, for instance, were also issued separately. Therefore, in this first checklist an arbitrary distinction has been used to draw the line: only those catalogues are included that have been found as separates, or that have been identified as separates in the sources consulted in compiling this checklist. An attempt has been made to account for all printed catalogues separately issued before 1801 that were listed in the sources consulted. I have attempted to locate as many others as possible. Both located and unlocated catalogues are included, therefore, although they are described differently.[1] The entries appear in chronological order, beginning with 1693, the date of the earliest-known example.

---

1. The checklist describes 278 catalogues that are located in collections and 8 others that are not extant but for which good evidence can be found that they were printed. All of these catalogues were printed in America, except item 20, which was printed in London for an American library. In addition, there are 138 entries for unlocated catalogues and another 265 references to other unlocated catalogues listed in McKay's *American Book Auction Catalogues* (and a few in Guerra's *American Medical Bibliography*). See p. xvi below for a discussion of the latter.

Significance of the Catalogues

Early book catalogues are important documents for both bibliographers and a wide range of cultural historians. This material is of interest to bibliographers and other scholars not only for the bibliographical descriptions themselves, but also because it supplies evidence for a study of the development of book-listing, pricing,[2] trade relationships, and other practices of the book trade of the time, and the development of library cataloguing techniques. The catalogues are especially important to bibliographers because they provide evidence that certain books once existed, even though no copies may be known today. They serve this function for European, English, and American publications.[3] Most useful for this purpose are those catalogues that give full titles or place and date of publication in their entries, or both.[4]

The contents of the catalogues listed here are also of great value to cultural historians interested in assessing reading tastes or the availability and distribution of particular books or particular subject classes of books. These catalogues are important to the study of reading tastes because they can help correct some long-standing misconceptions about what Americans read in the eighteenth century. The misconceptions originated from a tendency to judge what Americans read largely by what American printers printed, whereas the majority of books read in America were printed in and imported from England or Europe.[5] Two examples, one old and one new, from among

2. Thirty catalogues give price for some or all entries; see index under *prices*.

3. Twelve of the catalogues consist entirely of American publications (all involving various publishers), and eighteen others include separate sections devoted to American publications, in addition to five publishers' catalogues by individual American printers and one listing all Philadelphia publications; see index under *American publications* for itemized list.

4. Sixteen catalogues give full titles for all entries while approximately fifty more have a fair sprinkling of full titles (essentially a full transcription of the book's title-page). Thirty-five catalogues give place and date of publication in their entries and four others give only the date. See the index for itemized lists of these catalogues.

5. This fact has long been recognized even if its full implications have not been adequately studied. Lawrence Wroth noted that in the eighteenth century 'the function of the American bookseller . . . was largely the sale of the imported book.' 'Book Production and Distribution from the Beginning to the American Revolution,' part 1, *The Book in America*, ed. Helmut Lehmann-Haupt, 2d ed. (New York: Bowker, 1951), p. 46. For further discussion of this point, see Robert B. Winans, 'The Growth of a Novel-Reading Public in Late Eighteenth-Century America,' *Early American Literature* 9 (1975): 267–68.

many illustrate the problem. Hildeburn, in the introduction to his *Issues of the Press of Pennsylvania, 1685–1784*,[6] states that the books he lists show 'the growth of our literature and development of literary taste. Religion and politics, which engrossed the attention of our local writers during the first forty years, predominate to the end, but the leaven of fancy . . . worked spasmodically until 1760, when some poem or play came forth at least annually from a native pen.' As a description of the 'growth of our literature'—what Americans (or at least Pennsylvanians) wrote and published—this is fine. As a description of the 'development of literary taste,' it is useful but incomplete.

Although there is much less of a tendency now to make sweeping statements about reading tastes in the eighteenth century based solely on American publications, the unfortunate habit has not entirely disappeared. In 1973, Samuel J. Rogal brought out 'A Checklist of Eighteenth-Century British Literature Published in Eighteenth-Century America' explicitly as a record of literary taste.[7] He accurately notes that the many American editions of Pope's *Essay on Man*, Defoe's *Robinson Crusoe*, and Rowe's *Friendship in Death* indicate their great popularity. But his assertion that a lack of American editions of Pope's *Dunciad*, Swift's *Tale of a Tub*, *Battle of the Books*, and *Modest Proposal*, and Smollett's *Humphrey Clinker* indicates that they did not circulate among Americans is not true. A survey of the catalogues would show that *Tale of a Tub* and *Humphrey Clinker*, at least, were listed frequently from the time of their publication through to the end of the century and doubtless were widely read. So Rogal's expressed purpose 'to identify the most popular British writers presumably read by eighteenth-century Americans' (p. 232) is poorly served.

Previous Studies

Several previous studies have listed or discussed most of the kinds of catalogues treated in the present work.[8] These pioneering works, of

6. Charles R. Hildeburn, *A Century of Printing: The Issues of the Press of Pennsylvania, 1685–1784*, 1 (Philadelphia: Matlack and Harvey, 1885): vi.

7. *Colby Library Quarterly* 10 (1973): 231–57.

8. Clarence S. Brigham, 'American Bookseller's Catalogues, 1734–1800,' in *Essays Honoring Lawrence C. Wroth* (Portland, Me.: Anthoensen Press, 1951), pp. 31–67; George McKay, *American Book Auction Catalogues, 1713–1934: A Union List* (New York: New York Public

course, are generally incomplete in light of present knowledge. The present checklist attempts to fill the need for a more complete listing of each kind of printed book catalogue, to bring all of the different kinds together in one work, and to provide detailed information about the content of the catalogues.

Most of the catalogues are of course listed, along with many other publications, in Shipton and Mooney's *National Index of American Imprints through 1800: The Short-Title Evans* (Worcester: American Antiquarian Society, 1969) (*STE*), though without the kind and amount of information about them given here, and without easy access to catalogues as a separate class. But even the *STE*, the most complete of the general checklists of seventeenth- and eighteenth-century American publications, does not include 33 (12 percent) of the 277 extant catalogues listed here.

Explanation of Entries—Located Catalogues

This checklist[9] is organized chronologically, with all catalogues listed alphabetically by author within each year. Located catalogues are numbered sequentially. The first item in each entry is the author's name, given in the fullest and most correct form known, which is sometimes, therefore, an amplification or correction of the name as printed on the title-page. This is followed by the author's birth and death dates (or dates of flourishing), where known. These dates are taken from the *Short-Title Evans* and other bibliographical sources, including the printers file at the American Antiquarian Society. Institutions, such as social libraries, are listed under name, rather than the

Library, 1937); Jesse Shera, 'Check List of Circulating Library Book Catalogs, New England, 1765–1860,' in his *Foundations of the Public Library* (Chicago: University of Chicago Press, 1949), pp. 261–63 (other catalogues are also mentioned in his bibliography); C. Seymour Thompson, *The Evolution of the Public Library* (Washington, D.C.: Scarecrow Press, 1952); Jim Ranz, *The Printed Book Catalogue in American Libraries, 1723–1900* (Chicago: American Library Association, 1964); Charles A. Cutter, 'Library Catalogues,' in Bureau of Education, *Public Libraries in the United States of America: Their History, Condition, and Management* (Washington, D.C.: Government Printing Office, 1876), pp. 526–622 (checklist of catalogues, pp. 577–622); Louis Shores, *Origins of the American College Library, 1638–1800* (Nashville: George Peabody College, 1934).

9. Fredson Bowers, *Principles of Bibliographical Description* (Princeton: Princeton University Press, 1949) is the basis for the approach taken here.

city where they are located, although the city follows the name of the institution (unless included in it). Auction catalogues are listed under the name of the auctioneer, who is more truly the 'author' of the catalogue than the person whose books were being auctioned (under whose name these catalogues are usually listed), but the name of the latter is included in the index. Names not actually found on title-pages are supplied in square brackets.

The title of each catalogue is given in full (but not quasi-facsimile) transcription, without line endings. The use of the term *sic* to denote misspellings or other errors is eschewed. Type or woodcut ornaments on the title-page are not noted. Only the first word of the title, the first word of subsequent sentences, and proper nouns are capitalized. The place of publication, the printer, and the date of publication are supplied in square brackets in cases where they do not appear on the title-page.

The paragraph following the title transcription in each entry describes the collation, the pagination, and the contents of the volume.

The format listed is a true format designation, determined by the number of folds to each sheet and the orientation of the paper, rather than an approximate indication of leaf size; overall dimensions of a sample copy of the volume are appended to its location symbol at the end of the entry. Comparison of the format designation with the description of the signatures will indicate half-sheet or full-sheet imposition, half-sheet imposition being the all-but-universal rule in these publications. Catalogues printed on single sheets are designated as broadsides (printed on one side only) or broadsheets (printed on both sides), and the dimensions of the sheet and the number of columns are given.

The description of the gatherings follows the format designation. In the usual manner, the gathering is considered signed if any leaf of a gathering is signed, even though the first leaf is not. Unsigned extra preliminary and final gatherings are designated π and χ respectively, while other unsigned gatherings within a sequence are supplied a letter signature in square brackets. Extra preliminary leaves judged to be a part of other signatures are noted, as, for example, $\pi 1 [=E4]$ A–E^4 (–E4). Missignings and variants are noted in parentheses.

The total number of leaves given includes all blanks. However, the nature of the binding is ignored; thus unprinted paper wrappers and extra blank leaves supplied in binding and therefore not part of any printed sheet are not included in the description.

The pagination statement accounts for all pages, assigning implied numbers in square brackets to blank pages (except for extra binding leaves, as noted in the previous paragraph). Unnumbered preliminary pages are assigned lowercase roman numerals; in a few cases where unnumbered preliminary pages precede an existing group of roman-numbered pages, they are assigned, in square brackets, arabic numerals preceded by a superscript π. A figure representing the total number of pages is given in square brackets at the end of the pagination when the final page number does not indicate the true number of pages, usually owing to irregular pagination. Pagination variants are noted in parentheses.

In the description of the contents of each catalogue, only the page on which each section begins is given, the end of each section coming on the page before the initial page given for the next section. All blank pages are specified. The initial page of the actual catalogue section of the volume typically has a caption title, as do other sections in some catalogues, especially those of social libraries. But it has not seemed important to record these caption titles, nor running titles or heads, which are common.

The second paragraph of the annotations for each located catalogue identifies the class of catalogue (i.e., whether issued by a bookseller, social library, auctioneer, circulating library, college library, publisher, or another source), the number and type of entries in it, the manner of arrangement, a discussion of the date of attribution supplied for undated catalogues, and any other information about the catalogue that seems pertinent.

The number of entries in a catalogue given is approximate, except in cases where the entries are numbered. The number of entries is frequently larger than the number of actual titles of separate books entered in a catalogue, because a given title may be listed in more than one place. Lists of stationery (invariably spelled 'stationary' in the catalogues), supplies, and various other sorts of non-book items are not included in the total number of entries, although their presence is noted.

A description of the nature of the entries, based on length and form of main entry (i.e., by author or title), follows. Title entries may or may not include the author's name. Three terms—short, medium, and full—are used to describe the length, or completeness, of entries. Full entries give a complete or nearly complete transcription of the title-page, which means they usually are title entries. Medium entries contain less than a full transcription, but more than the minimum needed for identification. Short entries consist of the minimum information needed to identify a particular book; they are little more than catch-titles, and are more likely to be arranged by author than by title. Catalogues frequently contain mixtures of author and title entries, and short, medium, and full entries.

The following features, if present in entries, are also noted in the description: place and date of publication; price; name of donor of books (in library catalogues); and numbering system (accession or shelf numbers or a sequential numbering of the entries within the catalogue). Nearly all the catalogues indicate the number of volumes belonging to a title, and most indicate the format of the books, either by arranging them by format or by including a format designation in the entry. Since these last two features are so common, they are not noted in each description.

Each description, however, does specify the manner in which the catalogue entries are arranged or organized: random order, alphabetically (by author or title), by format, by subject, or by one of the many possible combinations of these, such as, to take an extreme example, 'by subject, by format within subjects, and alphabetically within format.' The word 'alphabetically,' as used in this checklist, refers to the style of partial alphabetization common in the eighteenth century (i.e., although all of the entries beginning with a given letter are printed together, the entries within any given letter group are not themselves in alphabetical order). The phrase 'in full alphabetical order' is used in the case of the few catalogues where the entries are fully alphabetized in modern fashion.

If the basic arrangement of the entries in a catalogue is by subject, a list of the subject headings is given (as phrased or spelled in the original). Catalogues that do not contain individual lists of such things as children's books, chapbooks, magazines, Bibles, and psalters typically carry a note to the effect that a 'large assortment' of these kinds of merchandise is available.

If the publication date of a catalogue is not given on the title-page but has been supplied, the rationale and evidence behind the assigned date are described. Except where other evidence is not available or is inconclusive, the dates assigned by previous bibliographers have not been uncritically accepted. An attempt has been made to determine independently or verify all assigned dates; in this process, revised dates have been assigned to seventeen catalogues. An analysis of the publication dates of all or a sample of the books listed in a catalogue frequently provided sufficient evidence for ascribing a publication date for the catalogue.[10]

Some entries in this catalogue contain additional information, such as the source of the attribution of the catalogue's printer when not named on the title-page, information on modern reprints of the catalogue, special features of the catalogue, publication information (mainly number of copies printed), and errors in the listing of the catalogue in previous bibliographies.

The final paragraph of annotations for each entry for a located catalogue begins with a list of citations of the catalogue in previously published major bibliographies and other source books (a list of the

---

10. For some undated catalogues, the earliest publication date for each entry in the catalogue was checked. This was done because, although the listing in the catalogue may in fact have been a reference to some recently published *n*th edition of the book, the information in the entry usually was inadequate to prove that it was any more recent than the first edition. Earliest publication date does not mean merely the earliest *American* publication, even if the book had been printed in America; it means the earliest publication of the book anywhere (usually in England), since most of the books listed in these catalogues were imported rather than printed here. One could then assume that the catalogue itself would have been published in the year of publication of the latest book listed in it, or in the next year. At least the catalogue could have been published no earlier than the date of its most recent entry.

This assumption was based first of all on informal observations made while working with many dated catalogues. It was formally tested by taking a typical dated catalogue (item 26— Garrat Noel, *Catalogue of Books*, New York, 1755) and checking the publication dates of all of its entries. This test showed that the latest publications listed in the catalogue were first published the same year as the catalogue, indicating that it was indeed 'up-to-date.'

Other undated catalogues contained far too many entries to make tracing the date of publication of each one at all practical. In these instances, only the publication dates of the novels were checked and used to date the catalogue. These books were the most popular form of literature at the time and new novels were published with great frequency; thus listings of them in the catalogues were likely to be more up-to-date than entries for other kinds of books.

abbreviations used in these citations and the sources they refer to begins on p. xxii). The Evans number for the catalogue, where one exists, is given first because Evans's *American Bibliography* is the primary bibliographic source for the period and because it provides easy access to those catalogues that have been reproduced on Readex Microprint cards in *Early American Imprints*. The citations for catalogues that do not appear in Evans begin with Bristol's *Supplement to Evans*, or the source that first listed them. Each entry notes *all* of the sources from among those given in the list below in which the catalogue appears; it has not seemed necessary to use the phrase 'Not in . . .' to call attention to catalogues that do not appear in sources where they might be expected to appear.[11]

Each entry concludes with a list of the locations of copies of the catalogue, using Library of Congress library symbols (a key to which begins on p. xxvii). Locations are given only for original copies. An asterisk following a location symbol identifies copies that I have examined. Comments on condition follow in parentheses, and for one of the copies of the catalogue overall dimensions (to the nearest half centimeter) are also given in parentheses. This list of locations is not exhaustive for only major collections on the east coast have been searched. I would appreciate being informed of the location of additional copies of any of these catalogues, or of the existence of catalogues not listed here. At least one copy of nearly every extant catalogue has been examined; for most items a majority of the extant copies have been seen.

Explanation of Entries—Unlocated Catalogues

This bibliography also contains a number of entries for catalogues that have been listed in previous bibliographies but are not now located. Entries for unlocated catalogues give only author, title, and place and date of publication, the information being taken directly

11. One source that might have been included with the others, the *National Union Catalog: Pre-1956 Imprints*, is not included because it is so inconsistent in its coverage. Approximately 40 percent of the extant catalogues in this checklist are omitted, and there is no apparent rationale governing inclusions or omissions. A few extra locations have been gleaned from *NUC* for some of those catalogues that are included in it, but by and large my lists of locations are more complete.

from the most reliable of the secondary sources that list the supposed catalogue. In some cases, where noted, the titles were constructed from more than one source to give a more likely or more informative title.

Unlocated catalogues appear in their proper chronological and alphabetical order, but, unlike located catalogues, are not numbered. They are assigned this lesser status because many if not most of them may be bibliographic ghosts. I have refrained from creating new ghosts. Entries for many of the unlocated catalogues derive from newspaper advertisements that state or imply the existence of such a catalogue. Many other newspaper advertisements could just as legitimately form the basis for additional entries. But I have not included such entries since I have grave doubts about their validity. In short, only those catalogues actually extant, or already listed in other sources, are described in this checklist.

The second paragraph of an entry for an unlocated catalogue lists the previous references to it, starting with the earliest since that source usually underlies the entries in all subsequent references. This paragraph may also cite the newspaper advertisements that were the initial basis for supposing the item was published. Although I have done a large amount of original research to complete this checklist, I have also relied on the work of others for certain kinds of information, including information about these advertisements. For advertisements of unlocated auction catalogues, George McKay's *American Book Auction Catalogues, 1713–1934* is nearly always the source of information. For advertisements of other kinds of unlocated catalogues, almost all of the references come from the Shipton-Mooney *Short-Title Evans*, or from *Early American Imprints*, to which *STE* is the printed key. All of the advertisements cited refer specifically to catalogues, rather than merely to the auctions or sales themselves. The accuracy of these references to newspaper advertisements has not been verified for this checklist.

Only 19 of the 376 eighteenth-century auction catalogues listed in McKay's *American Book Auction Catalogues* are known to exist as printed copies. McKay, however, did not limit his searches to printed catalogues. In his introduction, he notes that some advertisements state that a catalogue 'may be seen' at the place of sale. 'In such cases there may have been only one or a small number of manuscript lists which could be examined by prospective bidders' (p. 21). I believe that many of the eighteenth-century catalogues listed in McKay were probably of this sort, an opinion shared by Jesse Shera: 'Both Evans and McKay, especially the latter, list a large number of auction "catalogues" during these years [the 1770s and '80s], but doubtless most of them, if they existed at all, were only manuscript inventories.'[12]

Accordingly, only those McKay entries for unlocated auction catalogues that have also been listed by other bibliographers as having been printed receive a full entry in this checklist. Other unlocated auction catalogues are merely listed by their McKay number (with a reference, where known, to the auctioneer, in parentheses, and the previous owner of the books, in square brackets) in the proper year, after all of the regular entries for that year (i.e., 'See also McKay . . .'). Several entries for unlocated catalogues from Francisco Guerra's *American Medical Bibliography, 1639–1783* (New York: Lathrop Harper, 1962) have been treated in the same manner.

Chronological and Geographical Distribution of Catalogues

The three tables that follow show the chronological and geographical distribution of the catalogues, including supplements, listed in this checklist that either are known to be extant or are known from other evidence to have been printed.

These tables should hold no surprises for students of eighteenth-century American printing and book trades. Catalogues were published infrequently until the 1750s, after which came a period of steady if unspectacular growth, with a hiatus during the Revolutionary War, ending with a virtual explosion of catalogues in the 1790s. In fact, nearly as many extant catalogues were published between 1791 and 1801 as had been published in all the preceding years.[13] Of the different types of catalogues, those of booksellers by far outnumber the rest,

---

12. Jesse H. Shera, 'The Beginnings of Systematic Bibliography in America, 1642–1799: An Exploratory Essay,' in *Essays Honoring Wroth*, p. 269.

13. For further discussion of both the chronology and content of these and other catalogues, see my article 'The Beginnings of Systematic Bibliography in America up to 1800: Further Explorations,' *Papers of the Bibliographical Society of America* 72 (1978): 15–35.

although social library catalogues account for a not insubstantial number.

The vast majority of the catalogues were published in Pennsylvania, Massachusetts, and New York, with Pennsylvania the undisputed leader. The South, not unexpectedly, is poorly represented, not because it lacked books, or learning and culture, but rather because its scattered planters, located far from central market towns, most likely tended to order goods directly from England. A comparison of tables 2 and 3 indicates the large degree to which the book trades were concentrated in the large cities of the major colonies or states. Almost no catalogues were published in Pennsylvania outside of Philadelphia, only a few were published in New York outside of New York City (primarily in Albany), and the great bulk of Massachusetts catalogues were printed in Boston. Most of the early catalogues were printed in Boston, but by midcentury Philadelphia had taken the lead and held it thereafter, although at the end of the cen-

TABLE 1

American Catalogues of Books, 1693–1800,
by Type of Catalogue and Date of Publication

	1693 –1730	1731 –40	1741 –50	1751 –60	1761 –70	1771 –80	1781 –90	1791 –1800	Totals
Booksellers' catalogues	4	1	1	13	17	14	26	64	140
Social library catalogues	—	2	4	6	13	4	8	42	79
Auction catalogues	5	—	—	—	2	1	6	8	22
Circulating library catalogues	—	—	—	—	1	1	5	14	21
College library catalogues	2	1	1	2	—	1	1	3	11
Publishers' catalogues	—	—	—	—	—	1	—	5	6
Other catalogues	—	—	—	—	—	—	3	4	7
TOTALS	11	4	6	21	33	22	49	140	286

TABLE 2

American Catalogues of Books, 1693–1800, by Place of Publication (Colony or State) and Type of Catalogue

	Booksellers'	Social lib.	Auction	Circ. lib.	College lib.	Publishers'	Other	Totals
Pennsylvania	67	28	5	—	—	4	2	106
Massachusetts	38	11	10	13	5	1	2	80
New York	20	14	5	4	—	1	1	45
Connecticut	7	7	—	—	3	—	—	17
Rhode Island	2	5	1	1	1	—	1	11
New Jersey	—	3	—	—	1	—	1	5
South Carolina	1	4*	—	—	1	—	—	5
Maryland	—	2	—	2	—	—	—	4
New Hampshire	2	1	—	1	—	—	—	4
Vermont	—	1	—	—	1	—	—	2
Delaware	—	2	—	—	—	—	—	2
Virginia	2	—	—	—	—	—	—	2
Georgia	1	—	1	—	—	—	—	2
Kentucky	—	1	—	—	—	—	—	1
TOTALS	140	79	22	21	11	6	7	286

* Includes the 1750 Charleston Library Society *Catalogue*, published in London.

TABLE 3

American Catalogues of Books, 1693–1800, by Place and Date of Publication*

	1693 –1730	1731 –40	1741 –50	1751 –60	1761 –70	1771 –80	1781 –90	1791 –1800	Totals
Philadelphia	—	2	3	13	17	10	21	37	103
Boston	11	2	—	—	6	4	10	32	65
New York	—	—	1	6	5	3	4	19	38
New Haven	—	—	—	1	1	—	3	3	8
Providence	—	—	—	—	1	—	3	4	8
Worcester	—	—	—	—	—	—	2	3	5
Albany	—	—	—	—	—	—	—	5	5
Charleston	—	—	1†	—	1	2	—	1	5
Hartford	—	—	—	—	—	1	1	2	4
Portsmouth	—	—	—	—	—	—	—	4	4
Salem	—	—	—	—	—	—	—	3	3
Newburyport	—	—	—	—	—	—	—	3	3
Wilmington	—	—	—	—	1	—	1	—	2
Baltimore	—	—	—	—	—	—	—	2	2
Annapolis	—	—	—	—	—	1	1	—	2
Savannah	—	—	—	—	—	—	1	1	2
Burlington, N.J.	—	—	—	—	—	—	—	2	2
Norwich, Conn.	—	—	—	—	—	—	—	2	2
Bennington, Vt.	—	—	—	—	—	—	—	2	2
Poughkeepsie, N.Y.	—	—	—	—	—	—	—	2	2
Warren, R.I.	—	—	—	—	—	—	—	2	2

* This table lists only those cities in which two or more catalogues were published. In addition, in each of the following cities, one extant catalogue was published: New London, Conn. (1743), Woodbridge, N.J. (1760), Newport, R.I. (1764), Williamsburg, Va. (1772), Saybrook, Lime, and Guilford, Conn. (1787), Elizabethtown, N.J. (1790), and in the following between 1791 and 1800: Springfield, Mass., Leominster, Mass., Lexington, Ky., Carlisle, Pa., Washington, Pa., Danbury, Conn., Pittsfield, Mass., New Bedford, Mass., Newton, Mass., Trenton, N.J., and Petersburgh, Va.

†Includes Charleton Library Society *Catalogue*, published in London.

tury the number of catalogues printed in both cities was nearly even. Listing the catalogues by place of publication, however, tends to exaggerate the concentration in these major cities, since twenty-five of the catalogues represent institutions (mainly social libraries and a few booksellers) located outside the city where the catalogue was printed.

Acknowledgements

I would like to thank the National Endowment for the Humanities for a Summer Stipend and Wayne State University for a Faculty Research Award, both granted to me in 1975 for work on this project; my sisters Jean and Linda for some preliminary work in libraries that they were close to and I was not; Marcus A. McCorison, director and librarian of the American Antiquarian Society, and his marvelous staff, in particular Mary Brown, who was infinitely helpful as head of readers' services at the time I was working on this checklist, and most especially John B. Hench, who, as my editor, has whipped this work into better shape than it would otherwise possess; the staff members of all the other libraries where I worked, especially those at the New York Public Library Rare Book Room, the John Carter Brown Library, and the Library Company of Philadelphia, who were particularly helpful; and G. Thomas Tanselle, who supported me with valuable advice and encouragement throughout this project.

August 14, 1980
Ann Arbor, Michigan

WORKS CITED, AND ABBREVIATIONS USED

Alden, John E. 'John Mein, Publisher.' *Papers of the Bibliographical Society of America* 36 (1942): 199–214.

[Alden] Alden, John E. *Rhode Island Imprints, 1727–1800.* New York: R. R. Bowker, 1950.

American Antiquarian Society. 'Printers File.' A card catalog with detailed information about American printers before 1820.

[Bates] Bates, Albert Carlos. *Supplementary List of Books Printed in Connecticut, 1709–1800.* Publication no. 17. Hartford: Acorn Club, 1938.

[Bates II] Bates, Albert Carlos. *Second Supplementary List of Books Printed in Connecticut, 1709–1800.* Publication no. 18. Hartford: Acorn Club, 1947.

'Books in Williamsburg.' *William and Mary Quarterly* 15 (1906): 100–113.

Bowers, Fredson. *Principles of Bibliographical Description.* Princeton: Princeton University Press, 1949.

[Brigham] Brigham, Clarence S. 'American Booksellers' Catalogues.' In *Essays Honoring Lawrence C. Wroth* (Portland, Me.: Anthoensen Press, 1951), pp. 31–67.

[Bristol] Bristol, Roger P. *Supplement to Charles Evans' 'American Bibliography.'* Charlottesville, Va.: University Press of Virginia, 1970.

[Bristol, 'Additions'] Bristol, Roger P. 'Additions and Corrections to Bristol's Supplement to Evans.' *Proceedings of the American Antiquarian Society* 82 (1972): 45–53.

[Bristol, 'Additions' II] Bristol, Roger P. 'Additions and Corrections to Evans and to Bristol's Supplement Thereto.' *Proceedings of the American Antiquarian Society* 83 (1973): 261–73.

[Campbell] Campbell, William J. *The Collection of Franklin Imprints in the Museum of the Curtis Publishing Company, with a Short-Title Check List of All the Books, Pamphlets, Broadsides, &c. Known to Have Been Printed by Benjamin Franklin.* Philadelphia: Curtis, 1918.

[Cutter] Cutter, Charles A. 'Library Catalogues.' In U.S. Bureau of Education, *Public Libraries in the United States of America: Their History, Condition, and*

Management (Washington, D.C.: Government Printing Office, 1876), pp. 526–622.

[*EAI*] *Early American Imprints, 1639–1800 Series.* Ed. Clifford K. Shipton. New York: Readex Microprint Corporation, 1963–.

[Evans] Evans, Charles. *American Bibliography.* 14 vols. Chicago: privately printed, 1903–34 (vols. 1–12); Worcester, Mass.: American Antiquarian Society, 1955–59 (vols. 13–14).

[Ford] Ford, Worthington Chauncey. 'Broadsides, Ballads, &c. Printed in Massachusetts, 1639–1800.' *Collections of the Massachusetts Historical Society* 75 (1922): i-xvi, 1–483.

[Guerra] Guerra, Francisco. *American Medical Bibliography, 1639–1783.* Yale University Department of History of Science and Medicine, Publication no. 40. New York: Lathrop C. Harper, 1962.

Hallenbeck, Chester T. 'A Colonial Reading List from the Union Library of Hatboro, Pennsylvania.' *Pennsylvania Magazine of History and Biography* 56 (1932): 289–340.

'Harvard College Records.' *Publications of the Colonial Society of Massachusetts* 16 (1925).

[Hildeburn] Hildeburn, Charles R. *A Century of Printing. The Issues of the Press of Pennsylvania, 1685–1784.* 2 vols. Philadelphia: Matlack and Harvey (vol. 1) and J. B. Lippincott (vol. 2), 1885–86. Reprint. New York: Burt Franklin, 1968.

Houlette, William D. 'Plantation and Parish Libraries in the Old South.' Ph.D. dissertation, University of Iowa, 1933.

[Keep] Keep, Austin B. *History of the New York Society Library.* New York: DeVinne Press, 1908. Reprint. Boston: Gregg Press, 1972.

Landis, Charles I. 'The Juliana Library Company in Lancaster.' *Pennsylvania Magazine of History and Biography* 43 (1919): 24–52, 163–81, 228–50.

McCorison, Marcus A., ed. *The 1764 Catalogue of the Redwood Library Company at Newport, Rhode Island.* New Haven: Yale University Press, 1965.

[McCorison] McCorison, Marcus A. *Vermont Imprints, 1778–1820.* Worcester, Mass.: American Antiquarian Society, 1963.

[McKay] McKay, George L. *American Book Auction Catalogues, 1713–1934: A Union List.* New York: New York Public Library, 1937.

[McKay, 'Additions'] McKay, George L. 'Additions to a Union List of American Book Auction Catalogues,' *Bulletin of the New York Public Library* 50 (1946): 177–84.

[McMurtrie, *Albany*] McMurtrie, Douglas C. *A Check List of Eighteenth Century Albany Imprints*. University of the State of New York, *Bulletin*, no. 1155, 2 Jan. 1939; New York State Library *Bibliography Bulletin*, no. 80. Albany: University of the State of New York, 1939.

[McMurtrie, *Kentucky*] McMurtrie, Douglas C., and Albert H. Allen. *Check List of Kentucky Imprints. 1787–[1810]*. American Imprints Inventory, no. 5. Louisville: Historical Records Survey, 1939.

[Miller] Miller, C. William. *Benjamin Franklin's Philadelphia Printing 1728–1766*. Memoirs of the American Philosophical Society, vol. 102. Philadelphia: American Philosophical Society, 1974.

[Minick] Minick, Amanda Rachel. *A History of Printing in Maryland, 1791–1800, with a Bibliography of Works Printed in the State during the Period*. Baltimore: Enoch Pratt Free Library, 1949.

[Morsch] Morsch, Lucile M. *Check List of New Jersey Imprints, 1784–1800*. American Imprints Inventory, no. 9. Baltimore: Historical Records Survey, 1939.

[NUC] *The National Union Catalog: Pre-1956 Imprints*. London: Mansell, 1968–.

[Nichols] Nichols, Charles Lemuel. *Bibliography of Worcester. A List of Books, Pamphlets, Newspapers and Broadsides, Printed in the Town of Worcester, Massachusetts, from 1775 to 1848. With Historical and Explanatory Notes*. 2d ed. Worcester: privately printed, 1918.

[Ranz] Ranz, Jim. *The Printed Book Catalogue in American Libraries, 1723–1900*. ACRL Monograph no. 26. Chicago: American Library Association, 1964.

Rogal, Samuel J. 'A Checklist of Eighteenth-Century British Literature Published in Eighteenth-Century America.' *Colby Library Quarterly* 10 (1973): 231–57.

[Sabin] Sabin, Joseph. *Bibliotheca Americana: A Dictionary of Books Relating to America, from Its Discovery to the Present Time*. Completed by Wilberforce Eames and R. W. G. Vail. 29 vols. New York: Joseph Sabin (vols. 1–19), and Bibliographical Society of America (vols. 20–29), 1868–1936.

[Sealock] Sealock, Richard B. 'Publishing in Pennsylvania, 1785–1790, with a

List of Imprints Not Included in Evans' *American Bibliography*.' Master's thesis, Columbia University, 1935.

Shera, Jesse H. 'The Beginnings of Systematic Bibliography in America, 1642–1799: An Exploratory Essay.' In *Essays Honoring Lawrence C. Wroth* (Portland, Me.: Anthoensen Press, 1951), pp. 263–78.

[Shera]   Shera, Jesse H. *Foundations of the Public Library*. Chicago: University of Chicago Press, 1949.

[STE]   Shipton, Clifford K., and James Mooney. *National Index of American Imprints Through 1800: The Short-Title Evans*. 2 vols. Worcester, Mass.: American Antiquarian Society, 1969.

[Shores]   Shores, Louis. *Origins of the American College Library, 1638–1800*. Nashville: George Peabody College, 1934.

Sibley, John Langdon, and Clifford K. Shipton. *Biographical Sketches of Graduates of Harvard University*. 17 vols. to date. Cambridge, Mass.: Harvard University Press, 1873–1975.

Sills, R. Malcolm. 'The "Trumbull Manuscript Collections" and Early Connecticut Libraries.' In *Papers in Honor of Andrew Keogh* (New Haven: privately printed, 1938), pp. 325–42.

Silver, Rollo G. 'The Boston Book Trade, 1790–1799.' In *Essays Honoring Lawrence C. Wroth* (Portland, Me.: Anthoensen Press, 1951), pp. 279–304.

[Stark]   Stark, Lewis M., and Maud D. Cole. *Checklist of Additions to Evans' American Bibliography in the Rare Book Division of the New York Public Library*. New York: New York Public Library, 1960.

[Tapley]   Tapley, Harriet Silvester. *Salem Imprints, 1768–1825: A History of the First Fifty Years of Printing in Salem, Massachusetts, with Some Account of the Bookshops, Booksellers, Bookbinders and the Private Libraries*. Salem: Essex Institute, 1927.

[Thomas]   Thomas, Isaiah. *The History of Printing in America*. 2d ed. 2 vols. Albany: Joel Munsell, 1874.

[Thompson]   Thompson, Charles Seymour. *Evolution of the American Public Library, 1653–1876*. Washington, D.C.: Scarecrow Press, 1952.

[Trumbull]   Trumbull, James Hammond. *List of Books Printed in Connecticut, 1709–1800*. Publication no. 9. Hartford: Acorn Club, 1904.

Vital Records of Newton, Massachusetts, to the Year 1850. Boston: New-England Historic Genealogical Society, 1905.

[Waters]   Waters, Willard O. 'American Imprints, 1648–1797, in the Huntington Library, Supplementing Evans' *American Bibliography*.' *Huntington Library Bulletin* 3 (1933): 1–95; reprinted by Harvard University Press, 1933.

[Wheeler]   Wheeler, Joseph Towne. *The Maryland Press, 1777–1790*. Baltimore: Maryland Historical Society, 1938.

Winans, Robert B. 'The Beginnings of Systematic Bibliography in America up to 1800: Further Explorations.' *Papers of the Bibliographical Society of America* 72 (1978): 15–35.

Winans, Robert B. 'The Growth of a Novel-Reading Public in Late Eighteenth-Century America.' *Early American Literature* 9 (1975): 267–75.

[Wolf]   Wolf, Edwin, 2nd. 'The First Books and Printed Catalogues of the Library Company of Philadelphia.' *Pennsylvania Magazine of History and Biography* 78 (1954): 45–70.

Wolf, Edwin, 2nd. *The Library of James Logan of Philadelphia 1674–1751*. Philadelphia: Library Company of Philadelphia, 1974.

Wroth, Lawrence C. 'Book Production and Distribution from the Beginning to the American Revolution.' Part 1 of *The Book in America*, ed. Hellmut Lehmann-Haupt. 2d ed. (New York: Bowker, 1951).

The numbers in parentheses after the name of each library give the total number of catalogues located there; the asterisk indicates unique copies.

ENGLAND

BL   British Library (4): 19, 103, 131, 138

CALIFORNIA

CLCo   Los Angeles County Public Library (1): 138

CLU   University of California at Los Angeles (1): 219

CSmH   Henry E. Huntington Library, San Marino (11, 2*): 16, 29, 49, 57*, 58, 88, 90, 102*, 132, 246, 252

CSt   Stanford University Libraries, Stanford (1): 129

CU   University of California, Berkeley (1): 138

CONNECTICUT

CtHT-W   Watkinson Library, Trinity College, Hartford (2): 49, 51

CtHi   Connecticut Historical Society, Hartford (13, 5*): 16, 50, 76, 104*, 146*, 152, 190, 201*, 214, 221*, 237, 238, 245*

CtY   Yale University, New Haven (33, 7*): 8, 10, 13, 16, 19, 27, 29, 49, 76, 80*, 85, 99, 105*, 109*, 113*, 119*, 131, 133, 138, 142, 152, 173, 178*, 187, 190, 192, 203, 218, 229, 238, 247, 256*, 265

DELAWARE

DeWint   Henry Francis Dupont Winterthur Museum, Winterthur (1, 1*): 41*

DISTRICT OF COLUMBIA

DFo   Folger Shakespeare Library (3): 99, 260, 261

DLC   Library of Congress (41, 14*): 16, 20*, 30, 33*, 37*, 40, 44*, 47*, 49, 51, 58, 73, 74, 77*, 78, 81*, 85, 88, 95, 108*, 131, 136*, 138, 141*, 142, 151*, 152, 166, 177, 179, 191, 192, 198, 203, 218, 219, 228, 235*, 237, 241*, 262*

DNLM   U. S. National Library of Medicine (3): 101, 142, 192

ILLINOIS

ICN   Newberry Library, Chicago (5): 10, 13, 49, 58, 219

ICU   University of Chicago (1): 219

IU   University of Illinois, Urbana (5): 8, 10, 13, 40, 51

INDIANA

InI   Indianapolis–Marion County Public Library (1): 30

InU   Indiana University, Bloomington (1): 219

MASSACHUSETTS

MB   Boston Public Library (25, 5*): 1*, 8, 9*, 19, 26, 40, 49, 51, 87, 131,
138, 161*, 167, 168, 177, 180, 189, 191, 203, 205, 218, 219, 223*,
248, 277*

MBAt   Boston Athenæum (16, 1*): 15, 19, 27, 36, 50, 85, 129, 131, 138, 176,
189, 203, 219, 233, 243, 274*

MH   Harvard University, Cambridge (33, 5*): 3*, 8, 10, 10a* (Addendum), 13, 16, 49, 64, 85, 87, 88, 115, 123*, 124*, 125*, 129,
131, 138, 140, 152, 167, 176, 179, 183, 185, 189, 193, 203, 216,
233, 243, 248, 281

MHi   Massachusetts Historical Society, Boston (38, 6*): 7*, 8, 10, 16, 49,
54*, 69, 72*, 85, 87, 121, 129, 131, 138, 139, 140, 149, 153, 154,
164*, 165, 173, 174, 181, 182, 186, 187, 193, 195, 203, 208*, 220,
229, 247, 252, 255, 273, 282*

MSCV   Connecticut Valley Historical Society, Springfield (1, 1*): 225*

MSaE   Essex Institute, Salem (5, 1*): 172*, 186, 243, 270, 272

MWA   American Antiquarian Society, Worcester (118, 31*): 4*, 8, 10, 13,
15, 16, 21*, 23*, 27, 36, 38*, 40, 49, 50, 52*, 59*, 62*, 64, 69, 74,
75*, 83*, 85, 87, 88, 95, 97, 101, 107, 112*, 114*, 115, 116*, 118,
121, 127, 129, 131, 133, 137, 138, 143, 144*, 145*, 147*, 148, 149,
150, 152, 153, 154, 155, 156*, 157, 158, 165, 168, 170*, 171*,
173, 175, 177, 179, 180, 181, 182, 183, 184*, 185, 186, 187, 190,
191, 192, 194*, 197*, 198, 199, 203, 205, 209*, 212*, 214, 216,
217, 218, 219, 220, 222*, 224*, 228, 229, 232*, 233, 234, 236*,
237, 239, 243, 244, 246, 247, 248, 249*, 250*, 252, 255, 259*,
260, 261, 268, 270, 271, 272, 275, 279*, 280, 281

MWiW   Williams College, Williamstown (1): 195

MARYLAND

Maryland Diocesan Archives, Baltimore, on deposit at MdHi (1): 110

MdBE   Enoch Pratt Free Library, Baltimore (1): 110

MdBJ   Johns Hopkins University, Baltimore (1): 58

MdBP   Peabody Institute, Baltimore (1): 129

MdHi   Maryland Historical Society, Baltimore (9, 1*): 82*, 110, 131, 155, 177, 191, 218, 239, 253

MICHIGAN

MiD   Detroit Public Library (3): 51, 167, 231

MiU-C   William L. Clements Library, University of Michigan, Ann Arbor (19, 1*): 49, 131, 135, 138, 142, 143, 148, 155, 157, 158, 160, 168, 176, 179, 183, 185, 198, 246, 266*

MINNESOTA

MnU   University of Minnesota, Minneapolis (3): 260, 261, 276

NEW YORK

N   New York State Library, Albany (7): 49, 103, 155, 167, 176, 219, 231

NHi   New-York Historical Society, New York (21, 6*): 12*, 16, 27, 30, 49, 88, 90, 142, 163, 175, 179, 188*, 226*, 238, 242*, 251*, 255, 260, 271, 280, 283*

NN   New York Public Library (45, 11*): 2*, 27, 28*, 35*, 48*, 49, 50, 56*, 58, 61*, 65*, 74, 85, 87, 93, 107, 131, 133, 148, 150, 160, 163, 166, 176, 177, 179, 186, 191, 192, 203, 206*, 211*, 217, 218, 219, 244, 246, 254, 257*, 260, 261, 264, 265, 269*, 281

NNC   Columbia University, New York (1): 36

NNNAM   New York Academy of Medicine, New York (4, 1*): 49, 94*, 142, 192

NNPM   Pierpont Morgan Library, New York (3): 8, 10, 49

NNS   New York Society Library, New York (8, 2*): 31*, 43*, 88, 133, 150, 163, 179, 281

NORTH CAROLINA

NcD   Duke University, Durham (1): 275

NcU   University of North Carolina, Chapel Hill (2, 1*): 40, 284*

New Hampshire

Nh   New Hampshire State Library, Concord (2): 176, 219

NhD   Dartmouth College, Hanover (2): 246, 264

New Jersey

NjEli   Elizabeth Public Library, Elizabeth (1): 137

NjGbS   Glassboro State College, Glassboro (1): 49

NjHi   New Jersey Historical Society, Newark (4, 2*): 30, 162, 240*, 258*

NjP   Princeton University, Princeton (1): 281

NjR   Rutgers University, New Brunswick (3, 2*): 115, 169*, 263*

Ohio

OCl   Cleveland Public Library (1): 16

OO   Oberlin College, Oberlin (1): 138

OTM   Toledo Art Museum (1, 1*): 46*

Oklahoma

OkU   University of Oklahoma, Norman (2): 142, 192

Pennsylvania

P   Pennsylvania State Library, Harrisburg (1): 58

PBL   Lehigh University, Bethlehem (1): 219

PHi   Historical Society of Pennsylvania, Philadelphia (42, 20*): 15, 19, 24, 25*, 29, 32*, 34*, 39*, 40, 45*, 49, 51, 53, 55*, 58, 63*, 67, 68*, 70*, 74, 84*, 86*, 91*, 93, 98*, 99, 103, 122*, 135, 142, 148, 159*, 183, 192, 193, 202*, 203, 207*, 213*, 227*, 253, 267*

PMA   Allegheny College, Meadville (1): 219

PP   Free Library of Philadelphia (2): 19, 74

PPAK   Atwater Kent Museum, Philadelphia (1): 29

PPAmP   American Philosophical Society, Philadelphia (10): 49, 53, 74, 115, 131, 138, 203, 205, 219, 253

PPC   College of Physicians, Philadelphia (2): 142, 192

PPF   Franklin Institute, Philadelphia (1): 49

PPL   Library Company of Philadelphia (41, 5*): 15, 16, 19, 24, 29, 30, 40, 42*, 49, 51, 64, 67, 69, 74, 89, 93, 96*, 106*, 115, 126*, 128*, 129, 131, 138, 142, 149, 152, 153, 177, 179, 186, 191, 192, 198, 203, 218, 219, 229, 248, 254, 265

PPPrHi   Presbyterian Historical Society, Philadelphia (1): 99

PPiU   University of Pittsburgh (1, 1*): 120*

PU   University of Pennsylvania, Philadelphia (8, 2*): 5*, 17*, 19, 36, 49, 74, 152, 180

Rhode Island

RHi   Rhode Island Historical Society, Providence (8, 3*): 50, 66, 100*, 180, 199, 215*, 271, 278*

RNHi   Newport Historical Society (1): 50

RNR   Redwood Library and Athenæum, Newport (1): 50

RP   Providence Public Library (1): 49

RPA   Providence Athenæum (1): 66

RPB   Brown University, Providence (5, 1*): 50, 92*, 127, 180, 271

RPJCB   John Carter Brown Library, Providence (40, 7*): 6*, 16, 27, 49, 50, 58, 66, 74, 85, 93, 97, 101, 111*, 117*, 129, 130*, 131, 134*, 138, 142, 149, 168, 177, 179, 180, 185, 186, 187, 191, 192, 198, 200*, 204*, 218, 219, 246, 271, 273, 275, 276

South Carolina

ScC   Charleston Library Society (2): 73, 78

ScU   University of South Carolina, Spartanburg (1, 1*): 210*

Virginia

Vi   Virginia State Library, Richmond (1): 49

ViU   University of Virginia, Charlottesville (2): 49, 234

ViW   College of William and Mary, Williamsburg (1): 179

Vermont

Vt   Vermont State Library, Montpelier (1): 268

A Descriptive Checklist
of Book Catalogues
Separately Printed
in America
1693–1800

1 CAMBELL, DUNCAN, fl. 1693–1695

The library of the late Reverend and learned Mr. Samuel Lee. Containing a choice variety of books upon all subjects; particularly, comentaries on the Bible; bodies of divinity. The works as well of the ancient, as of the modern divines; treatises on the mathematicks, in all parts: history, antiquities; natural philosophy[,] physick, and chymistry; with grammar and school-books. With many more choice books not mentioned in this catalogue. Exposed at the most easy rates, to sale, by Duncan Cambell, bookseller at the dock-head over-against the conduit. Boston[:] Printed for Duncan Cambell bookseller at the dock-head over-[a]gain[s]t the conduit. 1693.

4°: [A]²B–D²E²(–E2); 9 leaves, pp. [i–ii], 1–16. [i]: title; [ii]: blank; 1: catalogue. Bookseller's catalogue: 1200 short author entries, in Latin and English, arranged (not entirely consistently) by subject, within subject by language (either Latin or English), and within language by format. The subject headings are divinity (by far the largest); physical books (medicine and science); philosophy; cosmography & geography; mathematical, astrological and astronomical books; history; school authors; juris prudentia; miscellanie; and three miscellaneous lots of consecutively numbered entries. Ms. note by Thomas Prince (according to MB) below the imprint: 'Mr. B. Green says—This was prin^d by his Broth Samuel's Letter, in Boston.' Evans attributes the printing to Benjamin Harris. As is the case generally in this checklist, authorship is assigned to the auctioneer/bookseller rather than the person who owned the books. Ten photostat facsimiles of this catalogue were produced in 1921 as no. 36 of the Photostat Americana Series of the Massachusetts Historical Society.

Evans 645.

MB* (21.5 × 17 cm. — bound).

See McKay 1 (Vincent)

———————— 1715/16 ————————

See McKay 2 (Moffatt) (=Guerra a-37)

———————— 1716 ————————

See McKay 3 (Dyke), 4

———————— 1717 ————————

2 [GERRISH, SAMUEL] d. 1741
   A catalogue of curious and valuable books, belonging to the late
Reverend & learned, Mr. Ebenezer Pemberton, consisting of divinity,
philosophy, history, poetry, &c. Generally well bound, to be sold by
auction, at the Crown Coffee-House in Boston, the second day of
July 1717. Beginning at three a clock afternoon, and so, de die in
diem, until the whole be sold. Also a valuable collection of pamphlets
will then be exposed to sale. The books may be viewed from the 25th
day of June, until the day of sale, at the house of the late Reverend
Mr. Pemberton, where attendance will be given. Boston: Printed by
B. Green, and may be had gratis, at the shop of Samuel Gerrish,
bookseller, near the Old Meeting-House in Boston. 1717.

8°: π1 A–C⁴D²; 15 leaves, pp. [i–ii], 1–28. [i]: title; [ii]: conditions of sale;
1: catalogue.

Auction catalogue: 1000 short author entries, in 45 lots, arranged by format, and
numbered consecutively within each format. McKay postulates that a separate
catalogue may have been prepared for a continuation of the sale of this library
(McKay 6). Fourteen photostat facsimiles of this catalogue were produced in
1941 as no. 140 of the Photostat Americana Second Series of the Massachusetts
Historical Society.

Evans 1921; McKay 5; *STE*, p. 307.
NN* (16.5 ×11.5 cm. — bound).

———————— 1718 ————————

[Fleet, Thomas, 1685–1758
Catalogue of very valuable books in most languages, lately brought

from England, to be sold by auction July 3d, by T. Fleet. Boston: Printed for, and to be had gratis of, B. Eliot. 1718.]

Advertised in the *Boston News-Letter*, June 9, 16, 23, 1718. Evans 1948; McKay 9; *STE*, p. 271.

[Gerrish, Samuel, d. 1741
Catalogue of books to be sold at auction, May 28, belonging to the estate of Grove Hirst esq. Boston: Printed for and to be had gratis of S. Gerrish. 1718.]

Advertised in the *Boston-News-Letter*, May 19, 26, 1718. Evans 1958; McKay 7; *STE*, p. 307.

3 GERRISH, SAMUEL, d. 1741

A catalogue of curious and valuable books, (which mostly belonged to the Reverend Mr. George Curwin, late of Salem, deceased) consisting of divinity, philosophy, history, poetry, &c. Generally well bound. To be sold by auction, at the house of Mr. Elisha Odlin, on the south side of the Town-House in Boston, on Tuesday the second day of September, 1718. Beginning at three a clock afternoon. The books will be shewn by Samuel Gerrish bookseller, near the Old Meeting House in Boston, from Thursday the 28th day of August, until the day of sale, where catalogues may be had gratis, and at the sign of the light house the place of sale. N.B. A parcel of pamphlets will be then also to be sold. Boston: Printed by J. Franklin, at his printing-house in Queen Street, over against Mr. Sheaf's school; where all sorts of printing work and engraving on wood, is done at reasonable prizes. 1718.

8°: π1 [=B2?] A⁸B²(–B2); 10 leaves, pp. [i–iv], 1–16. [i]: blank; [iii]: title; [iv]: conditions of sale, signed 'Samuel Gerrish'; 1: catalogue.

Auction catalogue: 565 short and medium author and title entries, with place and date of publication, arranged by format, and numbered consecutively within each format. Fifteen photostat facsimiles of this catalogue were produced in 1939 as no. 87 in the Photostat Americana Second Series of the Massachusetts Historical Society.

Evans 1953; McKay 10; *STE*, p. 307.

MH* (17.5 × 12 cm. — unbound; leaf B1 mutilated).

4 GERRISH, SAMUEL, d. 1741

A catalogue of rare and valuable books, being the greatest part of the library of the late Reverend and learned, Mr. Joshua Moodey, and part of the library of the Reverend & learned, Mr. Daniel Gookin, late of Sherbourn, deceas'd. With a valuable collection of books, imported in October last from London. Consisting of divinity philosophy history poetry miscellanies mathematicks voyages and travels. To be sold by auction, at the house of Mr. Elisha Odlin, on the south side of the Town-House in Boston, on Tuesday, the 23d day of December 1718. Beginning at three aclock afternoon. The books to be shewn by Samuel Gerrish bookseller, near the Old Meeting-House in Boston from Thursday the 18th day of December, until the day of sale. Boston: Printed by Samuel Kneeland, at the lower end of Queen-Street, for Samuel Gerrish, near the Old Meeting-House, where catalogues may be had gratis, 1718.

8°: π1[=²C2?] A–C⁴,²C²(–²C2); 14 leaves, pp. [i–ii], 1–26. [i]: title; [ii]: conditions of the sale; 1: catalogue.

Auction catalogue: 692 short to full author and title entries, some with notations of the condition of the book, arranged by format, and consecutively numbered within each format group.

Evans 1984; McKay 11; *STE*, pp. 307–8.

MWA* (18.5×11.5 cm. — bound).

See also McKay 8 (Gerrish)

———————— 1719 ————————

5 GERRISH, SAMUEL, d. 1741

A catalogue of curious and valuable books, consisting of divinity. philosophy. history. mathematicks. poetry. plays. voyages and travels. Generally well bound. To be sold by auction, at the Crown Coffee-House in King-Street Boston, on Monday the twenty sixth day of this instant October, 1719. Beginning every evening at half an hour after four a clock, until all be sold. The books will be shewn by Samuel Gerrish bookseller, near the Old Meeting-House, where catalogues may be had gratis; also at Mr. Henchman's, and at the place of sale. [Boston:] Printed by J. Franklin. 1719.

8°: $\pi 1[=C2?]$ A–B^4[C]^2(–C2); 10 leaves, pp. [i–ii], 1–18. [i]: title; [ii]: conditions of sale; 1: catalogue.

Auction catalogue: 780 short author entries, arranged by format, and numbered consecutively within each format.

Bristol 561; m.p. 39701; McKay 12; Guerra a-43; *STE*, p. 307.

PU* (17×11 cm. — unbound).

———————————————— 1720 ————————————————

6 [GERRISH, SAMUEL] d. 1741
[A catalogue of choice English books. Sold in the house of Andrew Cunningham, Jr. opposite to the north door of the Old Church, Boston. Boston: Printed by J. Franklin? 1720.]

8°: π^2 A–D^4?; 18? leaves, pp. [i–iv], 1–32? [i]: title (lacking in unique copy; based on McKay's entry); [ii]: blank?; [iii]: advertisement, giving conditions of sale, signed 'Samuel Gerrish'; 1: catalogue (the unique known copy lacks 31–32, but the nature of the entries on 30 indicates that the catalogue continues at least onto 31; 32, however, may be blank).

Bookseller's catalogue: 875 short and medium author entries, with date of publication, arranged by format and alphabetically within format, and numbered consecutively within each format. Although McKay lists this as an auction catalogue, it is not, as the advertisement on p. [iii] makes clear: Gerrish states that he intends 'to expose them to sale by retail, from the 11th to the 20th day of October 1720. . . . and the prizes of every book marked on the first leaf.'

Bristol 582; McKay 14; m.p. 39722; *STE*, p. 308.

RPJCB* (16×10.5 cm. — unbound; lacks leaves $\pi 1$ and D4, leaf A1 torn).

See also McKay 13 (=Guerra a-49)

———————————————— 1721 ————————————————

See McKay 15 (Fleet [Gore]), 16 ([Newton])

———————————————— 1722 ————————————————

See McKay 17 ([Stevens]), 18 (Fleet)

---------------------------- 1723 ----------------------------

7 GERRISH, SAMUEL, d. 1741

Catalogue of choice and valuable books, of divinity philosophy law mathematicks poetry history miscellanies medicine, &c. by some of the best authors ancient and modern, and generally well bound, and many of them extraordinary. Lately imported from London. To be sold at low prizes by retail, from Tuesday, October 22 · 1723. at 10 of the c[lock] am. until the 5. of November follo[wing] by S[amuel Gerrish] B[ookseller? . . .]. [Boston, 1723].

8°: [A]²B⁴,²B⁴,D–G⁴; 26 leaves, pp. [i–iv], 1–48. [i]: title; [ii]: advertisement to buyers, dated 'Boston, Sept. 28. 1723'; [iv]: note mentioning Bibles and other books not itemized in catalogue, and a list of three additional titles; 1: catalogue.

Bookseller's catalogue: 1450 short and medium author entries, with place and date of publication (p. [iii]: 'The Books were all printed in London, excepting where other places are mentioned'), arranged by format and alphabetically within format, numbered consecutively within each format, with two special subject lists (Latin books; collections of sermons and discourses) at the end of the quarto listings, and a separate list for law books at the end of the catalogue (full titles here, with date of publication, arranged by format).

Bristol 647; m.p. 39784; *STE*, p. 307.

MHi* (17.5×11 cm. — bound; bottom of leaves [A]1–2 torn away).

8 HARVARD COLLEGE. LIBRARY

Catalogus librorum bibliothecae Collegij Harvardini quod est Cantabrigiae in Nova Anglia. Bostoni Nov-Anglorum: Typis B. Green, academiae typographi. MDCCXXIII.

4°: [A]²B–Dd²; 54 leaves, pp. [π1–2] i–ii, 1–102, Dd2ʳ⁻ᵛ (variant: 86 misnumbered '84'). [π1]: title; [π2]: blank; i: 'Praemonitio ad Lectorem'; 1: catalogue; 100: 'Supplementum'; leaf Dd2: blank.

College Library catalogue: 2900 short and medium author entries (including 50 in the Supplementum), with place and date of publication (mostly 16th- and 17th-century books, from many European cities—a bibliographically valuable list), arranged by format and alphabetically within format, and numbered with location numbers. The catalogue was compiled by Joshua Gee, and 300 copies were printed ('Harvard College Records,' *Publications of the Colonial Society of Massachusetts* 16 [1925]: 475). The recto of leaf Dd2 in the separate MHi copy has the following ms. note: 'Dr. Mathers Catalogue for a Young Student's Lib^y.' Reproduced, along with the 1725 and 1735 supplements, in photostat facsimile as no. 13 of the Photostat Americana Second Series of the Massachusetts Historical Society in 1936.

Evans 2432; Sabin 30728; Cutter 1; Shores, p. 276; Ranz, p. 117; Guerra a-80; *STE*, p. 342.

CtY* (lacks leaf Dd2), IU, MB* (variant), MH*, MHi* (2 copies, one separate and one bound with 1725 Continuatio, the latter a variant), MWA* (21 × 17.5 cm. — bound; variant; lacks leaf Dd2), NNPM*.

See also McKay 19 (Gerrish), 20 (Gerrish [Belcher])

———————————————— 1724 ————————————————

[Gerrish, Samuel, d. 1741, and Daniel Henchman, fl. 1712–1761 Catalogue of the library of Rev. John Leverett, President of Harvard College, to be sold at auction, by Gerrish and Henchman, at the house of F. Holmes, November 9, 1724. Boston, 1724.]

Advertised in the *Boston News-Letter*, Oct. 8, Nov. 6, 1724. Above title is a combination of Evans and McKay entries. Evans 2544; McKay 21; *STE*, p. 308.

———————————————— 1725 ————————————————

9 GERRISH, SAMUEL, d. 1741

A catalogue of curious and valuable books, being the greatest part of the libraries of the Reverend and learned Mr. Rowland Cotton, late Pastor of the church in Sandwich, and Mr. Nathanael Rogers, late Pastor of a church in Portsmouth, in New-Hampshire, deceas'd. With a considerable number of choice new books, lately imported from London. The whole consisting of divinity, philosophy, history, law, mathematicks, poetry, voyages, travels, &c. To be sold by auction, in the house of Mr. Francis Holmes, at the Bunch of Grapes, just below the Town-House, in Boston, on Monday, the fourth day of October, 1725. at five a clock, p.m. By Samuel Gerrish, bookseller. Printed catalogues may be had gratis. [Boston, 1725.]

8°: π1[=C2?] A–B⁴[C]²(–C2); 10 leaves, pp. [i–ii], 1–18. [i]: title; [ii]: conditions of sale; 1: catalogue.

Auction catalogue: 695 short (mostly) and medium author entries, arranged by format, and numbered consecutively within each format.

Bristol 691; m.p. 39828; McKay 22; Guerra a–90; *STE*, p. 307.

MB* (17×10 cm. — unbound).

10 HARVARD COLLEGE. LIBRARY

Continuatio supplementi catalogi librorum bibliothecae Collegij Harvardini, quod est Cantabrigiae in Nova Anglia. [colophon:] Bostoni Nov-Anglorum: Typis B. Green, academiae typographi. MDCCXXV.

4°: Ee–Gg²; 6 leaves, pp. 103–12, Gg2^{r-v} [=12]. 103: title (caption); on 103: catalogue; on 112: colophon; leaf Gg2: blank. Usually bound with the 1723 catalogue.

College library catalogue: 170 short (mostly) to full author entries, with place and date of publication, arranged by format and alphabetically within format, and numbered with location numbers. This supplement was compiled by John Hancock, and a total of 300 copies were printed ('Harvard College Records,' *Pub. Col. Soc. of Massachusetts* 16 [1925]: 521–22). For photostat facsimile, see the 1723 Harvard catalogue, item 8 above.

Evans 2641; Sabin 30728; Shores, p. 14; *STE*, p. 342.

CtY*, ICN, IU, MH* (lacks leaf Gg2), MHi* (lacks leaf Gg2), MWA* (21 × 17.5 cm. — bound), NNPM*.

See also McKay 21A (Henchman? [Porter])

———————————— 1725 / 26 ————————————

See McKay 23 (Gerrish)

———————————— 1726 ————————————

See McKay 24 (Gerrish)

———————————— 1726 / 27 ————————————

See McKay 25 (Goffe) (=Guerra a–94)

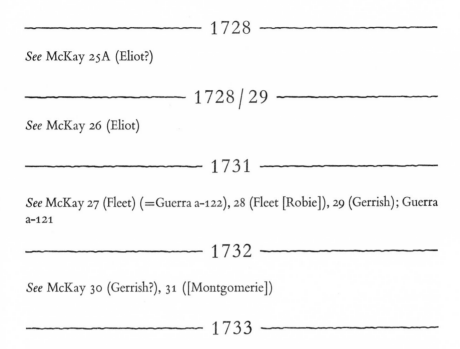

1728

See McKay 25A (Eliot?)

1728/29

See McKay 26 (Eliot)

1731

See McKay 27 (Fleet) (=Guerra a-122), 28 (Fleet [Robie]), 29 (Gerrish); Guerra a-121

1732

See McKay 30 (Gerrish?), 31 ([Montgomerie])

1733

11   LIBRARY COMPANY OF PHILADELPHIA

[Catalogue of books belonging to the Library Company of Philadelphia. Philadelphia: Printed by B. Franklin. 1733.]

'The first mention of the printing [of this catalogue, in the minutes of the Library Company] was on December 11, [1732,] when "B. Franklin was asked what his charge was for printing a Catalogue of the Books of the Library for each Subscriber. . . ." As of that date, it would appear that the catalogue had not yet been printed, although the intention to print dates from then. There is no record of the receipt of printed copies in the minutes, but presumably Franklin would have had them ready within a few weeks, so that actually they might have been finished before the end of 1732' (Edwin Wolf, 2nd, 'The First Books and Printed Catalogues of the Library Company of Philadelphia,' *PMHB* 78 [1954]: 47). The catalogue certainly was printed prior to May 30, 1733, when in another entry in the minutes Joseph Breintnall reported that, ' "Mr Franklin sending me a printed Catalogue, I added to it the Litterarias & Magazines which we lately received, and wrote on the Back the Books given by several Hands since the printing of the said Catalogue." ' (Wolf, 47–48). This latter entry is taken as evidence that the catalogue was 'a folio broadside, printed on one side of the sheet only.' Hildeburn 458; Evans 3714; Cutter 2 (dated 1732); Ranz, p. 15; Campbell 207; Miller 71; Guerra a-134; *STE*, p. 676.

—————————————— 1734 ——————————————

12 COX, THOMAS, fl. 1733–1744

A catalogue of books, in all arts and sciences, to be sold at the shop of T. Cox, bookseller, at the Lamb, on the south side of the Town-House in Boston. [Woodcut decoration, enclosing 'T. Cox.'] Boston: Printed and given gratis at the said shop. [1734.]

8°: [A]⁴B–D⁴; 16 leaves, pp. [i–ii], 1–29 [30]. [i]: title; [ii]: advertisement (see below); 1: catalogue; [30]: blank.

Bookseller's catalogue: 856 consecutively numbered, short author entries, arranged in no apparent order. Advertisement, p. [ii]: 'The following Catalogue contains a Compleat Account of all the Books that are to be Sold at Mr. Cox's Shop, which will be expos'd to Sale for Three Months from the Date of this Advertisement, and no longer, at the Expiration of which Time G. Vaux, who has been here for some Time on Mr. Cox's Account, intends to Return for London. Boston, June 30, 1734. The Conditions of Sale, are, the Lowest Price is mark'd on the first Leaf of each Book, from which there will be no Variation, Deduction, or Abatement on any Account whatever.'

Evans 3765; Brigham, p. 36; Guerra a-138; *STE*, p. 191.

NHi* (21.5×14.5 cm. — bound; leaf D4 torn).

See also McKay 32 ([Grainger])

—————————————— 1734/35 ——————————————

See McKay 32A ([Witherspoon])

—————————————— 1735 ——————————————

13 HARVARD COLLEGE. LIBRARY

Continuatio catalogi librorum, bibliothecae Collegij Harvardini. Ab anno 1725, ad annum 1735. [Boston, 1735.]

4°: Hh–Ii²[Kk]²; 6 leaves, pp. 113–24 [=12]. 113: title (caption); on 113: catalogue. Usually bound with the 1723 and 1725 catalogues, items 8 and 10 above. College library catalogue: 200 entries, as in the 1723 and 1725 catalogues. Date: this second supplement was compiled by James Diman, and 200 copies of it were printed in 1735 ('Harvard College Records,' *Pub. Col. Soc. of Massachusetts* 16 [1925]: 646); the latest publication date of books listed in the catalogue (discounting several misprints—one book is dated 1927 and another 1924) is 1735. For photostat facsimile, see the 1723 Harvard catalogue, item 8 above.

CtY*, ICN, IU, MH*, MWA* (21 × 17.5 cm. — bound).

14 LIBRARY COMPANY OF PHILADELPHIA

[Catalogue of books belonging to the Library Company of Philadelphia. Philadelphia: Printed by B. Franklin. 1735.]

Wolf suggests that this catalogue was 'probably printed on two or three folio pages instead of one. All we know of it are minutes [of the Library Company] of January 13, 1735, which "Ordered that B. Franklin print a Catalogue against the next Meeting, of all the Books in the Library," and of April 14 which delayed the printing until the arrival of the shipment ordered the previous fall. On April 12, 1736, payment of £6 16s. was authorized to Franklin "for Advertisements Receipts & Catalogues, at several Times printed." ' (Wolf, 'First Books and Printed Catalogues,' *PMHB* 78 [1954]: 49). Hildeburn 504; Evans 3950; Ranz, p. 15; Campbell 212; Miller 108; Guerra a-144; *STE*, p. 676.

See also McKay 33 (Edwards)

──────────────── 1737 ────────────────

See McKay 34

──────────────── 1737/38 ────────────────

See McKay 34A

──────────────── 1738 ────────────────

See McKay 34B (Fleet [Callender])

──────────────── 1738/39 ────────────────

See McKay 34C (Nichols)

──────────────── 1739 ────────────────

See McKay 34D (Nichols)

——————————————— 1740 ———————————————

See McKay 35 (Gerrish)

——————————————— 1741 ———————————————

15 LIBRARY COMPANY OF PHILADELPHIA

A catalogue of books belonging to the Library Company of Philadelphia. Communiter bona profundere deûm est. Philadelphia: Printed by B. Franklin, 1741.

8°: A–G⁴; 28 leaves, pp. [1–3] 4–55 [56]. [1]: title; [2]: blank; [3]: catalogue; [56]: account of the library (written by Franklin, according to Wolf).

Social library catalogue: 375 full title entries, with place and date of publication for most, and, for donated books, name of donor; arranged by format, and alphabetically within format, though not obviously so, since the order is based sometimes on a key word in the title of the book, and sometimes on its author. The minutes of the Library Company for April 13, 1741, indicate that 200 catalogues were printed (Wolf, 'First Books and Printed Catalogues,' *PMHB* 78 [1954]: 49). A facsimile of this catalogue was published in 1956 by the Library Company.

Evans 4787; Sabin 61784; Hildeburn 693; Cutter 3; Ranz, p. 117; Miller 246; Guerra a-183; *STE*, p. 676.

MBAt*, MWA* (15.5×10 cm. — bound), PHi*, PPL*.

——————————————— 1743 ———————————————

16 YALE COLLEGE. LIBRARY

A catalogue of the library of Yale=College in New-Haven. N[ew] London, printed by T. Green, 1743.

Small 8°: A–F⁴G²; 26 leaves, pp. [i–iv], 1–44 [45–48]. [i]: title; [ii]: blank; [iii]: 'Advertisement. To the Students of Yale-College' (signed 'T. Clap'); 1: catalogue; [45]: index; [48]: errata.

College library catalogue: 1100 short author entries, with location numbers, arranged by subject. Subject headings: languages; logic; rhetoric; oratory; poetry; mathematics; natural philosophy; botany; zoology; antient philosophy natural and moral; anatomy, physick, and chyrurgery; pneumatology; metaphysicks; geography; history; antiquities; voyages and travels; lives of famous men; chronology; ethics, or essays on morality; divinity (by far the largest category);

law-books; works on various kinds of subjects; treatises on various subjects; miscellaneous essays; political essays; plays and books of diversion. Facsimiles of this catalogue were printed in 1930 in Vienna, by the Institut für wissenschaftliche Hilfsarbeit, and in 1931 in New Haven by Yale.

Evans 5320; Sabin 105894; Cutter 4; Trumbull 1715; Shores, p. 279; Ranz, p. 117; Guerra a-196; *STE*, p. 1020.

CSmH, CtHi*, CtY* (7 copies, one an Ezra Stiles autograph copy; some imperfect), DLC* (sig. G unsigned), MH*, MHi* (lacks pp. 37–[48], supplied in photostat), MWA* (15.5×10 cm. — unbound; leaf G2 mutilated), NHi*, OCl, PPL*, RPJCB* (t.p. slightly mutilated).

——————————— 1743/44 ———————————

See McKay 36 (Cox) (=Guerra a-203), 37 (Church)

——————————— 1744 ———————————

17 FRANKLIN, BENJAMIN, 1706–1790

A catalogue of choice and valuable books, consisting of near 600 volumes, in most faculties and sciences, viz. divinity, history, law, mathematics, philosophy, physic, poetry, &c. which will begin to be sold for ready money only, by Benj. Franklin, at the Post-Office in Philadelphia, on Wednesday, the 11th of April 1744. at nine a clock in the morning; and, for dispatch, the lowest price is mark'd in each book. The sale to continue three weeks, and no longer; and what then remains will be sold at an advanced price. Those persons that live remote, by sending their orders and money to said B. Franklin, may depend on the same justice as if present. [Philadelphia: Printed by Benjamin Franklin. 1744.]

8°: A–B⁴; 8 leaves, pp. [1–3] 4–16. [1]: title; [2]: blank; [3]: catalogue.
Bookseller's catalogue: 445 consecutively numbered short and medium author entries, arranged by format. A facsimile of this catalogue was published in Philadelphia by the University of Pennsylvania in 1948.
Evans 5396; Sabin 61522; Hildeburn 867; McKay 38; Brigham, p. 37; Miller 346; Guerra a-204; *STE*, p. 280.
PU* (15.5×9 cm. — bound).

See also McKay 39 (Church), 40 (Church), 41 (Carlile), and 42 (Gerrish)

1744 / 45

[Catalogue of books to be sold at auction. And supplement. Philadelphia: Printed by B. Franklin? 1744/45.]

Advertised in the *Pennsylvania Gazette*, March 5, 12, 1744/45; the supplement, which McKay lists separately (44), was advertised on March 19. McKay suggests Joseph Goodwin as the possible auctioneer. No positive evidence that Franklin printed this item exists; see Miller. Hildeburn 923; Evans 5555; McKay 43; Miller 370; *STE*, p. 280 (Franklin given as 'author').

1745

See McKay 45 ([Evans])

1745 /46

See McKay 46 (Goodwin?) (=Guerra a-216)

1746

18 CORPORATION OF THE CITY OF NEW YORK. LIBRARY
[Catalogue of books. New York: Printed by James Parker. 1746.]

Austin Keep, in his *History of the New York Society Library* (New York: DeVinne Press, 1908; reprinted Boston: Gregg Press, 1972), pp. 75–76, mentions this catalogue, citing an advertisement in Parker's *New-York Weekly Post-Boy*, June 16, 1746, which notes that Parker, having ' "been at the Charge and Trouble of taking and printing a Catalogue of these Books," advertised free copies "to any Lovers of Reading, that will send and desire the same." ' In another advertisement, in a January 1747 issue of the same newspaper, now called the *New-York Gazette, Revived in the Weekly Post-Boy*, Parker specified that ' "Catalogues to be had for sending for." ' The only extant catalogue of this library is the one printed in 1766, item 57 below.

19 LIBRARY COMPANY OF PHILADELPHIA

Books added to the Library since the year 1741. [Philadelphia: Printed by B. Franklin. 1746.]

8°: A–D⁴; 16 leaves, pp. [1] 2–28 [29–32]. [1]: title (caption); on [1]: catalogue; [29]: rules; [32]: advertisement (membership in company still open).

Social library catalogue: 175 full title entries, with place and date of publication, arranged by format; donors of books named. Date: this catalogue was printed with and is usually bound with one or both of the following:

> The charter of the Library Company of Philadelphia. Philadelphia: Printed by B. Franklin, M,DCC,XLVI. 8°: A⁴.

> Laws of the Library Company of Philadelphia. Made, in pursuance of their charter, at a general meeting, held in the Library, on the third day of May, 1742. Philadelphia: Printed by B. Franklin, M,DCC,XLVI. 8°: [A]⁴B⁴.

This catalogue was compiled by John Sober and Lynford Lardner in 1746 (Wolf, 'First Books and Printed Catalogues,' 50), but the whole combination of charter, laws, and catalogue did not actually come from the press until early 1747 (see Wolf and Miller).

Evans 5853; Sabin 61787; Hildeburn 969; Guerra a-218; Miller 391; *STE*, p. 676.
BL, CtY* (b. with Charter and Laws), MB* (17.5 × 11.5 cm.; b. with Laws), MBAt* (b. with Charter, Laws, and 1741 Catalogue), PHi* (b. with Charter, Laws, and 1741 Catalogue), PP, PPL* (b. with Charter, Laws, and 1741 Catalogue), PU.

See also McKay, 'Additions,' p. 179 (Grymes [Potter]) (=Guerra a-217)

———————————————— 1747 ————————————————

See McKay 46A (Aarding or Harding)

———————————————— 1748 ————————————————

See McKay 47 ([Stoddard]), 48 ([Gee]), 48A (Church), 49 (Gerrish [Prince])

———————————————— 1749/50 ————————————————

See McKay 50

1750

20 CHARLESTON LIBRARY SOCIETY, Charleston, South Carolina

A catalogue of the books belonging to the Charles-Town Library Society, in Charles-Town, South-Carolina. London: Printed by W. Strahan for the Society. MDCCL.

8°: [A–C]⁴; 12 leaves, pp. [1–24]. [1]: title; [2]: blank; [3]: pamphlets (nos. 1–21); [4]: blank; [5]: books in folio (nos. 1–33); [6]: blank; [7]: folio (nos. 34–56); [8]: blank; [9]: quarto (nos. 14–27); [10]: blank; [11]: octavo (nos. 135–89); [13]: twelves (nos. 44–74); [14]: blank; [15]: books in twelves (nos. 1–43); [17]: books in quarto (nos. 1–13); [18]: blank; [19]: books in octavo (nos. 1–134); [24]: blank.

Social library catalogue: 356 short author entries, arranged by format, and numbered consecutively within each format. There are really two lists within each format, an original list and an additional one, bound, presumably incorrectly because of the lack of either signatures or page numbers, in a rather helter-skelter manner such that some of the latter lists precede the former. Though not printed in America, this catalogue clearly deserves a place in this checklist since it was published by an American library.

Ranz, p. 117.

DLC* (19.5 × 12.5 cm. — bound).

1750/51

[Catalogue of curious and valuable books sold at auction, Feb. 12, 1750/51. Philadelphia: Printed by B. Franklin and D. Hall. 1750/51.]

Based on an entry in Franklin and Hall's Ledger D for June 28, 1751; also advertised in the *Pennsylvania Gazette*, Jan. 2 through Feb. 26, 1750/51; see Miller. Miller 523; Bristol 11236.

See also McKay 50A ([Dale]), 50B

1751

[Vidal, Mr.

A catalogue of books to be sold at auction, beginning April 20, 1751. Philadelphia: Printed by William Bradford. 1751.]

Advertised in the *Pennsylvania Gazette*, April 11, 18, 1751. Attribution of 'author-ship' (auctioneer) from McKay. Hildeburn 1208; Evans 6649; McKay 52; *STE*, p. 138.

[Vidal, Mr.

A catalogue of books which will begin to be sold by auction on November 25, at Mr. Vidal's long room in Second Street. Philadelphia: Printed by William Bradford? 1751.]

Advertised in the *Pennsylvania Gazette*, Oct. 24, 31, Nov. 7, 1751. Miller includes this item as a product of Franklin's press. Hildeburn 1209; Evans 6650; McKay 53; Miller 522; *STE*, p. 138.

See also McKay 51 (Vidal)

──────────────── 1752 ────────────────

See McKay 53A ([Campbell])

──────────────── 1754 ────────────────

21 HALL, DAVID, 1714–1772

Imported in the last ships from London, and to be sold by David Hall, at the New-Printing-Office, in Market-street, Philadelphia, the following books, viz. [Philadelphia: Printed by B. Franklin and D. Hall. 1754.]

Broadside. 38×24 cm. 2 cols.

Bookseller's catalogue: 425 short author entries, arranged by format (set as continuous paragraphs, rather than having a separate line to each entry). Date: originally found bound in the 1754 volume of the *Pennsylvania Gazette* (after the issue of June 27) at MWA (now a separate broadside); could be no earlier than 1753, and probably no later than 1754, since the latest books listed in the catalogue are several first published in 1753.

Bristol 1649; m.p. 40686; Brigham, p. 37; Miller 590; Guerra a-273; *STE*, p. 334. MWA*.

22 NEW YORK SOCIETY LIBRARY

[A catalogue of the books belonging to the New-York Society Library. New-York: Printed by H. Gaine. 1754.]

Advertised in Hugh Gaine's *New-York Mercury*, Oct. 21, 1754, p. [1], col. 1: 'Catalogues of the above Books to be had of the Printer hereof, Price Four Coppers.' This advertisement offers fairly good evidence, leading Austin Keep to state unequivocally that such a catalogue was printed (*History of the New York Society Library*, p. 158).

23 NOEL, GARRAT, fl. 1752–1775
[Catalogue of books sold by Garrat Noel, at the Bible in Dock-street. New York, 1754.]

8°: [A]⁸; 8 leaves (first lacking in unique copy), pp. [1–16]. [1]: title (that given above is caption title from p. [3]); [2]: probably blank; [3]: catalogue.

Bookseller's catalogue: 450 short author entries, arranged by format. Date: Noel gave his address as Dock Street only from 1753–55; the latest novel listed in the catalogue is one first published in 1754 (many other novels listed appeared in 1750–53); therefore, 1754 is the most likely date.

MWA* (16×10.5 cm. — unbound; lacks t.p.).

24 UNION LIBRARY COMPANY OF PHILADELPHIA
A catalogue of books belonging to the Union-Library-Company of Philadelphia. To which is prefixed, the articles of the Company, with the names of the present members, and rules observed by the clerk in letting out books, &c. Philadelphia: Printed by James Chattin. 1754.

8°: [A]⁴B–C⁴E–H⁴I⁴(–I4) (F2 signed 'E2'); 31 leaves, pp. [1–3] 4–11 13 12 14–24 [25] 26–40 33 3 35 28 37–53 [54] [=62]. [1]: title; [2]: blank; [3]: articles; on 19: names of members; on 22: directions for the clerk; [25]: catalogue; [54]: blank.

Social library catalogue: 317 full title entries, with place and date of publication, arranged by format, and numbered consecutively within each format (numbers are probably accession numbers since no other order is apparent in the way the titles are listed). Despite the jumbled pagination, the text proceeds in correct order. The Union Library Company was founded in 1746 and was absorbed by the Library Company of Philadelphia in 1769 (Edwin Wolf, 'The First Books and Printed Catalogues of The Library Company of Philadelphia,' *PMHB* 78 [1954]: 52); see also its 1765 catalogue, item 55 below.

Evans 7295; Sabin 62353; Hildeburn 1346; Cutter 5; Guerra a–274; *STE*, p. 679. PHi*, PPL* (15×9.5 cm. — bound).

—— 1755 ——

25 BRADFORD, WILLIAM, 1719–1791

Books just imported from London, and to be sold by William Bradford, at his shop, adjoining the London Coffee-House in Market-Street. [Philadelphia: Printed by William Bradford. 1755.]

Broadside. 36.5 × 23.5 cm. 3 cols.

Bookseller's catalogue: 200 short author entries, arranged in no consistent order, but with some attempt to group like books together. Date: could be no earlier than 1755, and probably no later than 1756, since the latest books listed in the catalogue are several which were first published in 1755. Attribution of printer from Hildeburn and Evans. *NUC* reports a copy at MHi, but I found none there.

Evans 7368; Hildeburn 1401; Guerra a-275; *STE*, p. 109.
PHi*.

26 NOEL, GARRAT, fl. 1752–1775

A catalogue of books in history, divinity, law, arts and sciences, and the several parts of polite literature; to be sold by Garrat Noel, bookseller in Dock-street, New York. New-York: Printed by H. Gaine, in Queen-Street, between the Fly and Meal-Markets, 1755.

8°: [A]⁴B–C⁴; 12 leaves, pp. [1] 2–24. [1]: title; 2: catalogue; on 22: advertisement for *The Pious Country Parishioner*, 'Just Published, And to be Sold by Garrat Noel,' and *The Pious Indian Convert*; on 24: stationery.

Bookseller's catalogue: 550 short author entries, most of them in one alphabetical list, with a brief list of 'school books' at the end.

Evans 7519; Sabin 55403; *STE*, p. 615; Guerra a-280.
MB* (15.5 × 10 cm. — bound).

27 YALE COLLEGE. LIBRARY

A catalogue of books in the library of Yale-College in New-Haven. New-Haven: Printed by James Parker, at the Post-Office, 1755.

8°: a–f⁴; 24 leaves, pp. [π1–2] [i] ii, [1] 2–40 [41–44]. [π1]: title; [π2]: blank; [i]: 'Advertisement: To the Students of Yale-College' (signed 'T. Clap'); [1]: catalogue; [41]: index; [44]: blank.

College library catalogue: 1250 short author entries (a note on p. 40 claims 'The whole Number in the Library is about 3000,' meaning number of volumes), with location numbers (as explained in the advertisement, pp. [i]–ii), arranged by subject. Subject headings: as in the 1743 Yale catalogue (item 16 above), with one additional category, 'New Books, added.'

Evans 7598; Sabin 105895; Bates 2808; Cutter 6; Ranz, p. 117; Guerra a-277; *STE*, p. 1020.

CtY* (2 copies, one with 12 pp. of ms. additions at the end), MBAt* (lacks t.p.; leaf a2 mutilated), MWA* (16.5 × 10 cm. — unbound), NHi*, NN* (lacks t.p. [supplied in photostat] and leaf f4), RPJCB*.

See also McKay 53B (=Guerra a-278)

—————————————— 1756 ——————————————

28 HALL, DAVID, 1714–1772
    Lately imported, and to be sold by David Hall, at the New-Printing-Office, in Market-street, Philadelphia, the following books, viz. [Philadelphia: Printed by B. Franklin and D. Hall. 1756.]

Broadside. 39 × 24 cm. 2 cols.
Bookseller's catalogue: 400 short author entries, arranged by format (in paragraph style—see the 1754 Hall catalogue, item 21 above), plus a list of stationery. Date: catalogue is bound into the NN copy of the *Pennsylvania Gazette*, after the March 18, 1756, issue.
NN*.

—————————————— 1757 ——————————————

[Chattin, James, fl. 1752–1771
Catalogue of books to be sold by James Chattin. Philadelphia: Printed by James Chattin. 1757.]

Hildeburn 1520; Evans 7868; Guerra a-287; *STE*, p. 143.

29 LIBRARY COMPANY OF PHILADELPHIA
    The charter, laws, and catalogue of books, of the Library Company of Philadelphia. Communiter bona profundere deûm est. Philadelphia: Printed by B. Franklin, and D. Hall. MDCCLVII.

8°: [a]⁴b⁴c–d², A–C⁴D²E⁴F²G–R⁴S² (M2 signed M3); 78 leaves, pp. [1–2] 3–23 [24], ²1–27 [28] 29–127 [128] 129–132. [1]: title; [2]: blank; 3: charter; 9: laws; 21: account of the library; [24]: blank; ²1: catalogue (²[28] and ²[128] blank); ²129: account of a 'valuable Collection of ancient Medals.'

Social library catalogue: 850 full title entries, with place and date of publication, and, for donated books, name of donor; arranged by format and numbered consecutively within each format.

Evans 8006; Sabin 61788; Hildeburn 1521; Cutter 7; Miller 661; Ranz, pp. 117–18; Guerra a-291; STE, p. 676.

CSmH, CtY* (interleaved with blanks), PHi* (interleaved with blanks), PPAK, PPL* (2 copies, one, 19 × 12.5 cm. — bound, interleaved with blanks containing ms. additions).

See also McKay 53C (Wells [Rutledge]), 54 ([Parkman])

——————————— 1758 ———————————

30 LIBRARY COMPANY OF BURLINGTON,
Burlington, New Jersey

The charter, laws, and catalogue of books, of the Library Company of Burlington. Philadelphia: Printed by William Dunlap, at the Newest-Printing-Office, on the south side of the Jersey-Market, 1758.

8°: A–D⁴, ²A–I⁴; 52 leaves, pp. [1–2] 3–32, ²1–17 [18] 19–71 [72]. [1]: title; [2]: blank; 3: account of library; 7: charter; 15: laws; 30: rules; ²1: catalogue (²[18] blank); ²[72]: blank.

Social library catalogue: 700 full and medium title entries, most with place and date of publication, and, for donated books, name of donor; arranged by format, and numbered consecutively within each format. This catalogue was obviously modeled on the 1757 Library Company of Philadelphia catalogue, the previous item. The majority of the books were donated.

Evans 8096; Hildeburn 1577; Thompson, p. 254; Guerra a-292; STE, p. 125.

DLC*, InI, NHi* (lacks t.p., pp. 41–48, 69–71, which are supplied in photostat), NjHi (could not be located, 1974), PPL* (2 copies, one 18 × 12 cm. — bound, both interleaved with blanks containing ms. additions).

31 NEW YORK SOCIETY LIBRARY

A catalogue of the books belonging to the New-York Society Library. New-York: Printed and sold by H. Gaine, at the Bible and Crown, in Hanover-Square. [1758.]

8º: [A]⁴B–C⁴; 12 leaves, pp. [1–3] 4–20 (15 misnumbered '4'), ²[1] 2–3 [4]. [1]: title; [2]: conditions for the loan of books; [3]: catalogue; ²[1]: list of subscribers; ²[4]: blank.

Social library catalogue: 325 short author entries, arranged by format and alphabetically within format. Date: the New York Society Library account books, still in the possession of the Library, show an entry on June 6, 1758, for £ 3/5/0 'paid to Hugh Gaine for Printing Catalogues & Advertisements.' The Library published a facsimile of this catalogue in 1954.

Evans 8217; Ranz, p. 118; *STE*, p. 586.

NNS* (17×10.5 cm. — unbound).

See also McKay 55 ([Quincy]), 56 (Winter), 56A (Bradford)

———————————— **1759** ————————————

[Griffitts, William?

A catalogue of above 2000 volumes of valuable books, mostly new. Which will begin to be sold by auction on the 17th of January, 1759, at Mr. William Griffitts's store, on the Bank in Front and Water Streets, Philadelphia. Philadelphia: Printed by William Bradford. 1759.]

This title is a combination of Hildeburn and McKay entries. Advertised in the *Pennsylvania Gazette*, Jan. 11, 1759. Hildeburn 1622; Evans 8315; McKay 57; *STE*, p. 329.

32 HALL, DAVID, 1714–1772

Books imported in the last vessel from London, and to be sold by David Hall, at the New-Printing-Office, in Market-street, Philadelphia, viz. [Philadelphia: Printed by B. Franklin and D. Hall. 1759?]

Broadside. 39×25.5 cm. 3 cols.

Bookseller's catalogue: 450 short author entries, arranged (in paragraph style) by format, with a separate list of school books, and a list of stationery. Dated 1759 because Hildeburn found it bound into the 1759 volume of the *Pennsylvania Gazette* (after the issue of Feb. 22) at PHi where it is still to be found; the latest publications listed in the catalogue are several first printed in 1758. The editors of *STE* confused this item with the Hall 1760 catalogue at MWA (item 38 below) because the caption titles of the two are worded the same, and perhaps also because they could not locate this item at PHi; therefore, the 1760 Hall catalogue is the one listed in *STE* (p. 334) and reproduced on *EAI* under Evans 8362. See Miller 729 as well as 705. Guerra's entry for this item is also in error.

Evans 8362; Hildeburn 1620; Miller 705; Guerra a-298.

PHi* (bound with the 1759–60 *Pennsylvania Gazette*).

33 NOEL, GARRAT, fl. 1752–1775

A catalogue of books, in history, divinity, law, physic, arts and sciences, and the several parts of polite literature; to be sold, by Garrat Noel, and Company, booksellers and stationers, next door to the Merchant's Coffee-House, fronting the Meal-Market. New-York: Printed by H. Gaine, in Hanover-Square, MDCCLIX.

8°: [A]⁴B–C⁴? (C2–C4 lacking in unique copy); 12? leaves, pp. [1–3] 4–24? (all after 18 lacking in unique copy). [1]: title; [2]: blank; [3]: catalogue.

Bookseller's catalogue: probably 550 short author entries in full list (400 through p. 18), arranged alphabetically (lacking all after the middle of the Ps).

Evans 8447; Sabin 55403; Guerra a-300; *STE*, p. 615.

DLC* (15.5×10 cm. — unbound; imperfect as above).

See also McKay 58, 59, and 60 ([Thurman])

———————————————— 1760 ————————————————

34 BRADFORD, WILLIAM, 1719–1791

A catalogue of books. Just imported from London, and to be sold by W. Bradford, at the London-Coffee-House, Philadelphia, wholesale and retaile. With good allowance to those that take a quantity. [Philadelphia: Printed by William Bradford. 1760?]

8°: [A]⁴B⁴; 8 leaves, pp. [1–3] 4–16. [1]: title; [2]: blank; [3]: catalogue.

Bookseller's catalogue: 425 short author entries, most of them arranged in no apparent order (though occasionally a number of similar books are grouped together), with several brief subject lists on the last few pages (school books; plays; chapman's books). Date: the latest books listed in the catalogue are several first published in 1759, so the catalogue itself was probably published in 1759 or 1760, the latter being the usual date assigned. On the supposition that booksellers such as Bradford and Hall were printing one catalogue of their stock per year in this period, which seems likely from the available evidence, this catalouge may well have been printed in 1759 rather than 1760, since the next item bears the probable date of 1760. Over the title on the PHi copy is a ms. note: 'Wm Bradford October 17[??].' The last two digits in the date are frustratingly unreadable, although the most likely readings are 58, 68, or 88, none of which accords with the internal evidence. Because of the uncertainty of these speculations, the catalogue has been left with its usually assigned date.

Evans 8555; Hildeburn 1660; Guerra a-305; *STE*, pp. 109–10.

PHi* (20.5 × 14 cm. — bound).

35 BRADFORD, WILLIAM, 1719–1791

William Bradford, printer, bookseller, and stationer, at his store adjoining the London Coffee-House: has imported a collection of books among which are. . . . [Philadelphia: Printed by William Bradford. 1760?]

Broadsheet. 36 × 23.5 cm. 3 cols. each side.

Bookseller's catalogue: 112 consecutively numbered full title entries, arranged in no apparent order. Date: Bristol, *STE*, and NN date it [1764?], apparently on the basis of the address in the title; but Bradford was using the same address at least as early as 1755 (see item 25 above). The latest books listed in the catalogue are several first published in 1760, making that or 1761 the more likely date for the catalogue.

Bristol 2459; m.p. 41433; *STE*, p. 110.

NN*.

36 COLLEGE OF NEW-JERSEY [PRINCETON UNIVERSITY]. LIBRARY

A catalogue of books in the library of the College of New-Jersey, January 29, 1760. Published by order of the trustees. Woodbridge: Printed by James Parker, MDCCLX.

8°: [A]²B–E⁴; 18 leaves, pp. [i–iii] iv [5] 6–36. [i]: title; [ii]: blank; [iii]: 'The Design of the Publication'; [5]: catalogue.

College library catalogue: 804 short author entries, most with place and date of publication, arranged alphabetically, and by format within each letter, and numbered consecutively (by fives) as well as having location numbers. According to Sabin, Isaiah Thomas, in his *History of Printing* (no page given), stated that there was a New York edition of this catalogue; but neither Sabin nor anyone else ever saw one, and I in fact have been unable to locate the reference in Thomas's *History*. Princeton University printed a facsimile of this catalogue in 1949.

Evans 8683; Sabin 53088; Cutter 8; Shores, p. 277; Ranz, p. 118; Guerra a-314; *STE*, p. 702.

MBAt*, MWA* (18.5×12 cm. — unbound), NNC, PU.

37 DUNLAP, WILLIAM, d. 1779

Books and stationary, just imported from London, and to be sold by W. Dunlap, at the Newest-Printing-Office, on the south-side of the Jersey-Market, Philadelphia. [Philadelphia: Printed by William Dunlap. 1760.]

8°: [A]⁴; 4 leaves, pp. [[1-8]. [1]: title; [2]: blank; [3]: catalogue; on [8]: stationery.

Bookseller's catalogue: 475 short author entries, most of them arranged in no apparent order, with several brief subject lists at the end (tragedies; comedies; school books). Date: the DLC copy has a ms. signature and date at the top of the title: 'David Thompson 1761.' The catalogue could have been published no earlier than 1759, and probably no later than 1760, the usual date assigned, since the latest books listed in it are several which were first published in 1759. The layout of the catalogue and the caption title on p. [3] ('Books and Stationary just Imported, and to be sold by the Printer hereof') indicate that this catalogue may have been originally printed at the back of some book; but the true title-page it has in the issue described above shows that, in any case, it was also distributed separately. The catalogue described here appears as Evans 8587 in *STE* and on Microprint in *EAI*, though it is not the auction catalogue described by Evans. The auction catalogue was first noted by Hildeburn (1661) and also by McKay (61), who states that it is to be found at the end of *Father Abraham's Almanac . . . for . . . 1760* (Evans 8516). There is indeed a catalogue at the end of this almanac, but it is neither an auction catalogue nor is it the catalogue described above.

Evans 8587; *STE*, p. 235.

DLC* (16.5×10 cm. — unbound). Cf. Hildeburn 1661 and McKay 61.

38 HALL, DAVID, 1714-1772

Books imported in the last vessel from London, and to be sold by David Hall, at the New-Printing-Office, in Market-street, Philadelphia, viz. [Philadelphia: Printed by B. Franklin and D. Hall. 1760?]

Broadside. 38.5×17.5 cm. 2 cols.

Bookseller's catalogue: 350 short author entries, arranged (in paragraph style) by format, with a separate list of school books, plus a list of stationery. Date: could be no earlier than 1759 since the latest books listed in the catalogue are several first published in that year. The MWA copy was originally bound in the

1760 volume of the *Pennsylvania Gazette* (after the issue of Feb. 7), so 1760 is the usual date assigned. This catalogue is incorrectly listed in *STE*, p. 334, and reproduced in *EAI* as Evans 8362; see the entry for Hall's [1759?] catalogue, item 32 above. Curiously, the photocopy of this catalogue that appears in Miller omits the *s* at the end of the first word in the title, though in all other respects the Miller photocopy corresponds exactly with the original.

Bristol 11249; Brigham, p. 38; Miller 729; Guerra a-312.
MWA*.

39 LOCHNER, CHRISTOPH

Diese Neue Bücher und Waaren sind bey Christoph Lochner, Buchdrucker and Handelsmann, von Basel kommend, um einen billigen Preis bey der Quantität oder Einzeln zu bekommen, in seinem Laden, bey Mr. Dietrich, Tobackspinner in der Zweyten-strasse, zu Philadelphia. [Philadelphia, 1760.]

Broadsheet. 35.5×22 cm. 2 cols. each side.

Bookseller's catalogue: 240 short author entries, in German (mostly) and Latin, arranged in two groups (an unlabeled, miscellaneous group, and Theologischer Bücher), and by format within each group. Date: usually given as 1760 because of a ms. note at the bottom of the front of the broadsheet: 'Dieser Catologue ist aŭsgegeben ŭms [?] Jahr 1760.'

Evans 8579; Hildeburn 1659; *STE*, p. 222 (under title).
PHi*.

40 LOGANIAN LIBRARY, Philadelphia

Catalogus Bibliothecae Loganianae: being a choice collection of books, as well in the oriental, Greek and Latin, as in the English, Italian, Spanish, French and other languages. Given by the late James Logan Esq; of Philadelphia for the use of the publick. Numbered as they now stand in the library; built by him, in Sixth-street, over against the State-house Square. Philadelphia, printed by Peter Miller & Comp. in the year 1760.

8°: π1 A–O⁴P²; 59 leaves, pp. [i–ii], [1] 2–116 (variant: first 1 of 114 not struck). [i]: title; [ii]: blank; [1]: catalogue.

Social library catalogue: 2150 full and medium author entries, with place and date of publication, and location numbers; arranged by subject, by format within subject, and in full alphabetical order within format. Subject headings: divinity and ecclesiastical history; history, antiquities, geography, chronology, &c. (the largest category); voyages and travels; philology; orators, poets, fables, romances, &c.; philosophy; physick, mathematicks, and natural history; arts, liberal and mechanical, magick, &c.; medicine, surgery and chymistry; philosophical history; law; miscellaneous books. For the fullest information about this catalogue, see Edwin Wolf, 2nd, *The Library of James Logan of Philadelphia 1674–1751* (Philadelphia: The Library Company of Philadelphia, 1974). Wolf's book is, in a sense, a reprint of the catalogue described above, with the addition of some other books known to be in Logan's library. But it is also much more than a reprint because it gives accurate identification of author, title, and place and date of publication for each book (taken from the books themselves, most of which are still at the Library Company of Philadelphia), and annotations regarding Logan's notes in the books and his references to them in his writings, both public and private. A ms. catalogue of the Loganian Library for 1743–44 also exists at PPL, as well as the librarian's record book of loans and returns, 1794–1836.

Evans 8715; Sabin 41797 and 61797; Hildeburn 1662; Cutter 9; Ranz, p. 118; Guerra a-315; *STE*, p. 667.

DLC* (variant), IU, MB* (18.5×12 cm. — bound), MWA* (variant), NcU, PHi* (variant, also lacks pp. 51–54, 67–70), PPL* (4 copies, all variants).

41 RIVINGTON, JAMES, 1724–1802

A catalogue of books, lately imported, and sold by James Rivington, bookseller and stationer from London, at his store over against the Golden Key, in Hanover-Square, New-York. And also at his store next door to Messrs. Taylor and Cox, in Front-Street, Philadelphia. At both which places will be found, a constant supply of books, with all the new articles as they are published in Europe; and from whence all orders directed to him from the country, whether in a wholesale or retail way, will be punctually complied with. New-York: Printed by H. Gaine, printer and bookseller, at his Printing-Office at the Bible & Crown in Hanover-Square. MDCCLX.

8°: π1 [=H4] [A]⁴B–G⁴H⁴(–H4); 32 leaves, pp. [1–3] 4–64. [1]: title; [2]: blank; [3]: catalogue; on 63: advertisement for *London Magazine*.

Bookseller's catalogue: 1200 short to full author and title entries, arranged by subject. Subject headings: novels, poems, plays, translations, &c. (largest category); history, voyages, travels, &c.; divinity; physick, anatomy, surgery, &c.; law; philosophy, mathematics, &c.; architecture; trade and commerce; classics, school books and others omitted in the foregoing catalogue; miscellaneous. There are some interesting attributions of authorship in this catalogue, from a man very conversant with the London publishing world (having recently been a bookseller there).

Bristol 2176.

DeWint* (18×11 cm. — unbound).

See also McKay 62

——————— 1761 ———————

42 HALL, DAVID, 1714–1772

Lately imported, and to be sold by David Hall, at the New-Printing-Office, in Market-street, Philadelphia, the following books, viz. [Philadelphia: Printed by B. Franklin and D. Hall. 1761?]

Broadside. 40×25 cm. 2 cols.

Bookseller's catalogue: 400 short author entries, arranged (paragraph style) by format and alphabetically within format (some by author, some by key word in title); list of stationery items. Date: dated [1765] by Hildeburn, Evans, PPL, STE, and Miller, but unlikely to be that late. The latest book listed in the catalogue that can be fairly reliably dated is Hazelton's [Haselden's] Seaman's Assistant, the earliest edition of which, according to the British Museum catalogue, was published in 1761. However, since it is not certain that this edition of Haselden was the first, and since nearly all of the other books in the catalogue, including all the novels, were published in the middle 1750s (none later than 1756), there is a strong possibility that this catalogue was actually published in the late 1750s.

Evans 9997; Hildeburn 2141; Miller 839; STE, p. 334.

PPL*.

43 NEW YORK SOCIETY LIBRARY

A catalogue of the books belonging to the New-York Society Library. New-York: Printed by H. Gaine, at the Bible and Crown, in Hanover-Square. [1761.]

8°: A–C⁴; 12 leaves, pp. [1–3] 4–18, ²[1] 2–6 [=24]. [1]: title; [2]: conditions for loan of books; [3]: catalogue; ²[1]: list of subscribers.

Social library catalogue: 375 short author entries, in full alphabetical order. Date: dated 'Aug. 1761' in an eighteenth-century hand on the title-page. Library account books show an entry on Sept. 2, 1761, for £5 paid to 'Hugh Gain for 200 Catalogues.'

Bristol, 'Additions II,' 2241a; Keep, p. 170; Ranz, p. 118.

NNS* (15×9.5 cm. — unbound).

[Rivington, James, 1724–1802

A catalogue of books for sale by James Rivington. Philadelphia, 1761.]

Advertised in the *Pennsylvania Journal*, Feb. 26, 1761. The advertisement probably refers to Rivington's 1760 catalogue (item 41 above). Evans 8998; Guerra a-325; *STE*, p. 742.

See also McKay 62A, 62B (Wells? [Michie])

———————————— 1762 ————————————

44 NOEL, GARRAT, fl. 1752–1775

A catalogue of books, &c. sold by Garrat Noel, bookseller and stationer, from London, at his store next door to the Merchant's-Coffee-House, consisting of history, divinity, law, physic, surgery, military, miseellany, philosophy, mathematicks, antiquity, trade & commerce, husbandry, gardening, and farriery, clasicks and school books, novels, poems, plays, &c. At which place will be found a constant supply of books and stationary ware of all sorts, with all the new published articles, and where store-keepers, pedlars and others, may be furnished in a wholesale or retail way, and all orders directed to him will be punctually complied with. New-York: Printed by Hugh Gaine, in the year 1762.

8°: A–D⁴E²; 18 leaves, pp. [1–3] 4–36. [1]: title; [2]: advertisement for medicines; [3]: catalogue; on 32: stationery; on 33: list of maps, pictures, prints, &c.; on 34: advertisements for *The Lady's Preceptor* and *The Triumphant Christian*, both This Day . . . published'; 35: an unlabeled group of additional entries.

Bookseller's catalogue: 650 medium title, and short author, entries, arranged by subject. Subject headings: as given in the title, except the order is different; history also includes voyages, travels, lives &c.; and architecture, drawing, &c. are added to philosophy, mathematics and antiquity.

Evans 9222; Sabin 55403; Guerra a-332; *STE*, p. 615.

DLC* (20.5×12.5 cm. — bound).

45 RIVINGTON, JAMES, 1724–1802, AND SAMUEL BROWN, fl. 1755–1769

A catalogue of books, sold by Rivington and Brown, booksellers and stationers from London, at their stores, over against the Golden Key, in Hanover-Square, New-York: and over against the London Coffee-House, in Philadelphia. At both which places will be found, a constant supply of books, with all the new articles as they are published in Europe; and from whence all orders directed to them from the country, whether in a wholesale or retail way, will be punctually complied with. [Philadelphia?] M,DCC,LXII.

8°: π1 [A]⁴B–L⁴; 45 leaves, pp. [i–ii], 1–88. [i]: title; [ii]: blank; 1: catalogue (caption title, p. 1: 'Books of Entertainment, &c.'); on 83: additional catalogue of books from 'the Library of a Gentleman of genteel Taste, they are in good Condition, and will be sold at reasonable Rates'; on 88: advertisements for cutlery, jewelry, teas, and snuffs.

Bookseller's catalogue. Main catalogue: 782 consecutively numbered, short to full author and title entries, arranged in no apparent order, many with laudatory or descriptive comments and/or extracts, some rather lengthy (pp. 71–82, for instance, contain extracts from Rousseau's *New Heloise*). Additional catalogue: 185 short author entries, arranged by format. PHi supplies the imprint as [Philadelphia: Henrich Miller].

Evans 9259; Guerra a-334; *STE*, p. 742.

PHi* (18 × 11.5 cm. — bound).

See also McKay 63 ([Delancey]), 64

———————————— 1763 ————————————

46 ARNOLD, BENEDICT, 1741–1801

Benedict Arnold, has just imported (via New-York) and sells at his store in New-Haven, a very large and fresh assortment of drugs and chymical preparations; . . . [New Haven, 1763?]

Broadside. 30.5 × 9.5 cm. 3 cols.

Bookseller's and druggist's catalogue: a list of drugs, plus 150 short author entries for books, arranged in no apparent order. Date: dated [1765?] by Bristol and *STE*. Arnold kept a drug and book store for several years, starting in 1762. The latest books listed in the catalogue are a few first published in 1763 and many first published in 1762; therefore, 1763 seems like the most probable date.

The *Magazine of History* 26 (1924), extra no. 104, following p. 43, reprinted this catalogue, dating it [1760?]. Bristol and *NUC* give other locations, but these are either photocopies or the reprint.

Bristol 2548; m.p. 41515; *STE*, p. 34.

OTM.

47 GAINE, HUGH, 1726–1807

[A catalogue of books. New York: Printed by Hugh Gaine, 1763?]

8°: [A]⁴B–C⁴? (leaves A1, A2, and C4 are lacking in the only known copy); 12 leaves, pp. [1–3] 4–24 (probable; [1]–4, 23–24 lacking). [1]: title?; [2]: blank?; [3]?: catalogue; on 17: stationery and other articles; 18: a list of medicines 'prepared by the late Dr. Ward' and 'to be sold by H. Gaine,' with description and praise of each item.

Bookseller's catalogue: 250 medium and full title entries (in complete catalogue; 225 on intact pages), apparently loosely arranged in a few broad subject categories, though without any subject headings or divisions. Date: at least four of the novels listed were first published in 1763, so the catalogue itself could have been published no earlier than in that year, although DLC, *STE*, Guerra, and Bristol date it [1760].

Bristol 2131; m.p. 41125; Guerra a-311; *STE*, p. 297.

DLC* (22 × 13.5 cm. — bound; imperfect as above).

48 HALL, DAVID, 1714–1772

Imported in the last vessels from Europe, and sold by David Hall, at the New Printing-Office, in Market-street, Philadelphia, the following books, &c. [Philadelphia: Printed by Franklin and Hall. 1763?]

Broadsheet. 33 × 20 cm. 2 cols. each side.

Bookseller's catalogue: 900 short author entries, arranged in paragraphs, unlabeled, but each paragraph devoted to a different subject or group of subjects; also a list of stationery items, and mention of prints, magazines, and paper hangings. Subjects: Bibles; law; medicine; dictionaries; history, travel, novels, biography, belles lettres (i.e., miscellaneous, the largest grouping); religion; natural philosophy, natural history, mathematics, trade, navigation; farriery; architecture; military; household arts; classics and grammars; spelling books and psalters; children's books. Date: the catalogue was bound into the 1763 volume of the *Pennsylvania Gazette* at NN, after the issue of Nov. 3; it could have been published no earlier than 1763, and probably no later than 1764, since the latest novels listed in it are several first published in 1763.

Bristol 2411; m.p. 41386; Miller 787; *STE*, p. 334. NN*.

—————————— 1764 ——————————

49 LIBRARY COMPANY OF PHILADELPHIA

The charter, laws, and catalogue of books, of the Library Company of Philadelphia. Communiter bona profundere deûm est. Philadelphia: Printed by B. Franklin and D. Hall. M,DCC,LXIV.

8°: A–L⁸ (B3 and B4 signed 'A3' and 'A4', K2 unsigned); 88 leaves, pp. [1–2] 3–21 [22] 23–26, ²1–47 [48] 49–121 [122] 123–43 [144] 145–50. [1]: title; [2]: blank; 3: charter; 9: laws; 19: rules; [22]: blank; 23: account of the library; ²1: catalogue (²[48] and ²[122] blank); ²[144]: blank; ²145: catalogue of a collection of ancient medals; ²149: list of members, dated 'February, 1765.'

Social library catalogue: 1070 full title entries, most with place and date of publication, and, for donated books, name of donor; arranged by format, and numbered consecutively within each format. Both the Library Company minutes and the date of the list of members indicate that the publication of this catalogue was not actually completed until 1765; four hundred copies were printed (Wolf, p. 52).

Evans 9794; Hildeburn 1964; Cutter 10; Sabin 61788; Ranz, p. 118; Miller 810; Guerra a-355; *STE*, p. 676.

CSmH, CtY*, DLC, MB* (2 copies; one could not be located, 1975), MH (Law School Library), MHi*, MWA* (19.5×12.5 cm. — bound), MiU-C* (interleaved with blanks), NN*, NNNAM, NNPM*, PHi* (interleaved with blanks), PPAmP* (lacks pp. 53–54), PPL* (3 copies; one lacks pp. 25–36), RPJCB*. Additional locations (from Miller): CtHT-W, ICN, N, NHi, NNPM, NjGbS, PPF, PU, RP, Vi, ViU.

50 REDWOOD LIBRARY COMPANY, Newport, Rhode Island

A catalogue of the books belonging to the Company of the Redwood-Library, in Newport, on Rhode-Island. Newport: Printed by S. Hall. 1764.

8°: [B]⁴C⁴[D]⁴E⁴; 16 leaves, pp. [1–3] 4–23 [24] 25–28 [29–32]. [1]: title; [2]: blank; [3]: first catalogue (caption title: 'Books bought in London by John Thomlinson, Esq; with the Five Hundred Pounds Sterling given by Abraham

Redwood, Esq; to the Company of the Redwood-Library.'); [24]: blank; [25]: second catalogue (caption title: 'Books given by several Gentlemen.'); [29]: blank. Usually bound following:

Laws of the Redwood-Library Company. Newport: Printed by Samuel Hall. M,DCC,LXIV. 8°: [A]⁴; 4 leaves, pp. [1–3] 4–7 [8]. [1]: title; [2]: blank; [3]: laws; [8]: blank.

Social library catalogue: 866 short author entries in the two catalogues. The 751 entries in the first catalogue are arranged by format, and variously within format: the folio section begins with a miscellaneous group of theological and Greek and Latin books, followed by the bulk of the entries in alphabetical order; the quarto section begins with a miscellaneous group of dictionaries and Greek and Latin books, followed by the bulk of the entries in alphabetical order; the octavo section is arranged by subject; the duodecimo section is in alphabetical order. The subject headings in the octavo section are: classicks; history; divinity and morality; physick; law; natural history, mathematics, &c.; arts, liberal and mechanic; miscellanies, politics, &c. The 115 entries in the second catalogue are arranged by format, and alphabetically within format, with a brief list of pamphlets at the end. Alden notes that not only may the Laws and the Catalogue have been printed separately, but that the two parts of the Catalogue itself may have been separately printed. Alden also quotes an advertisement in the *Newport Mercury*, April 15, 1765, that shows that the publication of these items was not completed until 1765: ' "The Printer hereof has just printed the Laws and Catalogue of the Redwood library which will be ready to deliver to the Proprietors to-morrow. A few copies are to be disposed of to any other persons on applying to him." ' On this point, see also p. xviii of McCorison's introduction to the reprinted edition. This catalogue was reprinted, with annotated entries, and a valuable preface (by Wilmarth S. Lewis) and introduction, as, *The 1764 Catalogue of the Redwood Library Company at Newport, Rhode Island*, ed. Marcus McCorison (New Haven: Yale Univ. Press, 1965).

Evans 9764; Sabin 68532; Alden 304; Cutter 11; Ranz, p. 118; Guerra a-353; *STE*, p. 612.

CtHi* (lacks pp. [29–32]), MBAt*, MWA* (21.5×14 cm. — unbound), NN (pp. [3]–28 of Catalogue only), RHi*, RNHi (two copies; one copy has only pp. [1]–[24] of Catalogue), RNR, RPB, RPJCB.

———————————————— 1765 ————————————————

51 ASSOCIATION LIBRARY COMPANY OF PHILADELPHIA

A catalogue of books, belonging to the Association Library Company of Philadelphia: alphabetically digested. To which is prefixed, the articles of the said Company, &c. Philadelphia: Printed by William Bradford, at the corner of Market and Front-Streets. M.DCC.LXV.

8°: [A]⁴B–H⁴[I]²; 34 leaves, pp. [1–3] 4–20 [21] 22–68. [1]: title; [2]: blank; [3]: articles, including a list of members; [21]: catalogue. Page 23 contains page number and catchword only; pp. 34, 56, 60, 66 contain page number only.

Social library catalogue: 550 short to full author and title entries, about a third with place and date of publication, numbered with accession/shelf numbers, a separate sequence for each format; arranged alphabetically, by format within each letter, and more or less in accession number order within format; donors of books named. According to Wolf (p. 53), this library was absorbed by the Union Library Company (see item 55 below) in 1765, which in its turn merged with the Library Company of Philadelphia in 1769. The *STE* entry for this item incorrectly assigns it to the Library Company of Philadelphia.

Evans 10137; Sabin 61489; Hildeburn 2108; Cutter 12; Ranz, p. 118; Guerra a-371; *STE*, p. 676.

CtHT-W, DLC*, IU, MB* (20.5 × 13.5 cm. — bound), MiD, PHi*, PPL* (2 copies, one interleaved with blanks containing ms. additions).

52 BARCLAY, ANDREW, 1738–1823

A catalogue of books, lately imported from Britain; and to be sold by A. Barclay, second door north of the three King's Corn-hill Boston. [Boston, 1765?]

Broadside. 35 × 20.5 cm. 3 cols.

Bookseller's catalogue: 150 short author entries, arranged alphabetically, plus advertisements for Bibles, prayer books, spelling books, primers, singing books, etc.; stationery; and bookbinding. Date: could have been published no earlier than 1764, and probably no later than 1765, since the latest book listed in the catalogue was one first published in 1764. Barclay was at the address given in the title from 1765 to 1769; therefore, 1765 is the most probable date.

Bristol 2549; m.p. 41516; Ford 1340; Brigham, p. 40 (dated [1770]); *STE*, p. 60.

MWA*.

53 JULIANA LIBRARY COMPANY, Lancaster, Pennsylvania

The charter of the Juliana-Library-Company in Lancaster: and the laws of the said Company. Together with a catalogue of the books, and the prices thereof, with the numbers as they stand in the library-room. The whole being collected and revised by order of the directors for this present year, 1765. By Caleb Sheward, secretary. Wilmington, printed by James Adams, in Market-street, 1765.

4°: A–F²H–I²; 16 leaves, pp. [i–ii] iii 4–22 29 [30] 37–39 [40] 45–47 [48] [=32]. [i]: title; [ii]: blank; iii: charter; 8: laws; 21: catalogue ([30] and [40] blank); [48]: blank.

Social library catalogue: 190 short author entries, with prices and, for donated books, name of donor; arranged by format and numbered consecutively (by volumes) within each format. Despite the missing sig. G and the strange pagination, all of the printed part of the item appears to be intact; apparently provision was made for interleaving blank pages for expanding the catalogue (in the PHi copy, there is one cut-off stub of a leaf between pp. 22 and 29, and three between pp. [30] and 37). The editors of *STE* and *EAI* apparently could not locate a copy, and this item is therefore not reproduced in Microprint.

Evans 10034; Guerra a-364; *STE*, p. 406.

PHi* (20.5 × 16 cm. — bound), PPAmP* (extra whole blank leaf between [30] and 37 [=G1?]; leaves A2, B2, and F1 almost completely torn out).

54 MEIN, JOHN, fl. 1760–1775

A catalogue of Mein's Circulating Library; consisting of above twelve hundred volumes, in most branches of polite literature, arts and sciences; viz. history, voyages, travels, lives, memoirs, antiquities, philosophy, novels, divinity, physic, surgery, anatomy, arts, sciences, plays, poetry, husbandry, navigation, gardening, mathematics, law, &c. &c. &c. Which are lent to read, at one pound eight shillings, lawful money, per year; eighteen shillings per half-year; or, ten and eight pence per quarter; by John Mein, bookseller, at the London Book-Store, second door above the British Coffee-House, north-side of King-Street, Boston. This collection will be considerably enlarged from time to time, and the number of volumes will be more than doubled in less than a twelvemonth, if the publisher meets with due encouragement. At the above place the full value is given for any library or parcel of books, in any language or faculty; and books sold or exchanged. Boston: Printed [by McAlpine and Fleeming] in the year MDCCLXV. [Price, one shilling lawful money.]

8°: A–G⁴[H]²; 30 leaves, pp. [1] 2 [3] 4–57 (44 misnumbered '46'), ²1–2 [3]. [1]: title (brackets around last phrase in original); 2: conditions; [3]: main catalogue; ²1: miscellaneous list of books for sale, and references to the availability of classical books, dictionaries, children's books, chapbooks, plays, spelling books, psalters, primers, writing paper, medicines, and beer; [2][3]: advertisement (subscriptions being taken for *The Pulpit and Family Bible*, 'Just imported by J. Mein').

Circulating library and bookseller's catalogue: 750 short to full author (mostly) and title entries numbered consecutively by volume (1057 volumes), with price, and place and date of publication; arranged by subject. Subject headings: history, poetry, novels, &c. (by far the largest category); livres François; physic and surgery; divinity; law; husbandry, gardening, mathematics, &c. The attribution of printers is by MWA; MHi attributes it to McAlpine alone. See John E. Alden, 'John Mein, Publisher,' *PBSA* 36 (1942): 201–2. This catalogue is the first known catalogue of a circulating library in America. A note on p. [2]1 indicates that Mein also intended it as a sale catalogue. Another special feature of this catalogue is that most multivolume works have the contents of the separate volumes specified, some at great length. A number of facsimiles of this catalogue were produced in 1940 as no. 110 in the Massachusetts Historical Society Photostat Americana Second Series.

Evans 10069; Sabin 47406; Shera, pp. 135–36, 261; Guerra a-366; *STE*, p. 523. MHi* (20 × 12 cm. — unbound).

55   UNION LIBRARY COMPANY OF PHILADELPHIA

A catalogue of books, belonging to the Union Library Company of Philadelphia. Philadelphia: Printed by Henry Miller, in Second-street. M DCC LXV.

8°: a–c⁴, A–E⁴; 32 leaves, pp. [i–ii] iii–xxiv, 1–40. [i]: title; [ii]: blank; iii: charter; xi: laws; 1: catalogue.

Social library catalogue: 975 short to full author and title entries, with date of publication, numbered with accession/shelf numbers, a separate sequence for each format; arranged alphabetically, by format within each letter, and more or less in accession number order within each format. There are both title and author entries for many of the books listed; the accession/shelf numbers indicate that the actual number of titles in the library was around 650. The Union Library Company absorbed the Association Library Company (see item 51 above) in 1765 and the Amicable Library in 1766, and was itself absorbed by the Library Company of Philadelphia in 1769 (Wolf, pp. 52–53).

Evans 10139; Sabin 62353; Hildeburn 2109; Guerra a-372; *STE*, p. 679. PHi* (19 × 12.5 cm. — bound).

See also McKay 65 (Russell [Bollan])

——————————— 1766 ———————————

56 BOSTON, September 30, 1766. On Monday, the 13th of October next, will be offered to sale at a store in Union-Street, opposite to the Corn-Field, a valuable collection of books, a variety of maps and prints, with several optical and philosophical instruments, &c. at a very low price; which will continue on sale till the 15th of November, and no longer. Many articles are rated so low for the sake of closing some accounts of sales. N.B. There can be no abatement made, nor any credit given. [Boston, 1766.]

Broadside. 3 cols.

Bookseller's catalogue: 160 short author entries, with prices; arranged by subject, and more or less alphabetically within subjects; also, lists of 33 maps and prints, and 18 optical instruments. Subject headings: law books; history and biography; natural philosophy and mathematicks; divinity and morals; classicks; medical; poetry and amusement; architecture; penmanship; mixt. This is one of several catalogues somewhere between a 'regular' auction catalogue and a 'regular' bookseller's catalogue. The whereabouts of the original of this catalogue is not known; proof of its existence is a photoreproduction of it in the American Art Association auction catalogue for May 3 and 4, 1923, item 74. The American Art Association catalogue notes that Jeremiah Condy may be responsible for this catalogue. Isaiah Thomas, in his *History of Printing* 2: 228, locates the bookstore of Condy in 1758 as 'near Concert Hall,' and afterwards 'in Union Street, opposite the Sign of the Cornfield.' On the other hand, *STE* assigns this catalogue to 'Philip Freeman, 1712?–1789, bookseller.'

Bristol 2646; m.p. 41605 (not reproduced); *STE*, p. 106.

NN* (Am. Art Assoc. photo, not the original).

57 CORPORATION OF THE CITY OF NEW YORK. LIBRARY

A catalogue of the library, belonging to the Corporation of the City of New-York. New-York: Printed by John Holt, at the Exchange. M.DCC.LXVI.

8°: [A]⁴B–F⁴; 24 leaves, pp. [1–2] 3–48. [1]: title; [2]: advertisement (see below); 3: catalogue.

Social library catalogue: 1799 short and medium author entries, with place and date of publication, numbered consecutively throughout the catalogue (in increments of ten, on the basis of the number of volumes); arranged by format, and alphabetically within format. Few of the books listed were printed after 1715—most are seventeenth-century and quite a few are sixteenth-century (the earliest is dated 1523); most of the books were printed in London, but other European cities are also well represented. The collection is largely though not exclusively religious. The Corporation Library was set up in 1728 and continued in existence until plundered by British soldiers in the Revolution; see Keep, pp. 64–83, for its history.

Advertisement, p. [2]: 'This Library, in which are many antient, curious and valuable Books, stands in a very convenient Room in the City-Hall, fitted up for it, and for the very valuable modern Library belonging to the New-York Society, . . . the books of this Library will be lent out, upon very easy Terms, for the Improvement of the Inhabitants in Learning, Virtue, and Religion; according to the Order of the Worshipful the Magistrates [sic]: . . . by Thomas Jackson, Keeper of both libraries.'

Bristol 2694; m.p. 41648; Keep, p. 80; Waters 271; Guerra a-388; STE, p. 585. CSmH (17.5×10.5 cm. — bound).

58 JULIANA LIBRARY COMPANY, Lancaster, Pennsylvania

The charter, laws, catalogue of books, list of philosophical instruments, &c. of the Juliana Library-Company, in Lancaster. To which are prefixed, some reflections on the advantages of knowledge; the origin of books and libraries, shewing how they have been encouraged and patronized by the wise and virtuous of every age. With a short account of its institution, friends and benefactors. [a Latin quotation; an English quotation.] Published by order of the directors, Philadelphia: Printed by D. Hall, and W. Sellers. MDCCLXVI.

4°: π²A–G⁴; 30 leaves, pp. [π1–4], i–xi 12–29 [30] 31–35 [36] 37–47 [48] 49–56. [π1]: title; [π2]: blank; [π3]: dedication to Lady Juliana Penn; [π4]: blank; i: preface; 12: account of the library; 15: charter; 19: laws; [30]: blank; 31: catalogue ([36] and [48] blank); 55: list of philosophical instruments; on 56: advertisement, urging punctual payment of fees and careful usage of the books.

Social library catalogue: 210 medium and full author entries, with place and date of publication, and, for donated books, name of donor; arranged by format, and numbered consecutively (by volume) within each format group (probably accession numbers). The preface 'was likely prepared by Rev. Thomas Barton,' as was the account of the library (Charles I. Landis, 'The Juliana Library Company in Lancaster,' PMHB 43 [1919]: 46–47). The EAI Microprint reproduction omits p. 38.

Evans 10350; Hildeburn 2200; Thompson, p. 256; Guerra a-383; STE, p. 406.

CSmH, DLC* (2 copies; one has a few interleaved blanks), ICN, MdBJ, NN, P, PHi* (20.5 × 16 cm. — bound), RPJCB* (lacks t.p.—supplied in photostat; interleaved with blanks).

59 MEIN, JOHN, fl. 1760–1775

A catalogue of curious and valuable books, to be sold at the London Book-Store. [Boston: Printed by William McAlpine(?). 1766.]

8°: π1? A–F^{4}G^2; 27? leaves, pp. [i–ii?] [1] 2–52. [i]: title? (lacking in unique copy); [ii]: blank?; [1]: caption title, as given above; on [1]: first catalogue; 12: second caption title: 'The Following Books may be had at the London Book-Store, very cheap'; on 12: second catalogue; 52: drug and stationery items, and advertisement (imports new books, 'sells at the very lowest prices, for cash only.').

Bookseller's catalogue: total of 1741 consecutively numbered short author entries, 367 in the first catalogue, arranged by format, and 1375 (numbers 368–1741) in the second, arrangement not consistent, partly by format and partly by subject. Subject headings: [miscellaneous]; classics; law; physic and surgery; books of entertainment (the largest group); divinity; tragedies; comedies and operas; pretty little books for children; magazines; political pamphlets, poems, &c.; maps; Bibles, prayerbooks, &c. Date: Mein advertised the catalogue in the *Boston Evening-Post*, May 19, 1766. Attribution of printer is from Brigham.

Bristol 2686; m.p. 41642; Brigham, p. 38; cf. McKay 66; Guerra a-384; *STE*, p. 523.

MWA* (16.5 × 10.5 cm. — unbound).

60 NEW YORK SOCIETY LIBRARY

[Additional catalogue of books. New York: Printed by H. Gaine. 1766.]

The minutes of the Dec. 17, 1766, meeting of the Trustees of the Society Library (ms. at NNS) contain an order 'to pay Mr. Gain for the Additional Catalogue & for the advertisement he printed for this Library.' The advertisement, in the *New-York Gazette*, Sept. 19, 1765, states that the Society Library had 'a large well chosen collection of the most useful modern books, with a considerable late addition, of which a catalogue will be speedily published, that the subscribers may stitch in with their former catalogues.' Keep mentions the publication of this catalogue (*History of the New York Society Library*, p. 173); he could find no copy, however, and none has been found since.

See also McKay 66A (Foulke), 66B (Foulke [Jenney])

—————————— 1767 ——————————

61 BRADFORD, WILLIAM, 1719–1791, AND THOMAS, 1745–1838

William and Thomas Bradford, printers, booksellers and stationers, at their book-store, in Market-Street, adjoining the London Coffee-House: have for sale, the following books and stationary, . . . [Philadelphia: Printed by William and Thomas Bradford. 1767?]

Broadside. 39.5 × 25.5 cm. 4 cols.

Bookseller's catalogue: 300 short author entries, arranged inconsistently either by subject or key word in title, with two labeled categories at the end (school books; new plays); plus lists of stationery and blanks. Approximate list of unlabeled subject groups: medicine; law; religion; collected works of literary figures; history; travel; biography; magazines; poetry; novels; natural philosophy; moral philosophy; geography; trade; navigation. Date: bound into the 1767 volume of the *Pennsylvania Gazette* at NN; could have been published no earlier than 1767 since the latest books listed are a couple that were first published in that year (many of the books listed were first published in 1766).

Bristol 2743; m.p. 41699; Stark 383; *STE*, p. 110
NN*.

62 HALL, DAVID, 1714–1772

Imported in the last vessels from England, and to be sold by David Hall, at the New Printing-Office, in Market-street, Philadelphia, the following books, &c. [Philadelphia: Printed by David Hall. 1767?]

Broadsheet. 35 × 21 cm. 2 cols. each side.

Bookseller's catalogue: 725 short author entries, arranged (paragraph style) by subject; plus a list of stationery and drug items. Subject groupings, not actually labeled: law; medicine; history and biography; household arts; dictionaries; architecture; poetry and business; practical arts; religion; novels and other books of entertainment (this and the previous category are the largest); classics; French books. Date: originally bound in the 1767 volume of the *Pennsylvania Gazette* at MWA, after the issue of Nov. 26; the latest books listed in the catalogue are several first published in 1766, so the catalogue could have been issued no earlier than that, and may be no later than that.

Bristol 2767; m.p. 41719; Brigham, p. 39; Guerra a-401; *STE*, p. 334.
MWA*.

63 MILLER, JOHN HENRY, 1702–1782

Henrich Miller, Buchdrucker in der Zweyten-strasse, zwischen der Rees- und Wein-strasse, gegenüber Herrn John Lukens, dem General-Landmesser, hat folgende Bücher zu verkaufen: [Philadelphia: Gedruckt bey Henrich Miller. 1767.]

Broadside. 26 × 20 cm. 2 cols.

Bookseller's catalogue: 60 short and medium author entries, arranged by language (German [mostly]; Latin; English). Date: among the books listed is a 'Calendar auf das Jahr 1768,' evidence that the catalogue itself was published in 1767. A couple of Miller's own imprints are listed.

Evans 10690 (Bristol 2789 [m.p. 41738] is actually the same item); Guerra a-404; *STE*, p. 528.

PHi*.

[Noel, Garrat, fl. 1752–1775

Catalogue of books in history, divinity, law, arts and sciences and the several parts of polite literature, to be sold by Garrat Noel, bookseller. New York, 1767. 12°; 23 + pp.]

Advertised in the *New York Gazette*, Aug. 3, 1767. Evans 10718; Guerra a-405; *STE*, p. 615.

--------------------------- 1768 ---------------------------

[Bell, Robert, 1731?–1784

Catalogue of books to be sold at auction, May 4, 1768, by Robert Bell. Philadelphia: Printed by William Goddard. 1768.]

Advertised in the *Pennsylvania Chronicle*, May 2, 1768, according to McKay; *STE* says *Pennsylvania Gazette*. Hildeburn 2348; Evans 10831; McKay 71; *STE*, p. 72.

64 HALL, DAVID, 1714–1772

Imported in the last vessels from England, and to be sold by David Hall, at the New Printing-Office, in Market-street, Philadelphia, the following books, &c. [Philadelphia: Printed by David Hall. 1768?]

Broadsheet. 35 × 21 cm. 2 cols. each side.

Bookseller's catalogue: 725 short author entries, arranged (paragraph style) by subject; plus a list of stationery and drug items. Subject groupings, not actually labeled: miscellaneous, but mostly history and biography; law; medicine; household arts; dictionaries; architecture; religion; poetry and business; practical arts; novels and other books of entertainment; classics; French books; children's books. Date: originally bound in the 1768 volume of the *Pennsylvania Gazette* at MWA, after the Aug. 18 issue; the latest novel listed in the catalogue is one first published in 1767, so the catalogue itself could have been published no earlier than that, and likely no later than that, a supposition bolstered by an entry for 'The Daily Journal, or annual account book for 1768,' which, like an almanac, would have been most saleable in late 1767.

Bristol 2891; m.p. 41833; Sabin 29746; Brigham, p. 40; Guerra a-415; *STE*, p. 334.

MH, MWA*, PPL*.

65 LIBRARY COMPANY OF BRIDGETOWN, Mount Holly, New Jersey

A catalogue of books, belonging to the Library Company of Bridge-Town, (commonly called Mount-Holly) in New-Jersey. Philadelphia: Printed by William Goddard, in Market-Street. M.DCC.-LXVIII.

8°: [A]⁴B–F⁴; 24 leaves, pp. [i–ii] iii–xxxv [xxxvi], 1–11 [12]. [i]: title; [ii]: blank; iii: charter; xi: articles; xxxi: list of members; xxxiii: directions for the clerk; [xxxvi]: blank; 1: catalogue; [12]: blank.

Social library catalogue: 162 short author entries, with dates of publication, arranged in two format groups (folio; quarto, octavo, &c.), and numbered consecutively within each group.

Bristol 2908; m.p. 41849; Guerra a-417; Stark 397; *STE*, p. 545.

NN* (19.5×13 cm. — bound; sig. C, pp. xvii–xxiv, lacking).

66 PROVIDENCE LIBRARY, Providence, Rhode Island

Catalogue of all the books, belonging to the Providence Library. N.B. Those marked thus[*] are such books as were saved in the proprietors hands, when the late Library was burnt. Providence, N. E: Printed and sold by Waterman and Russell, at the New Printing-Office, at the Paper-Mill. M,DCC,LXVIII.

4°: [A]⁴B–C⁴; 12 leaves, pp. [1–2] 3–18 [19–20] 21–24. [1]: title (brackets in original); [2]: blank; 3: catalogue; [19]: second title:' Rules for governing the proprietors of, and institutions for rendering useful the books belonging to, the

Providence Library. Otium cum dignitate. Providence, New-England: Printed and sold by Waterman and Russell, at their New Printing-Office, at the Paper-Mill. M,DCC,LXVIII.'; [20]: blank; 21: rules.

Social library catalogue: 375 short author entries, with prices, arranged in full alphabetical order. According to Evans, this library merged with the Providence Athenæum in 1831. Microprint reproduction lacks title-page.

Evans 11051; Sabin 66330; Cutter 13; Alden 387; Thompson, p. 257; Guerra a-419; *STE*, p. 707.

RHi*, RPA*, RPJCB* (20×16 cm. — bound).

See also McKay 67 (Russell [Gridley]), 68 (Bleecker), 69 (Bleecker), 69A, 70 (Bleecker), 71A (Bell), 72 (Bell), and 73 (Bell)

———————————— 1769 ————————————

[Aitken, Robert, 1734–1802

Catalogue of books to be sold at auction by Robert Aitken. Philadelphia: Printed by John Dunlap. 1769.]

Advertised in the *Pennsylvania Journal*, Nov. 23, 1769. Hildeburn 2425; Evans 11140; McKay 75; *STE*, p. 11.

[Bell, Robert, 1731?–1784

Catalogue of the library of the late David James Dove. To be sold at auction by Robert Bell, May 8, 1769. Philadelphia: Printed by William Goddard. 1769.]

Advertised in the *Pennsylvania Chronicle*, May 8, 1769. Hildeburn 2427; Evans 11242; McKay 74; *STE*, p. 72.

[Bradford, Thomas, 1745–1838

Catalogue of a circulating library, kept by Thomas Bradford. Philadelphia: Printed by W. and T. Bradford. 1769.]

Advertised in the *Pennsylvania Journal*, Sept. 21, 1769. Hildeburn 2424; Evans 11189; *STE*, p. 109.

67 BRADFORD, WILLIAM, 1719–1791, AND
    THOMAS, 1745–1838
Imported in the last vessels from London, and to be sold by William and Thomas Bradford, printers, booksellers, and stationers,

at their book-store in Market-Street, adjoining the London Coffee-House; or by Thomas Bradford, at his house in Second-Street, one door from Arch-Street, and nearly opposite the sign of St. George, a large and neat assortment of books and stationary. [Philadelphia: Printed by W. and T. Bradford. 1769?]

Broadsheet. 40×24.5 cm. 4 cols. each side, although the verso also contains segments in 2 cols. and in 1 col.

Bookseller's catalogue: 475 short author entries, arranged by subject, plus lists of stationery and blanks. Subject groupings, some labeled (in quotes) and some not: religion; medicine; law; trade; belles lettres; history; travel; biography; 'Publication in 1768' (miscellaneous); 'New Novels in 1768'; 'New Plays and Farces'; periodicals; agriculture; more novels; household arts; military; dictionaries; geography; natural philosophy; surveying; mathematics; astronomy; arithmetic; bookkeeping; 'Cl[a]ssics'; 'Plays'; 'School Books'; 'Seamen['s] ... Books, Charts and Stationary.' Date: usually dated 1769; several of the subject headings and the fact that the latest novels listed in the catalogue were first published in 1768 indicated that the catalogue could not have been published before 1768, though that date is as likely as 1769. MHi has a photostat copy of this catalogue which they incorrectly date [1775]. Attribution of printer from Hildeburn.

Evans 11190; Hildeburn 2452; Guerra a-425; *STE*, p. 110.
PHi*, PPL*.

68 CATALOGUE of books, to be sold, by public auction, at the City Vendue-Store, in Front-Street: notice of the time of sale will be given in the public papers. [Philadelphia: Printed by W. and T. Bradford. 1769?]

Broadside. 40×25 cm. 4 cols.

Auction catalogue: 350 short author entries, arranged in no apparent order (though a large group of law books heads the list). Date: could have been published no earlier than 1768, and probably no later than 1769, since the latest books listed in the catalogue are several first published in 1768; 1769 is the date usually assigned. Attribution of printer from Hildeburn.

Evans 11202; Hildeburn 2426; McKay 77; Guerra a-424; *STE*, p. 138.
PHi*.

69 HALL, DAVID, 1714–1772
David Hall, at the New Printing-Office, in Market-street, Philadelphia, has to dispose of, wholesale and retail, the following books, &c. [Philadelphia: Printed by D. Hall and W. Sellers. 1769.]

Broadsheet. 35 × 21 cm. 2 cols. each side.

Bookseller's catalogue: 850 short author entries, most of them arranged (paragraph style) by format, with a separate list at the end for school-books; plus lists of stationery and medicines. Date: dated 1769 because it was originally bound in the 1769 volume of the *Pennsylvania Gazette* at MWA; could have been published no earlier than 1768, and probably no later than 1769, since the latest novels listed in the catalogue are several first published in 1768. Attribution of printer from Hildeburn.

Evans 11282; Hildeburn 2450 and 2542 (dated [1770]; these two entries refer to the same item); Brigham, p. 40; Guerra a-430; *STE*, p. 334.

MHi* (slightly mutilated), MWA*, PPL*.

70 MILLER, JOHN HENRY, 1702–1782

Catalogus von mehr als 700 meist Deutschen Büchern, welche entweder zusammen oder einzeln zu verkaufen sind. Wo selbige zu sehen sind, solches kan man erfahren bey Henrich Miller, Buchdrucker in der Rees-strasse, gegenüber Morävian=Alley, zu Philadelphia; bey welchem dieser Catalogus zu haben ist, wie auch bey Herrn Christoph Saur, in Germantaun. [Philadelphia: Gedruckt bey Henrich Miller. 1769?]

8°: A–B⁸; 16 leaves, pp. [1–32]. [1]: title; [2]: catalogue.

Bookseller's catalogue: 730 short and medium author entries, in German (mostly) and Latin, numbered consecutively, and arranged by format, with one page of 'neue Bücher sind bey Henrich Miller . . . um billige Preise zu haben' on p. [32]. Attribution of printer from Hildeburn and Evans.

Evans 11339; Hildeburn 2428; Guerra a-437; *STE*, p. 528.

PHi* (20 × 12.5 cm. — bound).

See also McKay 73A (Bell), 76 (Russell [Knight])

───────────────── 177? ─────────────────

71 KNOX, HENRY, 1750–1806

[London Book-Store, a little southward of the Town-House in Cornhill, Boston. Boston, 177?]

Bookseller's catalogue. 3pp. The title above is that given on the MWA accession slip. This catalogue was purchased and received by MWA from book dealer

Benjamin Tighe, Athol, Mass., on Oct. 13, 1967; several of the staff of MWA recalled seeing it at that time, but apparently it disappeared shortly thereafter and its location is not now known.

---------- 1770 ----------

[Bell, Robert, 1731?–1784

Catalogue of books to be sold at auction, October 25, 1770. Philadelphia: Printed for Robert Bell. 1770.]

Advertised in the *Pennsylvania Chronicle*, Oct. 22, 1770. Hildeburn 2506; Evans 11562; McKay 82; *STE*, p. 72.

[Bell, Robert, 1731?–1784

A catalogue of new and old books consisting of history, divinity, biography, surgery . . . sold at a house upon Hunter's Quay. . . . New York, 1770.]

Advertised in the *New York Gazette*, Feb. 5, 1770. McKay 78; Bristol 3143; m.p. 42059; Guerra a-444; *STE*, p. 72.

72 BELL, ROBERT, 1731?–1784

A catalogue of new and old books, which will be exhibited by auction, by Robert Bell, bookseller and auctionier, on Wednesday the 4th of July, 1770, and will continue selling for eight or ten evenings successively; at the Royal Exchange Tavern, King-street, in the Town of Boston. [Boston, 1770.]

Broadsheet. 37.5 × 23 cm. 2 cols. each side. Preceding the catalogue, on the recto, is some introductory material, including a note on the hours of sale, a 'Eulogium on Books,' and 'Conditions of Sale by Auction'; following the catalogue, on the verso, are a proposal to publish Robertson's *History of Charles the Fifth* by subscription, and a note that a supplementary catalogue will be published 'Tuesday Next' (apparently never issued).

Auction catalogue: 183 short (mostly) to full author entries, with prices, numbered consecutively but arranged in no apparent order; plus 25 entries for charts, maps, and plans, also numbered consecutively (183–207), with prices. MHi has only a negative photocopy of this item, with the following ms. notation regarding the original on the back, which they could not explain: 'Misc NewsPapers (Bowdoin XII, June 25) Deposited by Am. Ac. of Arts & Sciences, 1/7/19.'

Bristol 3144; m.p. 42060; Ford 1507; McKay 79A; Guerra a-445; *STE*, p. 72.
MHi* (photocopy).

[Bell, Robert, 1731?–1784

Catalogue of old physical and surgical authors to be sold at the prices
marked therein. Philadelphia: Printed for Robert Bell. 1770.]

Advertised in the *Pennsylvania Journal*, Oct. 11, 1770. Hildeburn 2507; Evans
11563; Guerra a-443; *STE*, p. 72.

[Bell, Robert, 1731?–1784

Catalogue of second hand Greek and Latin classics for sale by Robert
Bell. Philadelphia: Printed for Robert Bell. 1770.]

Advertised in the *Pennsylvania Journal*, Oct. 11, 1770. Hildeburn 2505; Evans
11564; *STE*, p. 72.

73 CHARLESTON LIBRARY SOCIETY, Charleston, South Carolina

A catalogue of books, belonging to the incorporated Charles-town Library Society, with the dates of the editions. ΨΥΧΗΣ ΙΑΤΡΕΙΑ. Physick of the soul. Charlestown: Printed for the Society, by Robert Wells: MDCCLXX.

4°: [A]²B–I²; 18 leaves, pp. [1–3] 4–36. [1]: title; [2]: blank; [3]: catalogue.
Social library catalogue: 814 short and medium author entries, with place and
date of publication; arranged by format and alphabetically within format, and
numbered consecutively within each format. An edition of rules and bylaws
was also published in 1770 (Bristol 3166, at DLC); in addition, a separate edition of rules and bylaws was published in 1762 (Evans 9087, at CSmH), and a
4th edition of them was published in 1785 (Evans 18951, at BL).
Evans 11596; Thompson, p. 254; Ranz, p. 118; Guerra a-447; *STE*, p. 142.
DLC* (22.5 × 17 cm. — bound), ScC.

74 LIBRARY COMPANY OF PHILADELPHIA

The charter, laws, and catalogue of books, of the Library Com-
pany of Philadelphia. With a short account of the library prefixed.
Communiter bona profundere deûm est. Philadelphia: Printed by
Joseph Crukshank, in Second-street. M,DCC,LXX.

8°: A–Q⁴QQ⁴R–Uu⁴[Xx]²; 178 leaves, pp. [1–2] 3–13 [14] 15–33 [34] 35–38, ²[1–318]. [1]: title; [2]: blank; 3: account of library; 9: list of members; [14]: blank; 15: charter; 21: laws; [34]: blank; 35: rules; ²[1] or E4ʳ: catalogue (F2ᵛ, F4ᵛ, L4ᵛ, N2ᵛ, O1ᵛ, O3ᵛ, Q1ᵛ, Q3ᵛ, QQ4ʳ⁻ᵛ, S4ᵛ, U3ᵛ, X1ᵛ, Y3ᵛ, Cc2ᵛ, Dd2ᵛ, Ff2ᵛ, Hh4ᵛ, Ll3ᵛ, Mm3ᵛ, Mm4ᵛ, Nn3ᵛ, Oo1ᵛ, Pp4ᵛ, Qq2ᵛ, Rr3ᵛ, Ss1ᵛ, Ss3ᵛ, Tt4ᵛ, Uu3ᵛ: all blank).

Social library catalogue: 2233 separate books, in full title and full author entries (total number of entries is much larger because of extensive double listing by both author and title), with accession number, place and date of publication, and, for donated books, name of donor; arranged alphabetically (sometimes by author, sometimes by subject, that is, key word in title), by format within each letter, and more or less in accession number order within format. Wolf (p. 54) calls this 'the first of the modern catalogues of the Company,' and notes that present accession numbers are additions to the series established in this catalogue.

Evans 11820; Sabin 61788; Hildeburn 2511; Cutter 14; Ranz, p. 118; Guerra a-457; *STE*, p. 676.

DLC*, MWA* (22×13.5 cm. — bound), NN*, PHi* (2 copies), PP, PPAmP* (presentation copy from library directors to Benjamin Franklin, with ms. additions), PPL* (6 copies; one lacks sig. Tt; another repeats sig. Cc and reverses the order of sigs. Tt and Ss, is interleaved with blanks, and has ms. additions), PU, RPJCB*.

See also McKay 79 (Bell), 80 (Bell), and 81 (Russell [Bernard])

———————— **1771** ————————

[Bell, Robert, 1731?–1784
Catalogue of books to be sold at auction, December 2, 1771. Philadelphia: Printed for Robert Bell. 1771.]

Advertised in the *Pennsylvania Chronicle*, Dec. 2, 9, 1771. Hildeburn 2638; Evans 11982; McKay 86; *STE*, p. 72.

[Bell, Robert, 1731?–1784
Catalogue of books to be sold at auction, October 7, 1771. Philadelphia: Printed for Robert Bell. 1771.]

Advertised in the *Pennsylvania Chronicle*, Oct. 7, 1771. Hildeburn 2637; Evans 11981; McKay 85; *STE*, p. 72.
NUC, 45: 9, incorrectly locates a copy at PPL.

75 GAINE, HUGH, 1726–1807

Just imported in the last vessels from London, and to be sold, by Hugh Gaine, at his book store and printing-office, at the Bible and Crown, in Hanover-Square. [New York: Printed by Hugh Gaine. 1771.]

Broadside. 52.5×42 cm. 4 cols.

Bookseller's catalogue: 275 short author entries, arranged by subject; plus a list of stationery items. Subject groupings, not actually labeled: religion; poetry; novels; travel; history; biography; mathematics; arithmetic, astronomy, book-keeping, navigation, and surveying; trade; law; medicine; dictionaries and grammars; classics; miscellaneous. Date: MWA copy has on verso a ms. copy of a petition of Charles Phelps of New York to Gov. Tompkins for a land grant, dated July 23, 1771. The catalogue could not have been published earlier than 1771 since the latest novel listed in it was first published in that year.

Bristol 3346; m.p. 42237; Brigham, p. 40; Guerra a-473; *STE*, p. 297.
MWA*.

76 NOEL, GARRAT, fl. 1752–1775, AND EBENEZER HAZARD, 1744–1817

A catalogue of books, sold by Noel and Hazard, at their book and stationary store, next door to the Merchants Coffee-House, where the public may be furnished with all sorts of books and paper. As also, blank books, and every other kind of stationary ware, at reasonable rates, by wholesale and retail. Country stores are supplied on reasonable terms for cash, with Bibles, common prayer books, testaments, psalters, Watts's Psalms and Hymns, primmers, Child's New Plaything, Dilworth's Spelling Book, and School-master's Assistant, Entick's Spelling Dictionary, Best Young Man's Companion, paper of all sorts, ink-powder, slates, slate pencils, bonnet and press paper, &c. &c. &c. New-York: Printed by Inslee and Car. M,DCC,LXXI.

8°: A–E⁴; 20 leaves, pp. [1–3] 4–31 [32–33] 34–40 (35 misnumbered '34'). [1]: title; [2]: blank; [3]: main catalogue; on 29: 'Medly of Things' (mostly stationery, but including fishing tackle and shaving equipment); [32]: blank; [33]: caption title: 'A Supplement to Noel and Hazard's Catalogue of Books, Stationary, &c.'; on [33]: supplementary catalogue; on 37: lists of stationery, paper, pamphlets, maps, and 'A Miscellany of Things'; on 40: advertisement for Davies' *Sermons,* 'Just Published.'

Bookseller's catalogue. Main catalogue: 725 short and medium author entries, arranged by subject, and then alphabetically within each subject. Subject headings: history, voyages, and travels, &c.; divinity; law; physic, surgery, anatomy, &c.; novels, poems, plays, &c.; philosophy and mathematics; trade, navigation, architecture, &c.; husbandry, gardening, fariery, &c.; classics, school books, &c.; miscellaneous; pamphlets; maps, plans, draughts, &c.; chapmen's books. Supplementary catalogue: 125 short author entries, arranged alphabetically. A note on p. 31 indicates that the supplementary catalogue was probably printed separately and later than the main one: 'N.B. An Appendix will be added to the foregoing Catalogue, on every new Importation.' The latest publication date for any of the entries in the supplement is 1771, so it was probably published later that same year or early in 1772.

Evans 12168; Guerra a-478; *STE*, p. 615.

CtHi* (21.5 × 14 cm. — unbound), CtY* (lacks t.p.).

[Templeton and Stewart
Catalogue of a large and elegant assortment of new books on divinity, law, history, physic. . . . New York, 1771.]

Advertised in the *New York Gazette*, May 27, June 3, 1771. Title based on McKay's entry. McKay 84; Bristol 3394; m.p. 42284; Guerra a-482; *STE*, p. 823.

See also McKay 83 (Applegate)

———————————— 1772 ————————————

77 CHARLESTON LIBRARY SOCIETY, Charleston, South Carolina
Appendix to the catalogue of books, belonging to the incorporated Charlestown Library Society. ΨΥΧΗΣ ΙΑΤΡΕΙΑ. Charlestown: Printed for the Society, by Robert Wells. MDCCLXXII.

4°: π1[=B2?] A⁴[B]²(–B2); 6 leaves, pp. [1–3] 4–11 [12]. [1]: title; [2]: blank; [3]: catalogue; [12]: blank.
Social library catalogue: 71 entries, as in the 1770 Charleston Library Society catalogue (item 73 above).
Bristol 3436; m.p. 42327; Guerra a-498; *STE*, p. 142.
DLC* (22.5 × 17 cm. — bound).

78 CHARLESTON LIBRARY SOCIETY, Charleston, South Carolina

A catalogue of books, given and devised by John Mackenzie Esquire, to the Charlestown Library Society, for the use of the College when erected. Charlestown: Printed for the Society, by Robert Wells. MDCCLXXII.

4°: [A]⁴B–C⁴; 12 leaves, pp. [1–3] 4–24. [1]: title; [2]: blank; [3]: catalogue.

Social library catalogue: 408 short and medium author entries, with place and date of publication; arranged by format, and then alphabetically within each format, and numbered consecutively (in increments of five) within each format.

Bristol 3437; m.p. 42327 (following the previous item); Guerra a–503; Ranz, p. 118.

DLC* (22.5 × 17 cm. — bound), ScC.

79 COX, EDWARD, fl. 1766–1778, AND EDWARD BERRY, fl. 1766–1772

A catalogue of a very large assortment of the most esteemed books in every branch of polite literature, arts and sciences. Viz. history, voyages, travels, lives, memoirs, antiquities, philosophy, novels, divinity, physic, surgery, anatomy, arts, sciences, plays, poetry, husbandry, architecture, navigation, gardening, mathematicks, law, &c. &c. Which are to be sold by Cox & Berry at their store in King-Street, Boston. N.B. All new books of merit, magazines and reviews, imported by every opportunity from London.———[Boston, 1772?]

8°: A–E⁴F²; 22 leaves, pp. [1–3] 4–44. [1]: title: [2]: list of non-book items for sale; [3]: catalogue; 41: list of 5 books, with a paragraph-length comment in praise of each, 'To be had very Cheap'; on 42: advertisements for medicines; 44: advertisements for *The Frugal Housewife*, 'To be Sold by Cox and Berry,' and 'A Compendium of Church Musick; Containing a great Variety of Favourite Anthems,' which is 'In the Press and speedily will be published.'

Bookseller's catalogue: 1400 short author entries, most of them in one alphabetical list, with several separate subject lists at the end (law; physic, surgery and anatomy; physical pamphlets; French books; Bibles and prayer books; old folio's and quarto's; school books; little books for the instruction and amusement of children). Date: the first Boston edition of *The Frugal Housewife*, advertised on p. 44, was printed in 1772, so the catalogue could be no earlier than that. MWA also uses the other book advertised on p. 44 to help date the catalogue, noting that, although they have found no book with that exact title, 'on Dec.

30, 1771 under the heading of Newburyport, Dec. 24, 1771 Daniel Bayley issued proposals for publishing a "Collection of favorite anthems" which AAS. thinks may have been the title refered [sic] to in this catalogue.'

Bristol 3446; m.p. 42336; Brigham, p. 41; Guerra a-500; STE, p. 191; Stark 475a. MWA* (22 × 13.5 cm. — bound), NN*.

80 KNOX, HENRY, 1750–1806

A catalogue of books, imported and to be sold by Henry Knox, at the London Book-Store, a little southward of the Town-House, in Cornhill, Boston, MDCCLXXII. [Boston, 1772.]

4°: [A]⁴B–D⁴; 16 leaves, pp. [1–2] 3–32. [1]: title; [2]: blank; 3: catalogue; 31: stationery; on 32: advertisements (makes blank books, receives magazines, supplies libraries and other quantity buyers).

Bookseller's catalogue: 600 short (mostly) to full author entries (a few with descriptive and laudatory comments), most of them in one alphabetical list, with a separate, brief list of school books and classical authors at the end. The unique copy of this catalogue, at CtY, is inlaid in a Beinecke Library copy of Francis S. Drake's *Life and Correspondence of Henry Knox* (Boston: Samuel Drake, 1873), between pp. 12 and 13. Evans 12424 describes a Knox catalogue dated 1772, but the editors of *EAI* and *STE* were only able to locate a 1773 Knox catalogue (see item 87 below), to which they assigned number 12424, assuming that Evans was mistaken about the date. The 1773 Knox catalogue, therefore, appears as Evans 12424 on Microprint and in *STE*, and the catalogue described above does not appear in either place.

Evans 12424.
CtY* (18 × 11.5 cm. — unbound).

[MacGill, Robert
Catalogue of a small collection of books. Consisting of history, entertainment, new novels, song books, some law books, and a few divinity books. For sale by Robert MacGill. Williamsburg: Printed by William Rind. 1772.]

Advertised in Rind's *Virginia Gazette*, according to *STE*. Evans 12441; *STE*, p. 441.

81 VIRGINIA GAZETTE OFFICE, Williamsburg, Virginia

A catalogue of books to be sold at the Post Office, Williamsburg. [Williamsburg: Printed by John Purdie and William Hunter?, 1772.]

Broadside. 38×24 cm. 2 cols.

Bookseller's catalogue: 425 short author entries, arranged (paragraph style) by format and alphabetically within each format. Date: most likely date is 1772 since the latest novels listed in the catalogue were several first printed in that year, and many of the novels listed were published in 1771. On the back of one of the DLC copies is a series of handwritten account book entries under the date 'Mar: 29 1774,' which is probably why Evans dated the catalogue [1774]. DLC dates it [176–]; *STE* and *EAI* follow Evans. Evans, *STE*, and *EAI* list this item under John Dixon and William Hunter, since they were the proprietors of the *Virginia Gazette* in 1774; in 1772 John Purdie and William Hunter were the publishers. Evans gave the location correctly as DLC, but *STE* and *EAI* state that the 'copy reported cannot be located,' so the catalogue is not reproduced on Microprint. William D. Houlette, in 'Plantation and Parish Libraries in the Old South' (Ph. D. diss., Univ. of Iowa, 1933), prints the contents of this catalogue, dating it 1775. 'Books in Williamsburg,' *WMQ* 15 (1906): 100–113, prints the contents of a similar catalogue published in the Nov. 25, 1775, issue of the *Virginia Gazette*.

Evans 13252; *STE*, p. 227.

DLC* (2 copies).

[Woodhouse, William, 1740?–1795
Catalogue of new and old books for sale by William Woodhouse. Philadelphia: Printed by Robert Bell. 1772.]

Advertised in the *Pennsylvania Chronicle*, Sept. 19, 1772. Hildeburn 2755; Evans 12629; Guerra a–512; *STE*, p. 1012.

See also McKay 87 (Bell), 87A (Russell [Sheafe]), 87B (Russell), 87C (Langford), 88 (McDavitt), 88A (Russell)

——————— 1773 ———————

82 AIKMAN, WILLIAM, fl. 1773
[A catalogue of Aikman's circulating library. Annapolis, 1773?]

12°: A–E⁶F⁴; 34 leaves, pp. [1–4] 5–67 [68]. [1]: title (lacking); [2]: blank?; [3]: conditions; [4]: blank; 5: catalogue; [68]: blank. May also be lacking several pages at the end since there is a catchword, 'Supplement,' on p. 67.

Circulating library catalogue: 854 consecutively numbered medium and full author and title entries, arranged alphabetically. Date: dated [1773?] by MdHi because other evidence suggests that Aikman's library was only in existence before 1775, and because the Town and Country Magazine for 1771 is listed on p. 66.

MdHi* (17.5×11.5 cm. — unbound; imperfect as above).

83 BELL, ROBERT, 1731?–1784

Philadelphia, July 15th 1773. Robert Bell's sale catalogue of a collection of new and old books, in all the arts and sciences, and in various languages, also, a large quantity of entertaining novels; with the lowest price printed to each book; now selling, at the book-store of William Woodhouse, bookseller, stationer, and bookbinder, in Front-street, near Chesnut-street, Philadelphia. In this collection are included a number of elegant and uncommon books, very scarce and rarely to be met with, being the library of a gentleman who lately left this country—Also to be sold, three pair of large walnut book-cases, either separate or together. Said Bell gives ready money for any library or parcel of books. [Philadelphia: Printed by Robert Bell. 1773.]

8°: A–F⁴; 24 leaves, pp. [1] 2–44 [45–48]. [1]: title (caption); on [1]: catalogue; [45]: advertisements for several books 'Lately published by Robert Bell' (Robertson's *History of Charles the Fifth*, Porteus' *Death: A Poetical Essay*, and Shipley's *Sermon for conciliating the Affections of Britons and Americans*); [47]: 'Conditions' relating to printing by subscription Bacon's *New Abridgement of the Law*; [48]: continuation of catalogue.

Bookseller's catalogue: 947 consecutively numbered, short (mostly) and medium author entries, with prices; arranged by format.

Evans 12670; Hildeburn 2856 (probably—title varies); Brigham, p. 42; Guerra a-513; *STE*, p. 72.

MWA* (19.5×12.5 cm. — bound).

84 GEYER, ANDREAS

Andreas Geyer, Buchbinder in der Zweyten-strasse, nahe bey der Arch-strasse, hat mit den allerletzten Schiffen aus Deutschland folgende Bücher bekom̄en, welche er für billige Preise verkaufen wird, näml. [Philadelphia: Gedruckt bey Henrich Miller. 1773?]

Broadside. 24.5×19 cm. 2 cols.

Bookseller's catalogue: 60 short author entries in German, arranged in no apparent order. Date: taken from Hildeburn and Evans; internal evidence provides no verification because the books are nearly all standard, long-in-print religious books. Attribution of printer from Hildeburn.

Evans 12789; Hildeburn 2883; Guerra a-518; *STE*, p. 308. PHi*.

85 HARVARD COLLEGE. LIBRARY

Catalogus librorum in Bibliotheca Cantabrigiensi selectus, frequentiorem in usum Harvardinatum, qui gradu baccalaurei in artibus nondum sunt donati. Bostoniae: Nov. Ang. Typis Edes & Gill, M,DCC,LXXIII.

8°: [A]⁴B–C⁴D²; 14 leaves, pp. [1–4] 5–27 [28]. [1]: title; [2]: blank; [3]: 'Monitum' (explanation of catalogue, in Latin); [4]: blank; 5: catalogue; [28]: blank.

College library catalogue: 800 short author entries, with location numbers, arranged in full alphabetical order. As the title indicates, this is a selected list for undergraduates, compiled by James Winthrop.

Evans 12805; Sabin 30728; Cutter, 15; Shores, p. 173; Ranz, p. 118; Guerra a-519; *STE*, p. 342.

CtY* (uncut), DLC*, MBAt* (2 copies), MH* (lacks t.p.), MHi*, MWA* (22.5×14 cm. — unbound), NN*, RPJCB* (2 copies: copy 1 has defective printing on p. 15; copy 2 has ms. additions).

86 HASENCLEVER, FRANCIS

Francis Hasenclever, in dem Hause worin Leonhard Melchior ehedem gewohnt hat, in der Zweyten-strasse, halbwegs zwischen der Rees- und Arch-strasse, zu Philadelphia, hat neulich folgende schöne Sammlung von Büchern aus Deutschland erhalten, welche er um die billigsten Preise verkaufen will, näml. [Philadelphia: Gedruckt bey Henrich Miller. 1773?]

Broadsheet. 34.5×21.5 cm. 2 cols. each side.

Bookseller's catalogue: 225 short author entries, in German, arranged in no apparent order. Date: from Hildeburn and Evans. Attribution of printer from Hildeburn.

Evans 12808; Hildeburn 2889; Guerra a-520; *STE*, p. 346. PHi*.

87 KNOX, HENRY, 1750–1806

A catalogue of books, imported and to be sold by Henry Knox, at the London Book-Store, a little southward of the Town-House, in Cornhill, Boston, MDCCLXXIII. [Boston, 1773.]

4°: [A]⁴B–E⁴; 20 leaves, pp. [1–2] 3–40. [1]: title; [2]: blank; 3: catalogue; on 39: stationery and other articles.

Bookseller's catalogue: 800 short (mostly) to full author entries, most of them in one alphabetical list, with a separate, brief list of school books and classical authors at the end. Catalogue entries occasionally include comments praising the book. This catalogue appears in *STE* and on Microprint as Evans 12424, though that number should be assigned to the 1772 Knox catalogue (see item 80 above).

[Evans 12424]; Brigham, p. 42; Guerra a-521; *STE*, p. 401.

MB*, MH*, MHi*, MWA* (21.5 × 14.5 cm. — bound), NN*.

88 NEW YORK SOCIETY LIBRARY

The charter, and bye-laws, of the New-York Society Library; with a catalogue of the books belonging to the said Library. New-York: Printed by H. Gaine, printer, bookseller and stationer, at the Bible and Crown in Hanover-Square, M,DCC,LXXIII.

8°: [A]⁴B–D⁴E²; 18 leaves, pp. [1–3] 4–14 [15] 16–35 [36]. [1]: title; [2]: blank; [3]: charter; 12: laws; [15]: catalogue; [36]: blank.

Social library catalogue: 400 short author entries, arranged alphabetically, and by format within each letter.

Evans 12895; Sabin 54545; Ranz, p. 119; Guerra a-525; *STE*, p. 610.

CSmH, DLC*, MH*, MWA* (18.5 × 11.5 cm. — unbound), NHi (could not be located, 1975), NNS.

89 REINHOLDT, GEORG CHRISTOPH, fl. 1763–1793

Georg Christoph Reinholdt, Buchbinder in der Markt-strasse, neben dem Wirthshause zum Schwarzen Bären, zu Philadelphia, hat folgende Bücher zu verkaufen: [Philadelphia: Gedruckt bey Henrich Miller. 1773.]

Broadside. 35 × 21 cm. 2 cols.

Bookseller's catalogue: 130 short and medium author entries, in German, arranged by format. Date: from Hildeburn and Evans. Attribution of printer from Hildeburn.

Evans 12971; Sabin 69118; Hildeburn 2922; Guerra a-531; *STE*, p. 718.

PPL*.

90 SMITH, SOLOMON, fl. 1772–1779, AND JOSEPH
COIT, 1750–1779

Hartford, 5ᵗʰ July, 1773. Just imported from London, and to be
sold, at a moderate advance, by Smith and Coit, at their store east of
the Court-House in Hartford, a universal assortment of drugs and
medicines, painter's colours, and grocery articles; together with the
following books, &c. [Hartford, 1773.]

Broadside. 37.5×30 cm. 5 cols.

Bookseller's catalogue: 375 short author entries, arranged by subject and alphabetically within subject; plus a list of stationery. Subject headings: divinity;
psalmody; law; physic, surgery, &c.; school books; history; miscellany.

Bristol 3644; m.p. 42505; Waters 339; *STE*, p. 788.

CSmH, NHi*.

See also McKay 89 (Dellap), 90 (Russell), 91 (Bartlett), 91A (Russell), 91B
(Russell [Hall]), 91C (Gould)

──────────────── 1774 ────────────────

[Bell, Robert, 1731?–1784

Catalogue of books to be sold at auction, March 14, 1774. Philadelphia: Printed by Robert Bell. 1774.]

Advertised in the *Pennsylvania Gazette*, Mar. 9, 1774. Hildeburn 2989; Evans
13138; McKay 93; *STE*, p. 72.

[Bell, Robert, 1731?–1784

Catalogue of books to be sold at auction on December 16th, 1774.
Philadelphia: Printed by Robert Bell. 1774.]

Advertised in the *Pennsylvania Gazette*, Dec. 14, 1774. Hildeburn 2991; Evans
13140; McKay 95; *STE*, p. 72.

[Bell, Robert, 1731?–1784

Catalogue of books to be sold at auction on May 19th, 1774. Philadelphia: Printed by Robert Bell. 1774.]

Advertised in the *Pennsylvania Gazette*, May 11, 18, 1774. Hildeburn 2990; Evans
13139; McKay 94; *STE*, p. 72.

[Bell, Robert, 1731?–1784

Catalogue of new and old books, to be sold by auction, by Robert Bell, bookseller, and professor of book-auctioneering, on Monday the seventh of February, 1774. Philadelphia: Printed by Robert Bell. 1774.]

Advertised in the *Pennsylvania Gazette*, Feb. 9, 1774. Hildeburn 2988; Evans 13137; McKay 92; Guerra a-540; *STE*, p. 72.

91 HALL, WILLIAM, 1752–1834

William Hall, at the New Printing-Office, in Market-street, Philadelphia, has to dispose of, wholesale and retail, the following books, &c. [Philadelphia: Printed by Hall and Sellers. 1774?]

Broadsheet. 35.5 × 22 cm. 2 cols. each side.

Bookseller's catalogue: 650 short author entries, most of them arranged (paragraph style) by format (with a tendency to group like books together within each format), with two brief, separate lists, at the end, of school books and French books, plus lists of stationery, paper, and medicines. Date: dated 1774 by Hildeburn and Evans; could be no earlier, and probably not much later, than 1772 since the latest novels listed in the catalogue are several first published in 1772. David Hall died in 1772 and his son William took over his business then.

Evans 13312; Hildeburn 3027; Guerra a-547; *STE*, p. 335. PHi*.

92 SPARHAWK, JOHN, 1730–1803

A catalogue of books, &c. to be sold by John Sparhawk, at the London Book-Store, in Philadelphia. [Philadelphia, 1774?]

12°: A–C⁶D⁴; 22 leaves, pp. [1] 2–44. [1]: title (caption); on [1]: catalogue; on 42: stationery; on 42: 'Some curious hard ware'; on 44: medicines. It is likely that a title-page leaf, probably printed as part of sig. D, and perhaps a final (blank) leaf are lacking in the unique copy.

Bookseller's catalogue: 1150 short (mostly) to full author entries, arranged by format, and, within each format, alphabetically. Date: dated [1773?] by Bristol, *STE*, and RPB, but the catalogue could have been printed no earlier than 1774, since the latest novels listed in it are several first published in that year.

Bristol 3646; m.p. 42507; *STE*, p. 779. RPB* (16.5 × 10 cm. — unbound).

See also McKay 94A (Russell), 94B (Russell)

1775

[Bell, Robert, 1731?–1784

Catalogue of books to be sold at auction by Robert Bell, January 18, 1775. Philadelphia: Printed by Robert Bell. 1775.]

According to McKay, advertised in the *Pennsylvania Gazette*, Jan. 11, 18, 1775, stating sale to begin Jan. 16; *STE* locates the ad in the *Pennsylvania Journal*. Hildeburn 3180; Evans 13829; McKay 96; *STE*, p. 72.

93 LIBRARY COMPANY OF PHILADELPHIA

The second part of the catalogue of books, of the Library Company of Philadelphia. Communiter bona profundere deûm est. Philadelphia: Printed by R. Aitken, bookseller, opposite the London Coffee-House, Front-Street. M,DCC,LXXV.

8°: A–H⁴I²; 34 leaves, pp. [1–3] 4–5 [6] 7–67 [68]. [1]: title; [2]: blank; [3]: rules; [6]: catalogue; [68]: blank.

Social library catalogue: 375 books, listed in a mixture of full author and full title entries (the actual number of entries is much greater because of extensive cross-referencing), with place and date of publication, and, for donated books, name of donor; arranged alphabetically and, within each letter, by format, and numbered with a separate sequence of accession numbers for each format.

Evans 14392; Sabin 61788; Hildeburn 3179; Guerra a-575; *STE*, p. 676.

NN* (bound with 1770 Charter), PHi* (bound with 1770 Charter), PPL* (21 × 13 cm. — unbound), RPJCB* (bound with 1770 Charter).

See also McKay 96A (Bell)

1777

94 BELL, ROBERT, 1731?–1784

Books in physic, surgery, and chemistry, now selling at Bell's Book-Store. [Philadelphia: Printed by Robert Bell. 1777.]

8°: [A]²; 2 leaves, pp. [1–4]. [1]: caption title: 'Epilogue. Written by Mr. Garrick. Spoken by Mrs. Abington.', followed by the epilogue itself: 'In Parliament, whene'er a question comes, ... You that say No would damn it—the Ayes have it.'; [2]: title of catalogue (caption); on [2]: catalogue of medical books; [4]:

another caption title: 'At Bell's Book Store in Third-Street Philadelphia, may be had: Great variety of new and old Books in the Arts and Sciences; Likewise, Hebrew, Greek, Latin, English and French Classics; With History, Divinity, Law, Plays, Novels; and Instructive Entertainment.', followed by a general catalogue.

Bookseller's catalogue. Medical catalogue: 58 short to full author entries, consecutively numbered, and arranged in no apparent order. General catalogue: 40 short author entries, consecutively numbered, and arranged by subject (obviously intended as a selective and representative list). This catalogue was probably not published separately; it was printed at the back of Bell's 1777 Philadelphia edition of John Burgoyne's *The Maid of the Oaks*; it is listed here only because Bristol treats it as a separate item.

Bristol 4436; m.p. 43225; Guerra a-598; *STE*, p. 72.
NNNAM* (20 × 12 cm. — unbound).

[Bell, Robert, 1731?–1784
Catalogue of books to be sold at auction by Robert Bell, December 18th, 19th and 20th. Philadelphia: Printed by Robert Bell. 1777.]

Advertised in the *Pennsylvania Evening Post*, Dec. 12, 16, 1777. Hildeburn 3530; Evans 15241; McKay 97; *STE*, p. 72.

See also McKay 96B (Bowman)

———————— 1778 ————————

[Bell, Robert, 1731?–1784
Catalogue of a small collection of sentimental food to be exhibited at auction by Robert Bell, on the 15th, 16th and 17th of January. Philadelphia: Printed by Robert Bell. 1778.]

Advertised in the *Pennsylvania Ledger*, Jan, 14, 1778. Hildeburn 3686; Evans 15731; McKay 98; *STE*, p. 72.

[Bell, Robert, 1731?–1784
Catalogue of books in Bell's Circulating Library, containing above 2000 volumes. Philadelphia: Printed by Robert Bell. 1778.]

Advertised at the end of Zimmermann, *Strictures on National Pride* (Philadelphia: Bell, 1778)—Evans 16176. Hildeburn 3690; Evans 15734; *STE*, p. 72.

[Bell, Robert, 1731?–1784

Catalogue of books to be sold at auction, by Robert Bell, April 23, 24 and 25. Philadelphia: Printed by Robert Bell. 1778.]

According to *STE*, advertised in the *Royal Pennsylvania Gazette*, Apr. 24, 1778; McKay says *Pennsylvania Ledger*, Apr. 22. Hildeburn 3689; Evans 15732; McKay 100; *STE*, p. 72.

[Bell, Robert, 1731?–1784

Catalogue of books to be sold at auction, May 21, 22 and 23. Philadelphia: Printed by Robert Bell. 1778.]

According to *STE*, advertised in the *Royal Pennsylvania Gazette*, May 19, 1778; McKay says *Pennsylvania Ledger*, May 20. Hildeburn 3688; Evans 15733; McKay 101; *STE*, p. 72.

[Bell, Robert, 1731?–1784

Jewels and diamonds for sentimentalists, now on sale at Bell's Book-Store, next door to St. Paul's Church, Philadelphia. Philadelphia: Printed by Robert Bell. 1778.]

Advertised at the end of *Miscellanies for Sentimentalists* (Philadelphia: Bell, 1778) —Evans 15914. Hildeburn 3726; Evans 15735; *STE*, p. 72.

95   BELL, ROBERT, 1731?–1784

Robert Bell, bookseller, provedore to the sentimentalists, and professor of book-auctioniering in America, is just arrived from Philadelphia; with a small collection of modern, instructive, and entertaining books, which he will exhibit by auction, to the sentimentalists of the town, this evening, and to morrow evening; but no longer— At the time of the exhibition, they will then, instantaneously, either be sold or sacrificed, according to the taste of the company, by way of experiment. Hours of exhibiting from seven to nine each evening. Memorandum. Those who behold with their eyes, sentimental entertainment, going off reasonable, and do not improve this very great chance of purchasing the books by the assistance of the magical mallet, will probably wish in vain for such another opportunity. Catalogue of books with the prices printed, at which they ought to sell. [Philadelphia: Printed by Robert Bell. 1778?]

Broadsheet. 35×21.5 cm. Recto, title and catalogue (2 cols.); verso, numerous quotations, intended to encourage the buying of books.

Auction catalogue: 37 short to full author entries, consecutively numbered but otherwise unordered, with prices ('at which they ought to sell'). A memorandum notes the availability of books of all sorts at Bell's regular bookstore. Most of the books listed are Bell publications; others are apparently also Philadelphia editions, though not published by Bell. Date: the catalogue could have been published no earlier than 1778, since a third of the books listed in it were published by Bell in that year, but it might possibly have been published in 1779 since American (non-Bell) editions of two of the books listed in it first appeared in that year, although English editions of them were available earlier. This catalogue may be the one referred to by Hildeburn 3686, Evans 15731, and McKay 98, and listed as unlocated on p. 62 above.

Bristol 4643; m.p. 43414; Brigham, p. 43; *STE*, p. 72. DLC* (dated [178–?]), MWA*.

[Dellap, Samuel, fl. 1773–1793
Catalogue of books to be sold at auction at Samuel Dellap's auction room, on Jan. 15th, and six or seven following evenings. Philadelphia: Printed for Samuel Dellap, 1778.]

Advertised in the *Pennsylvania Evening Post*, Jan. 13, 1778. Hildeburn 3687; Evans 15781; McKay 99; *STE*, p. 216.

———————— 1779 ————————

96 AITKEN, ROBERT, 1734–1802
    J. M. [initials surrounded by type ornaments] R. Aitken, printer, book-binder, and bookseller, opposite the Coffee-House, Front-Street, Philadelphia, [all from 'R. Aitken' surrounded by type ornaments] 1779 [date also surrounded by type ornaments] performs all kinds of printing-work, plain and ornamental, he binds books in the most elegant manner; and has for sale, books in all languages, arts, and sciences; also, a neat assortment of stationary, and some patent medicines. The following books printed by R. Aitken, are to be sold single or by the dozen. [Philadelphia: Printed by Robert Aitken, 1779.]

Broadside. 40.5×23.5 cm. 1 col.

Publisher's catalogue: 19 short author and title entries, arranged in no apparent order.

Evans 16179; *STE*, p. 11.

PPL*.

[Catalogue of a collection of books, about 900 volumes, to be sold at Sheriff's sale, March 4. Philadelphia, 1779.]

Advertised in the *Pennsylvania Gazette*, Feb. 24, Mar. 3, 10, 1779. Hildeburn 3859; Evans 16221; McKay 102, *STE*, p. 138.

See also McKay 102A (Tongue)

———————————————— 1780 ————————————————

[Brown, William

Catalogue of a collection of valuable books to be sold by auction at the house of David Franks, Nov. 1, 1780. Philadelphia: Printed by Robert Bell. 1780.]

Advertised in the *Pennsylvania Gazette*, Nov. 1, 1780. Attribution of 'authorship' (auctioneer) from McKay; Hildeburn gives no author, and Evans and *STE* list it under Robert Bell. Hildeburn 4002; Evans 16710; McKay 104; *STE*, p. 72.

[A catalogue of the library of the late Reverend Francis Alison, D.D. To be sold at auction August 31, 1780. Philadelphia: Printed by John Dunlap? 1780.]

Advertised in the *Pennsylvania Packet*, July 18, 29, Aug. 1, 1780. Hildeburn 4003; Evans 16691; McKay 103; *STE*, p. 13 (under Alison).

See also McKay 102B (Duncan), 102C ([Semple]), 104A (Bell), 104B (Duncan)

———————————————— 1781 ————————————————

[Bayard, John, fl. 1781–1784

Catalogue of books to be sold at auction, October 23. Philadelphia: Printed by Robert Bell. 1781.]

According to McKay, advertised in the *Pennsylvania Packet*, Oct. 18, 20, 23, 1781; *STE* says *Pennsylvania Journal*, Oct. 17. Hildeburn, Evans, and *STE* list this catalogue under Robert Bell, but the advertisement gives Bayard as the auctioneer, though Bell's Book-store was the place of sale. Hildeburn 4086; Evans 17094; McKay 105; *STE*, p. 72.

97 FOSTER, THEODORE, 1752–1828

Providence, November 24, 1781. As a small acknowledgement of the grateful sentiments of esteem and respect, entertained by the subscriber, for the worthy freemen and inhabitants of the Town of Foster, he begs them to accept a book-case, and the books enumerated in the following catalogue, free of charge, for the use of the Town, and they will oblige their friend, and most obedient humble servant, Theodore Foster. Catalogue of books belonging to the Town of Foster. [colophon:] Providence: Printed by Bennett Wheeler. [1781.]

Broadside. 27×34 cm. 2 cols.

Town library catalogue: 30 consecutively numbered short to full author and title entries, most of a political or historical nature. The original of this item was in the library of Henry Russell Drowne of New York, which was destroyed by fire in 1935.

Evans 19410; Alden 854; Guerra a-684; *STE*, p. 276.

MWA*, RPJCB* (both are photostats of Drowne copy).

See also McKay 104C (Duncan [Middleton]), 104D (Russell), 105A (Bayard), 105B (Russell [Vassall]), 105C (Yancey), 105D (Bell)

———————————— 1782 ————————————

[Bailey, Francis?, 1735?–1815

Catalogue of a collection of books belonging to the Rev. Robert Smith, of South Carolina, and Mr. James Cannon, deceased, late of this city. To be sold at auction, April 24th. Philadelphia: Printed by Francis Bailey. 1782.]

Advertised in the *Freeman's Journal*, Apr. 24, 1782. Hildeburn 4189; Evans 17723; McKay 107; *STE*, p. 43.

[Bayard, John, fl. 1781–1784

Catalogue of a gentleman's very valuable library to be sold at auction, Oct. 17–26th. Philadelphia: Printed by Robert Bell. 1782.]

Advertised in the *Pennsylvania Gazette*, Oct. 15–17, 19, 1782. For the sequel to this catalogue, see the next item. Hildeburn 4191; Evans 17470 (assigned to Bell); McKay 110; *STE*, p. 66.

98 BAYARD, JOHN, fl. 1781–1784

A few more numbers belonging to the gentleman's very valuable library, which will be sold by auction, at the City Vendue Store, on the evening of Saturday the 26th of October, 1782. [Philadelphia: Printed by Robert Bell, 1782.]

Broadside. 28.5 × 24 cm. 2 cols.

Auction catalogue: 51 consecutively numbered items (numbers 527–77), 10 of them maps, and 41 short author book entries, arranged in no apparent order. The list of maps and books is signed 'John Bayard, Auctionier' [*sic*], and this is followed by an advertisement: 'Now Selling at Bell's Book-Store... Emma Corbett.' The title and numbering system of this broadside clearly imply a previous catalogue, probably the preceding, unlocated item. Bell is assigned as printer because of the presence of his advertisement.

McKay 111; Bristol 5521; m.p. 44174; *STE*, p. 66.

PHi* (catalogued under Bell).

[Bell, Robert, 1731?–1784

Catalogue of books to be sold at auction, Jan 30th. Philadelphia: Printed by Robert Bell, 1782.]

Advertised in the *Freeman's Journal*, Jan. 30, 1782. Hildeburn 4192; Evans 17468; McKay 106; *STE*, p. 72.

[Bell, Robert, 1731?–1784

Catalogue of books to be sold at auction, May 1st. Philadelphia: Printed by Robert Bell. 1782.]

Advertised in the *Freeman's Journal*, May 1, 1782. Evans 17469; McKay 108; *STE*, p. 72.

[Bell, Robert, 1731?–1784
Catalogue of books to be sold at auction, November 2d. Philadelphia: Printed by Robert Bell. 1782.]

Advertised in the *Freeman's Journal*, Nov. 2, 1782. Evans 17471; McKay 112; *STE*, p. 72.

[Catalogue of a curious and valuable collection of books, to be sold on Oct. 11th. Philadelphia, 1782.]

Advertised in the *Freeman's Journal*, Oct. 9, 1782. Hildeburn 4190; Evans 17488; McKay 109; *STE*, p. 138.

See also McKay 105E (Bayard), 106A (Bayard), 107A (Bayard), 108A (Bayard), 108B (Bayard), 112A (Bayard)

––––––––––––––––––– 1783 –––––––––––––––––––

[Bailey, Francis?, 1735?–1815
Catalogue of a collection of scarce and valuable books, belonging to a gentleman just arrived from Europe, with the price of each book affixed. Philadelphia: Printed by Francis Bailey. 1783.]

Advertised in the *Freeman's Journal*, June 25, 1783. Hildeburn 4282; Evans 17868 (assigns no author); *STE*, p. 43.

[Bayard, John, fl. 1781–1784
Con[tinuation of book auction begun Jan. 21, 1783?]. Philadelphia, 1783. Broadsheet.]

A fragment of such a catalogue was supposedly located at the Cadmus Book Shop in New York City at the time McKay compiled his list of auction catalogues; present location unknown. McKay 10127.

[Bell, Robert, 1731?–1784
Catalogue of books to be sold at auction, December 3d. Philadelphia: Printed by Robert Bell. 1783.]

Advertised in the *Pennsylvania Packet*, Dec. 2, 4, 6, etc., 1783. Mentioned in McKay 112H, but not treated as a separate entry. Evans 17835; *STE*, p. 72.

[Bell, Robert, 1731?–1784

Catalogue of books to be sold at auction, February 19th. Philadelphia: Printed by Robert Bell. 1783.]

According to McKay, advertised in the *Pennsylvania Packet*, Feb. 20, 22, 25, 1783; *STE* says *Pennsylvania Gazette*, Feb. 19. Hildeburn 4283; Evans 17831; McKay 112C; *STE*, p. 72.

[Bell, Robert, 1731?–1784

Catalogue of books to be sold at auction, May 6th. Philadelphia: Printed by Robert Bell. 1783.]

Advertised in the *Pennsylvania Packet*, May 3, 6, 8, 1783. Evans 17832; McKay 112D; *STE*, p. 72.

[Bell, Robert, 1731?–1784

Catalogue of books to be sold at auction, November 13th. Philadelphia: Printed by Robert Bell. 1783.]

Advertised in the *Pennsylvania Packet*, Nov. 13, 15, 18, Dec. 2, 4, etc., 1783. Evans 17834; McKay 112H; *STE*, p. 72.

[Bell, Robert, 1731?–1784

Catalogue of books to be sold at auction, October 30th. Philadelphia: Printed by Robert Bell. 1783.]

Advertised in the *Pennsylvania Packet*, Oct. 28, 30, Nov. 1, 4, 6, 8, 1783. Evans 17833; McKay 112G; *STE*, p. 72.

99 BELL, ROBERT, 1731?–1784

Just published and now selling, at Bell's Book-Store, in Third-Street, price one quarter of a dollar. A catalogue of a large collection of new and old books, in arts, sciences, and entertainment, for persons of all denominations, with the selling price printed to each book; now on sale, at said Bell's Book-Store, near St. Paul's Church, in Third-Street. Philadelphia: Printed by Robert Bell, in Third-Street. M,DCC,LXXXIII.

8°: [A]⁴B–L⁴; 44 leaves, pp. [1–9] 10–88 (80 misnumbered '66'). [1]: title; [2]: advertisements for 'New Publications' by Bell (12 books—full title entries, with prices); [9]: catalogue; on 87: advertisement for book to be published; 88: list of 21 charts and maps, with prices.

Bookseller's catalogue: 2421 consecutively numbered medium and short author entries, with prices, arranged alphabetically. There are actually two alphabetical lists: one, pp. [9]–80; the other, pp. 81–87. A note that appears at the end of each letter group in both the first and second lists mentions a supplement to be published in 'a few weeks.'

Evans 17830; Sabin 61520 and 61751; Hildeburn 4281; Guerra a–708; *STE*, p. 72.
CtY* (lacks ⅔ of leaf L4), DFo* (lacks pp. [1–6], 77–88), PHi* (22 × 14.5 cm. — bound), PPPrHi.

100 CARTER, JOHN, 1745–1814

Just imported from London, and to be sold by John Carter, at the Printing-Office, at Shakespear's Head, an assortment of books and stationary, among which are the following articles, viz. [Providence: Printed by John Carter, 1783.]

Broadside. 47 × 19 cm. 1 col.

Bookseller's catalogue: 125 short author entries, arranged in three groups (paragraph style): a large, unlabeled group; chapman books; gilt books for children. Date: the bottom left of the sheet carries the date, 'Providence, November 22, 1783.'

Bristol 5693; m.p. 44353; Alden 947; *STE*, p. 136.
RHi*.

[Prichard, William, fl. 1782–1809
Catalogue of the circulating library of William Prichard. Philadelphia, 1783.]

Advertised in the *Freeman's Journal*, Oct. 1, 1783. Hildeburn 4284; Evans 18143; *STE*, p. 702.

[Rhode Island College (Brown University). Library
Catalogue. Providence, 1783.]

Cutter 16. There is a ms. 'Catalogue of books ordered from England in 1783' at RPB, to which Cutter's entry probably refers.

See also McKay 112B (Bayard), 112E (Bell), 112F (Greenleaf)

———————— 1784 ————————

[Bell, Robert, 1731?–1784

Catalogue of books to be sold at auction, April 15. Philadelphia: Printed by Robert Bell. 1784.]

Advertised in the *Pennsylvania Gazette*, Apr. 14, 1784. Evans 18349; McKay 115; *STE*, p. 72.

[Bell, Robert, 1731?–1784

Catalogue of books to be sold at auction, April 22. Philadelphia: Printed by Robert Bell. 1784.]

Advertised in the *Pennsylvania Gazette*, Apr. 21, 1784. Evans 18350; McKay 116; *STE*, p. 72.

101 BELL, ROBERT, 1731?–1784

New and old, medical, surgical, and chemical works, lately imported, and now selling at Bell's Book-Store, near St. Paul's Church in Third-Street, Philadelphia; with the lowest price printed to each book. [Philadelphia: Printed by Robert Bell, 1784.]

8°: K2–4 L⁴; 7 leaves, pp. [75–88] [=14]. [75]: title (caption); on [75]: medical catalogue: on [87]: second caption title: 'New, and Old Miscellaneous Works, now on Sale at Bell's Book-Store in Third-Street, Philadelphia. With the Selling Price Printed to each Book.'; on [87]: miscellaneous catalogue.

Bookseller's catalogue: total of 394 entries. Medical catalogue: 352 consecutively numbered (omitting 168–182) medium and full author (mostly) and title entries, with prices, arranged alphabetically. Miscellaneous catalogue: 55 consecutively numbered (353–407) short and medium author and title entries, with prices, arranged alphabetically. This catalogue was printed with, and bound at the end of, Bell's 1784 Philadelphia edition of John Elliot's *The Medical Pocket-Book* (Evans 18456—copy at MWA); the text of this book ends on K1ᵛ, p. 74, and the catalogue begins immediately on K2ʳ. This catalogue is listed here because there are several reasons to believe that it was also issued separately. A note at the bottom of p. [80], the last page of sig. K, states: 'A Continuation of this Catalogue will be published on Monday next.' Apparently, sig. L, which picks up the alphabetical sequence of the medical catalogue in the middle of the H's, where it had been left at the end of sig. K, was published later and added to the beginning of the catalogue. In addition, an advertisement for the catalogue in the *Pennsylvania Gazette*, Jan. 14, 1784, implies that it was distributed separately. Finally, RPJCB possesses the first three leaves (K2–4) of this catalogue, which it lists as a separate item, and to which it assigns Evans number 18351, though Evans's entry has a different (assumed) title. *STE* suggests that rather than being a separate item, Evans 18351 probably refers to the catalogue at the back of Elliot's *Medical Pocket-Book*, described above.

Evans 18351 (?—not on m.p. under this number; can be found on m.p. at the end of 18456); Hildeburn 4452 (probably; title varies); *STE*, p. 72.

DNLM (bound with Elliot's *Medical Pocket-Book*), MWA (bound with Elliot's *Medical Pocket-Book*), RPJCB* (fragment, as noted; 20.5 × 13 cm. — unbound).

102 BELL, ROBERT, 1731?–1784

Thursday the 8th of April, 1784. Auction of books, will commence this evening, at Bell's Book-Store, near St. Paul's Church, in Third-Street, and the sale by auction will be continued, for several evenings successively, when a considerable variety of the most excellent authors in arts, sciences, and entertainment, will be instantaneously sold, or sacrificed, according to the taste of the company. Hours of sale, each evening from seven to nine o'clock. Printed catalogues of the books to be had at the place of sale. Conditions of sale.————To prevent insipidity, as soon as the magical mallet hath consigned the book to the highest bidder, the money to be paid upon the spot. [Philadelphia: Printed by Robert Bell, 1784.]

Broadsheet. 27.3 × 20.5 cm. 2 cols. each side.

Auction catalogue: 227 consecutively numbered, short author entries, arranged by format. Note at bottom of verso: 'A Continuation of this Catalogue will be published next Wednesday, the 14th of April 1784 [see the first unlocated Bell catalogue of 1784, p. 71 above]. And the sale by Auction will be continued on the Evenings of Thursday, Friday, and Saturday.' Not reproduced on Microprint.

Evans 18348; Hildeburn 4448; McKay 114; *STE*, p. 72.
CSmH*.

103 BOINOD, DANIEL, AND ALEXANDER GAILLARD, d. 1784

Catalogue des livres qui se trouvent chez Boinod & Gaillard. Les livres éclairent la multitude, humanisent les hommes puissants, charment le loisir des riches, instruisent toutes les classes de la société. Raynal. Philadelphia: [Printed by Charles Cist,] MDCCLXXXIV. [Se vend à un quart de dollar.]

8°: π⁴ A–P⁴; 60 leaves, pp. [i–viii], [1] 2–117 [118–20]. [i]: cover-title: 'Catalogue.'; [ii]: blank; [iii]: title (brackets around last sentence in original); [iv]: introduction: 'Aux Américains Libres.' 'To the Free Americans.' —bilingual (French on [iv] and [vi]; English on [v] and [vii]); [viii]: blank; [1]: catalogue of French books; 82: catalogue of Latin books; on 103: catalogue of English books; 113: catalogue of German books; 115: catalogue of Dutch books; [118]: blank.

Bookseller's catalogue. All segments of the catalogue give place and date of publication. Catalogue of French books: 1600 full title entries, arranged in full alphabetical order. Catalogue of Latin books: 475 short to full author entries, arranged by subject, and then in full alphabetical order within each subject. Subject headings: auctores classici Graeci & Latini; libri philosophici; libri historici, politici & juridici; libri medici, anatomici, chymici, & historiae naturalis. Catalogue of English books: 175 full title entries, arranged in full alphabetical order. Catalogue of German books: 42 short and medium author entries, arranged in full alphabetical order. Catalogue of Dutch books: 68 short and medium author entries, arranged in full alphabetical order. Printing is attributed to Cist because he normally did the printing for these publishers.

Evans 18371; Sabin 61519; *STE*, p. 99.

BL (the copy reproduced on m.p.; lacks sig. P, pp. 113–[120]), N, PHi* (22×13.5 cm. — unbound), PPL.

[Boinod, Daniel, and Alexander Gaillard, d. 1784

A catalogue of French, Latin, English, German, and Dutch books for sale by Boinod and Gaillard. Philadelphia: Printed by Charles Cist. 1784.]

Advertised in the *Pennsylvania Journal*, Jan. 17, 1784; advertisement probably refers to the preceding item. Hildeburn 4451; Evans 18372; *STE*, p. 99.

[Boyd, Alexander

Catalogue of a collection of modern erudition, to be sold at auction by Alexander Boyd. Philadelphia, 1784.]

Advertised in the *Freeman's Journal*, Feb. 25, 1784. Hildeburn 4450; Evans 18379; McKay 118; *STE*, p. 108.

[Boyd, Alexander, and John Bayard, fl. 1781–1784

Catalogue of books to be sold at auction, on March 11, 12 and 13, by Alexander Boyd and John Bayard, auctioneers. Philadelphia, 1784.]

Advertised in the *Pennsylvania Gazette*, Mar. 10, 1784. Hildeburn 4449; Evans 18380; McKay 113; *STE*, p. 108.

[Jackson and Dunn, Philadelphia
Catalogue of books for sale by Jackson and Dunn. Philadelphia: Printed by Robert Aitken. 1784. 12°; 10 pp.]

According to *STE*, 'entry from Aitken's accounts,' from which Evans presumably took the format and number of pages. Hildeburn 4446; Evans 18540; *STE*, p. 383.

[Murphy, William, fl. 1784
An addition to Murphy's catalogue of library-books, containing a scarce and valuable collection of the best ancient and modern authors extant. Baltimore: Printed by William Goddard. 1784.]

A circulating library catalogue, from an unspecified advertisement in the *Maryland Journal*. Evans 18616; Wheeler 331; *STE*, p. 546.

[Prichard, William, fl. 1782–1809
A catalogue of a very valuable and scarce collection of books, in various languages, arts and sciences, chiefly in good condition, many of them in elegant bindings, and consist of the most celebrated authors, in law, physic, divinity, history, philosophy, mathematics, husbandry, gardening, navigation, arithmetic, poetry, plays, novels, voyages, travels, classics, dictionaries, grammar, &c. &c. Which are now selling (the lowest prices marked in the catalogue) by William Prichard, bookseller and stationer at the American Circulating Library, opposite Letitiae-Court, Market-Street, Philadelphia, who gives a generous price for any library or parcel of books. Philadelphia, 1784.]

Advertised in the *Freeman's Journal*, June 9, 1784. Title from Evans. Hildeburn 4447; Evans 18740; *STE*, p. 702.

104 UNION LIBRARY SOCIETY OF
WETHERSFIELD, Connecticut
The constitution and by-laws of the Union Library Society of Wethersfield, with a catalogue of books, the property of said Society. Hartford: Printed by Hudson & Goodwin. M,DCC,LXXXIV.

4°: [A]⁴B⁴C²; 10 leaves, pp. [1–3] 4–19 [20]. [1]: title; [2]: blank; [3]: constitution; 9: by-laws; 12: catalogue; on 19: receipt form for the purchase of shares in the Society; [20]: blank.

Social library catalogue: 175 short author entries, arranged alphabetically.

Evans 18882; Sabin 103063; Bates 2005; Thompson, p. 259; *STE*, p. 990. CtHi* (20.5×14 cm. — unbound).

1785

105 BEERS, ISAAC, 1742?–1813

[Quotation on pleasure of books, from 'Knox's Essays'] Isaac Beers, has just imported from London, a large assortment of books and stationary, which he has now ready for sale, at his book-store, in New-Haven, viz. . . . [colophon:] New-Haven: Printed by Thomas and Samuel Green. [1785?]

Broadside. 47×28.5 cm. 4 cols.

Bookseller's catalogue: 400 short author entries, arranged by subject and alphabetically within subjects. Subject headings: divinity; history, travels, &c.; law; physick, surgery, &c.; mathematicks, astronomy, navigation, school-books, &c.; miscellaneous (largest category). Date: dated [1785?] by CtY; the latest novels listed are two first published in 1784, so the catalogue itself could have been published no earlier, and probably not much later.
CtY*.

[Campbell, Samuel, 1763?–1836

A catalogue of a valuable collection of books, in elegant bindings, and genuine London and Edinburgh editions. New York: Printed by Francis Childs and Co., for Samuel Campbell. 1785.]

Advertised in the *New York Daily Advertiser*, Sept. 17, 1785. Evans 18947; *STE*, p. 131.

106 CLARKSON, MATTHEW, 1758–1825, AND
EBENEZER HAZARD, 1744–1817

For sale at public vendue, on Thursday the 10th day of March, at the late dwelling house of Pierre Eugene du Simitiere, Esq. in Arch-street, between Third and Fourth-streets, where the State Lottery Office is now kept, the American Musæum. This curious collection was, for many years, the principal object of Mr. Du Simitiere's attention, and has been thought worthy of notice by both American and European literati: it consists of the following articles, which will be sold in lots, viz. . . . [colophon:] Philadelphia, printed by Charles Cist, at the corner of Fourth and Arch-streets. [1785.]

Broadside. 61.5×47 cm. 4 cols.

Auction catalogue: 270 short author and title entries, arranged in lots by subject (subject headings: almanacs and registers [not itemized]; architecture; catalogues of books and curiosities [not itemized]; dictionaries and grammars; drawing; divinity; geography and astronomy; heraldry; history; mathematics; miscellany; occult philosophy; natural history; physic and surgery; poetry; voyages and travels; books and papers relat. to America; newspapers); plus lots consisting of coins, curiosities, drawings and prints, horti sicci, and American money. The broadside is signed: 'Matthew Clarkson, Ebenezer Hazard, Administrators.' Date: Du Simitiere died in October 1784, and the sale was held on Mar. 10, 1785 (see *Pennsylvania Packet*, March 8, 9, 10, 1785). The title given by McKay is misleading, but the item referred to is the one described here.

Evans 18402; Hildeburn 4481; McKay 118A; *STE*, p. 154.
PPL*.

107 PRICHARD, WILLIAM, fl. 1782–1809

A catalogue of a scarce and valuable collection of books, in various languages, arts, and sciences; instructive and entertaining: consisting of history, biography, voyages, philosophy, politics, husbandry, letters, mathematics, novels, poetry, philosophy, travels, navigation, trade, gardening, plays, architecture, debates, classics, law, physic, divinity, &c. which are now selling by William Prichard, bookseller and stationer, at the American Circulating Library, opposite Letitia-Court, Market-Street. Philadelphia. Who gives a generous price for any library or parcel of books. [Philadelphia, 1785.]

8°: π^2[=F3, 4?] A–E⁴ [F]⁴ (–F3, 4); 24 leaves, pp. [i–iv], [1] 2–43 [44]. [i]: title; [ii]: blank; [iii]: advertisement (thanks public for encouragement and will endeavor to continue in their favor); [1]: catalogue; [44]: blank.

Bookseller's catalogue: 982 consecutively numbered short and medium (mostly) author entries, with prices, arranged by subject, and by format within each subject. Subject headings: history, biography, poetry, arts and sciences:—English, French, Italian, &c. (by far the largest category, it actually contains all subjects except those following, with some attempt to group like books together); divinity; libri classici; French school-books; law; new pamphlets, magazines, &c.; American poetical productions. Note on p. [iv]: 'In a few Days will be published, an Additional Catalogue to the Circulating Library'—no copy known. Date: could be no earlier than 1785, and probably no later than 1786, since the latest novels and magazines listed in the catalogue are several first published in 1785. Evans 19205; Hildeburn 4447 (?—dated 1784 and title varies); *STE*, p. 702. MWA, NN* (22×13.5 cm. — bound).

108 SPOTSWOOD, WILLIAM, 1753?–1805

Just published, a catalogue of new books, sold wholesale and retail by W. Spotswood, printer & bookseller; Front-street, west-side, between Market and Chesnut-streets, next door but one to the Custom-House. [Philadelphia, 1785.]

Broadside. 44×25 cm. 2 cols.

Bookseller's catalogue: 30 medium and full author entries, arranged alphabetically, plus advertisements for stationery and medicines. Date: could be no earlier than 1785, and probably no later than 1786, since the latest books listed in the catalogue are several first published in 1785.
DLC*.

See also McKay 118B (Boyd), 118C, 118D (Parker), 'Additions,' p. 179 (Pritchard)

––––––––––––––––––– 1786 –––––––––––––––––––

109 BEERS, ISAAC, 1742?–1813

A catalogue of books, stationary and other articles, sold by Isaac Beers, at his book-store in New-Haven. New-Haven: Printed by Meigs & Dana, 1786.

12°: [A]⁴B²C⁴D²E²; 14 leaves, pp. [i–iii] iv [5] 6–27 [28]. [i]: title; [ii]: blank; [iii]: 'Sentiments' (quotations encouraging reading); [5]: catalogue; [28]: blank.

Bookseller's catalogue: 800 short and medium author entries, arranged by subject and alphabetically within subjects. Subject headings: history, biography, voyages, travels, &c.; divinity, ecclesiastical history, &c.; law; physic, surgery, chemistry, &c.; poetry; arts & sciences, mathematics, astronomy, navigation, trade & commerce, English dictionaries, agriculture & geography; novels & romances; classics, Greek, Latin, Hebrew,—books for learning French, grammars, &c.; miscellanies; books of instruction for children & young people, and for the use of schools; small histories &c. commonly called Newberry's books; tragedies; comedies; music; miscellaneous articles (mostly stationery). Note on

p. 27: 'An Appendix will be added to the foregoing upon every New Importation.' See item 113 below.

Bates 1902; Bristol 6242; m.p. 44852 (not reproduced); *STE*, p. 70.
CtY* (15×9 cm. — unbound).

[Campbell, Samuel, 1763?–1836

A catalogue of books, in divinity, sermons, and ecclesiastical history, to be sold at the most reasonable prices. (Catalogues to be had gratis.) New York: Printed for Samuel Campbell's new book store, no. 41, Hanover-Square, four doors east from the corner of the Old Slip. 1786.]

'From an advertisement,' according to *STE*. Evans 19537; *STE*, p. 131.

[Campbell, Samuel, 1763?–1836

Samuel Campbell's sale catalogue for 1786. Containing above five thousand volumes, being a choice collection of books, in every branch of science and literature, all new, the best editions, in good bindings (except otherwise expressed in the catalogue) and will be sold at the most reasonable prices at Samuel Campbell's new book and stationary store, no. 44, Hanover-Square, corner of Old-Slip. New York: Printed by Francis Childs, for Samuel Campbell. 1786.]

'Entry from an advertisement,' according to *STE*. Evans 19538; *STE*, p. 131.

[Catalogue of jewels and diamonds for sentimentalists! Lately returned from the eastward. At the bookstore of the late deceased [Robert Bell] will begin the sale of a number of said decedents jewels and diamonds for sentimentalist! Philadelphia: Printed by Francis Bailey? 1786.]

'Entry from advertisements,' according to *STE*. Evans 19544; *STE*, p. 138.

110 CLARK, STEPHEN

A catalogue of the Annapolis Circulating Library, consisting of near fifteen hundred volumes, in agriculture, arithmetic, astronomy, biography, chymistry, commerce, gardening, geography, geometry, history, husbandry, law, military affairs, mathematics, navigation, painting, physic, rhetoric, surgery, surveying, voyages, travels, plays, novels, magazines, &c. Which are lent to read, by Stephen Clark, bookseller, stationer and bookbinder, in Church-street, Annapolis, where may be had, all new books, stationary wares of all sorts, school-books, jewellery, plated wares, watches, and a great many other articles of store-goods too tedious to mention. Books bought, sold, or exchanged. [Annapolis: Printed by Frederick Green, 1786.]

8°: [A]⁴B–C⁴ˣC⁴D–E⁴F²(–F²); 25 leaves, pp. [1–7] 8–49 [50]. [1]: half-title: 'A catalogue of the Annapolis Circulating Library'; [2]: blank; [3]: title; [4]: blank; [5]: conditions; [6]: blank; [7]: catalogue; [50]: stationery and errata.

Circulating library catalogue: 705 consecutively numbered, short to full author and title entries, arranged by a strange combination of subject and format: history, &c. folio, quarto and octavo; histories, voyages, travels, &c.; divinity, agriculture, &c. octavo; trade, physic, medicine, chirurgery, &c.; letters, miscellanies, poems, &c.; law; astronomy, navigation, geography, &c.; travels, trials, cookery, &c.; dictionaries. octavo; histories, voyages, travels, &c. duodecimo; miscellaneous periodical poems, &c. duodecimo; memoirs, lives, letters, &c.; translations from the classics; gardening, poems, plays, &c.; divinity, physics, &c. duodecimo; novels, romances, &c. (the largest category, in alphabetical order by title); arithmetic, &c.; poems, &c.; French books, in duodecimo; voyages, travels, miscellanies, &c. octavo. Date: dated [1783] by Evans, Wheeler, and Guerra but it could have been no earlier than 1786, and probably not much later, since the latest novel listed in the catalogue is one first published in 1786, and quite a few of the novels listed date from 1784–85. Attribution of printer from Wheeler, whose collation of this item appears to be incorrect.

Evans 17872; Wheeler 284; Guerra a-709; *STE*, p. 153.

MdHi* (lacks pp. [1–2], 47–[50]; 15.5×9.5 cm. — unbound), Maryland Diocesan Archives, on deposit at MdHi*.

111 MARTIN, WILLIAM

Catalogue of Martin's Circulating Library, at no. 45, Main-street, Boston. [Boston:] Printed by Edmund Freeman. M,DCC,LXXXVI.

8°: [A]⁴B⁴; 8 leaves, pp. [1–3] 4–16. [1]: title; [2]: terms; [3]: catalogue.

Circulating library catalogue: 450 short author entries, arranged alphabetically.

Bristol 6312; m.p. 44915; Shera, pp. 149, 261; *STE*, p. 450.

RPJCB* (18.5×12.5 cm. — bound).

[Prichard, William, fl. 1782–1809
Catalogue of books by auction at Prichard's Auction-Room, in Pew-

ter Platter-Alley, under the great lamp, December 6, 1786. Philadelphia: Printed by Eleazer Oswald. 1786.]

Advertised in the *Pennsylvania Packet*, Dec. 7–9, 1786. Evans 19938; McKay 120; *STE*, p. 702.

[Prichard, William?, fl. 1782–1809

Catalogue of books by auction, at the old City Vendue-Store, in Front-street, between Market and Arch-streets; the sale will be continued this evening the 25th [January, 1786] instant, from 6 o'clock till 9. The collection consisting of great variety of ancient and modern authors, with every species of useful and entertaining literature. Philadelphia: Printed by Carey and Co. 1786.]

Advertised in the *Pennsylvania Packet*, Jan. 12, 14, etc., 1786. Attribution of 'authorship' (auctioneer) from McKay. Evans 19543; McKay 119; *STE*, p. 138 (under title).

[Roberts, Thomas

Catalogue of a very extensive assortment of books and stationary. Charleston: Printed by Childs, Haswell and M'Iver, for Thomas Roberts. 1786.]

'Entry from an advertisement,' according to *STE*. Evans 19966; *STE*, p. 743.

[Wright, S., and Co., Charleston, South Carolina

A catalogue of new books amongst which are some of the best authors. Charleston: Printed by Childs, M'Iver & Co. for S. Wright & Co. 1786.]

'Entry from an advertisement,' according to *STE*. Evans 20163; *STE*, p. 1016.

112 YOUNG, WILLIAM, 1755–1829

William Young's catalogue for 1787. Books. Voyages, history, arts and sciences, divinity, church history, natural history, poetry, translations, travels, antiquities, mathematics, philosophy, geography, novels, music, miscellanies. English, French, Latin, and Greek school books and classics, small histories, and gilt books for children. Stationary. Imperial, medium, royal, demy, and foolscap writing paper.

Blank books ready made, or furnished to order. Memorandum books, slates, patent pencils, ink-powder, ink-stands, quills, wax, wafers, &c. &c. Printing work performed by Young and M'Culloch, the corner of Chesnut and Second-streets, Philadelphia. [Philadelphia: Printed by Young and M'Culloch, 1786.]

8°: π^2A–B⁴[C]⁴D²; 16 leaves, pp. [i–ii], [1–3] 4–30. [i]: title; [ii]: list of 12 'Books just Published'; [1]: 'Cash for Rags'—a plea to bring in rags, signed and dated: 'William Young. Philadelphia, October 20, 1786.'; [3]: catalogue; 30: advertisement for *Father Tammany's Almanac for 1787*, 'Just Published by Young & M'Culloch.'

Bookseller's catalogue: 775 short author entries, numbered consecutively (by fives) through 695, most of them in one fully alphabetical list, with a separate brief list of school books and classics at the end. Attribution of printer from MWA. Evans 20173; Sabin 106123; Brigham, p. 44; *STE*, p. 1023.
MWA* (17.5×11 cm. — bound).

See also McKay 119A (Rousselet), 119B (Procter), 119C (Hinkley)

────────── **1787** ──────────

113 BEERS, ISAAC, 1742?–1813

Appendix. To Beers's catalogue of books. August, 1787. [New Haven: Printed by Meigs and Dana, 1787.]

12°: [A]⁴; 4 leaves, pp. [1] 2–7 [8]. [1]: title (caption); on [1]: catalogue; [8]: blank.

Bookseller's catalogue: 200 short author entries, as in Beers's 1786 catalogue, item 109 above, with which this item is bound at CtY, but with these subject headings: divinity; history, voyages & travels; law; physic surgery &c.; novels, romances, &c.; miscellaneous; poetry; books for learning French; tragedies; comedies; magazines.
Bates 1901; Bristol 6446; m.p. 45035 (not reproduced); *STE*, p. 70.
CtY* (15×9 cm. — bound).

114 CAMPBELL, SAMUEL, 1763?–1836

Samuel Campbell's sale catalogue for 1787. Containing above ten thousand volumes, being a choice collection of books, in every branch of science and literature, all new, the best editions, in good bindings and will be sold at the most reasonable prices, at Samuel

Campbell's new book and stationary store, no. 44, Hanover Square, corner of the Old Slip, New-York. Gentlemen by applying soon, will the more readily procure the books they want; though it is proposed to keep this catalogue complete, by supplying the place of such books as may be sold off, besides making the addition of all new publications of merit. Orders will be thankfully received, and executed with the utmost care and punctuality, with a very handsome allowance made to those who purchase quantities. New-York: Catalogues delivered (gratis) by Samuel Campbell. MDCCVXXXVII [i.e., 1787].

12°: π1[=D2?] A–C⁶[D]²(–D²); 20 leaves, pp. [1–3] 4–40. [1]: title; [2]: index; [3]: catalogue; on 37: stationery; 38: music and prints; 39: list of 16 books 'printed for Samuel Campbell'; on 40: advertisement for primers and almanacs.

Bookseller's catalogue: 1007 consecutively numbered short to full author entries, arranged by subject, and then by format within each subject. Subject headings: history, voyages, travels, miscellanies, and biography; divinity, sermons, and ecclesiastical history; physic, surgery, anatomy, chemistry, and midwifery; arts and sciences, architecture, agriculture, arithmetic, bookkeeping, mathematics, geography, &c.; law; poems, poetical translations, dramatic works, song books, fables, &c.; novels and romances; English dictionaries, grammars, school books, &c., for the English classes; books for the Latin classes; books for the French classes; books for the Greek classes; pamphlets, tracts, &c.; tragedies, comedies, farces, &c.; chap books and small histories; Newbery's books, for little masters and misses; books omitted.

Evans 20260; Brigham, p. 44; *STE*, p. 131.

MWA* (19×11.5 cm. — bound).

[Dellap, Samuel, fl. 1773–1793

Catalogue of books by auction . . . at Samuel Dellap's Auction-Room, in Third, the corner of Chesnut-street. October 20, 1787. Philadelphia: Printed by Dunlap and Claypoole. 1787.]

Advertised in the *Pennsylvania Packet*, Oct. 19, 20, 22–24, 1787. Evans 20329; McKay 122; *STE*, p. 216.

[Duplessis, Peter Le Barbier?

Catalogue of the sale by public auction, at Mr. Duplessis' Long-Room, in Church-Alley, near Third-Street, above Market-Street. The libraries of Sam. Wharton, Esq, & Sam. Garrigues, bankrupts, being a collection of most valuable books in elegant bindings, and good preservation. On Friday, the 20th [April] instant at ten o'clock in the forenoon, will begin the sale, &c. Philadelphia: Printed by Eleazer Oswald. 1787.]

Advertised in the *Pennsylvania Packet*, Apr. 19, 20, 1787. Evans 20884; McKay 121; *STE*, p. 235.

115 FRIENDS' LIBRARY, Philadelphia
Catalogue of books in Friends' Library [Philadelphia: Printed by Joseph James, 1787.]

8°: [A]⁴B–D⁴; 16 leaves, pp. [1] 2–32. [1]: title (caption); on [1]: catalogue.

Social library catalogue: 850 medium author and title entries, arranged by format, and alphabetically within each format, and numbered consecutively within each format. The number of entries given here counts individual titles within numerous 'Collections of Tracts.' A large majority of the books are of a religious nature. Note on p. 2: 'The Books set down in this Catalogue, and marked with an Asterisk, were the Gift of our much esteemed Friend, Anthony Benezet, late deceased' [in 1784]. Date: Evans, *STE*, and MH date it [1795]; MWA and NjR date it [1794], probably on the basis of a ms. note on the NjR copy dated 'Jan. 24, 1794.' But Friends' Minutes at PPL show that the date was 1787 and the printer was Joseph James.

Evans 29312; *STE*, p. 676.

MH* (has additional, blank preliminary leaf), MWA* (19.5×12 cm. — unbound), NjR*, PPAmP*, PPL*.

116 GAINE, HUGH, 1726–1807
Catalogue of books and stationary, &c. sold by Hugh Gaine, at his book store and printing-office, at the Bible, in Hanover-Square. New-York: Printed by Hugh Gaine, at the Bible, in Hanover-Square, M,DCC,LXXXVII.

12°: [A]⁴B²C⁴D²; 12 leaves, pp. [1–3] 4–24. [1]: title; [2]: blank; [3]: catalogue; on 22: stationery; on 23: patent medicines; on 23: jewelry.

Bookseller's catalogue: 750 short author entries, most of them in one alphabetical list, with two brief, subject lists at the end (small histories, or chapmen books; plays).

Bristol 6495; m.p. 45073; Brigham, p. 45; *STE*, p. 297.

MWA* (18.5×12 cm. — bound).

117 GUILD, BENJAMIN, 1749–1792

A catalogue of a large assortment of books consisting of the most celebrated authors in history voyages travels geography antiquities philosophy novels divinity physick surgery anatomy arts sciences husbandry architecture navigation mathematicks law periodical publications poetry plays musick, &c. &c. To be sold by Benjamin Guild at the Boston Book-Store, no. 59 Cornhill, Boston. [Boston, 1787?]

8°: [A]⁴B–D⁴; 16 leaves, pp. [1–3] 4–32. [1]: title; [2]: list of stationery and note about supplying libraries and country traders; [3]: catalogue.

Bookseller's catalogue: 925 short (mostly) and medium author entries, most of them in one fully alphabetical list, with several brief subject lists at the end (children's books; plays; instrumental musick; vocal musick; charts). Date: Evans and STE date it [1790]; RPJCB dates it [1786?] because they examined the catalogue and found no items listed in it that had been published later than 1785. But the Printers File at MWA indicates that Guild bought the Boston Book-Store from Ebenezer Batelle in 1787 and moved it to no. 59 Cornhill in that year. The most likely date, therefore, is 1787.

Evans 22545; STE, p. 331.

RPJCB* (22.5×14.5 cm. — unbound).

118 GUILD, BENJAMIN, 1749–1792

Addition to a catalogue of a large assortment of books . . . [as in previous item] &c. &c. To be let or sold by Benjamin Guild at the Boston Book-Store, no. 59 Cornhill, Boston. [Boston, 1787?]

8°: [A]⁸; 8 leaves, pp. [1–3] 4–16. [1]: title; [2]: conditions of the circulating library; [3]: catalogue.

Circulating library and bookseller's catalogue: 375 short and medium author (mostly) and title entries, arranged in full alphabetical order. Date: dated [1788?] by MWA, Bristol, and STE, but since many of the novels listed in the catalogue were first published in 1785 or 1786, only a few in 1787, and none in 1788, and since this catalogue is clearly a supplement to the previous item, 1787 seems to be the most likely date.

Bristol 6711; m.p. 45266; Brigham, p. 50 (dated [1791]); STE, p. 331.

MWA* (22×13.5 cm. — bound).

119 LIBRARY OF SAYBROOK, LIME, AND GUILFORD, Connecticut

A catalogue of books, which belong to the Library of Saybrook, Lime, and Guilford. [1787?]

Broadside. 41.5 × 25.5 cm. 3 cols.

Social library catalogue: 230 short author entries, arranged alphabetically. Date: Shera, p. 103, dates it [ca. 1760], and CtY dates it [ca. 1765?], but at least one of the books listed in the catalogue was first published as late as 1784. Shera also notes that 'in 1787 the collection was valued at £167/7/–, it then having sixty folios, twenty-four quartos, and three hundred and seven volumes of other sizes' (p. 33; Shera cites the Trumbull Manuscript Collections at CtY, and Bernard Steiner, *History of the Plantation of Menunkatuck* [Baltimore: author, 1897], pp. 410–11). Since the number of volumes listed in the catalogue described above corresponds with these figures, this catalogue probably was printed in 1787. The majority of the entries are of a religious nature. The catalogue is in the Trumbull Manuscript Collections at CtY, and is mentioned in R. Malcolm Sills, 'The "Trumbull Manuscript Collections" and Early Connecticut Libraries,' in *Papers in Honor of Andrew Keogh* (New Haven: privately printed, 1938), pp. 330, 333. Shera, pp. 33, 103, Plate II (photoreproduction); Thompson, p. 258. CtY*.

[Prichard, William, fl. 1782–1809
Catalogue of a collection of modern books. Will be exposed for sale, to the highest bidder, selected from several invoices of the latest importations from London, Dublin and Glasgow. Prichard's Auction Room, November 17, 1787, and every night this week. Philadelphia: Printed by Eleazer Oswald. 1787.]

Advertised in the *Independent Gazette*, Nov. 17, 1787. Evans 20661; McKay 123; *STE*, p. 702.

120 PRICHARD, WILLIAM, fl. 1782–1809

A catalogue of ancient and modern books, for 1787, in various languages, arts, and sciences, which are now selling at the prices affixed, by William Prichard, printer and bookseller, in Market Street between Front and Second Streets; where libraries are bought and books exchanged. Philadelphia: Printed by W. Prichard and P. Hall, in Market Street, between Front and Second Streets. [1787.]

8°: [A–E]⁴; 20 leaves, pp. [1–2] 3–32, ²1–8. [1]: title; [2]: blank; 3: main catalogue; 32: stationery and jewelry, and advertisement (Prichard and Hall do all kinds of printing); ²1: caption title ('Prichard's Sale Catalogue'); on ²1: supplementary catalogue.

Bookseller's catalogue. Main catalogue: 1309 short author entries (1209 consecutively numbered books and 100 unnumbered pamphlets), with prices, arranged by subject and by format within subjects. Subject headings: history, biography, &c. arts and science:—English, French, Italian &c.; novels; poetry; divinity; law; physic; agriculture and botany; school books, Greek, Latin and French; English school books; livres Francois; pamphlets. Supplementary catalogue: total of 370 entries, without prices; 78 consecutively numbered entries for prints framed; entries for prints unframed (16), musical instruments (20), music in books (100 short title entries), music in sheets, songs, etc. (32 short title entries), guns and swords (5), and odd volumes (120 short author entries) are unnumbered. Not reproduced on Microprint.

Evans 20660; Sabin 65481; *STE*, p. 702.

PPiU* (20×11.5 cm. — bound).

[Prichard, William, fl. 1782–1809

Catalogue of two extensive libraries of books late the property of gentlemen, deceased, consisting of many scarce and valuable authors. Prichard's Auction Room, next door to the Post-Office, in Chesnut-street. November 28 to December 5, 1787. Philadelphia: Printed by Eleazer Oswald. 1787.]

Advertised in the *Pennsylvania Packet*, Nov. 28, et seq., 1787. Evans 20662; McKay 124; *STE*, p. 702.

[Prichard, William, fl. 1782–1809

Prichard's Auction Room. December 8th. Lovers of literature will have an opportunity of augmenting their libraries with some of the best editions of the most approved and valuable authors. Philadelphia: Printed by Eleazer Oswald. 1787.]

Advertised in the *Pennsylvania Packet*, Dec. 8, 11, 1787. Evans 20663; McKay 125; *STE*, p. 702.

[Prichard, William, fl. 1782–1809

Prichard's Auction Room, next door to the Post Office, on Wednesday evening, the 19th [December] instant and every succeeding evening this week, where will be sold the most valuable collection of ancient and modern authors, that were ever yet dispatched beneath the stroke of the mallet on this side of the Atlantic. Philadelphia: Printed by Eleazer Oswald. 1787.]

Advertised in the *Pennsylvania Packet*, Dec. 17, etc., 1787. Evans 20664; McKay 126; *STE*, p. 702.

121 THOMAS, ISAIAH, 1749–1831

Catalogue of books to be sold by Isaiah Thomas, at his bookstore in Worcester, Massachusetts. Consisting of many celebrated authors in history, voyages, travels, geography, antiquities, philosophy, novels, miscellanies, divinity, physick, surgery, anatomy, arts, sciences, husbandry, architecture, navigation, mathematicks, law, periodical publications, poetry, plays, musick, &c. &c. MDCCLXXXVII. Printed at Worcester by Isaiah Thomas.

12°: [A]⁴[B]²C⁴D–E²; 14 leaves, pp. [1–2] 3–26 [27–28]. [1]: title; [2]: blank; 3: catalogue; on 24: stationery; [27]: advertisement for Thomas's various services (supplies libraries, books bought and exchanged, printing and binding performed); [28]: blank.

Bookseller's catalogue: 550 short author entries, arranged by subject. Subject headings: divinity; history, miscellanies, &c.; novels, sentimental works, &c.; tragedies and comedies; physick, surgery, &c.; architecture; dictionaries; geography and arithmetick; classical and school books; children's books; chapman's books. *STE* incorrectly dates the catalogue MDCCXXXVIII.

Evans 20745; Sabin 95400; Nichols 125; Brigham, p. 45; *STE*, p. 829.

MHi*, MWA* (20 × 12 cm. — bound).

See also McKay 120A (Prichard), 120B (Barkley), 120C (Prichard), 120D (Prichard), 120E (Smith), 120F (Smith), 121A (Barclay), 121B (Hayt), 121C (Prichard), 122A (Prichard), 122B (Procter), 122C (Dellap), 123A (Hayt), 124A (Prichard), 'Additions,' p. 179

——————————————— 1788 ———————————————

[Bradford, William, 1719–1791
Catalogue of books just imported from London, and to be sold by W. Bradford. Philadelphia: Printed by William Bradford, October, 1788.]

Probably from a newspaper advertisement. Evans 20980; *STE*, p. 110.

122 DOBSON, THOMAS, 1751–1823

Thomas Dobson, bookseller and stationer, at the new stone house, in Second street, below the Market, the seventh door above

Chesnut street,—has for sale, wholesale and retail, . . . [Philadelphia: Printed by Thomas Dobson, 1788.]

Broadside. 43 × 38 cm. 3 cols.

Bookseller's catalogue: 115 short to full author (mostly) and title entries, with prices, arranged in no apparent order, plus a list of stationery articles. An advertisement at the bottom of the sheet, noting the availability of 'a very General Assortment of Books' in many subject areas, indicates that this catalogue was probably intended as a representative sampling of Dobson's stock. Date: the catalogue lists 'Doctor Percival's Father's Instructions to his Children . . . (will be speedily published.)' and '(In the Press) A New American Edition of Nicholson's Introduction to Natural Philosophy,' both of which were printed by Dobson in 1788.

Bristol 6696; m.p. 45252 (not reproduced); Sealock 147; *STE*, p. 227. PHi* (with Nead Papers).

123 FOLSOM, JOHN WEST, 1758–1825
Catalogue of books, sold by John W. Folsom, no. 30, Union-Street, near the Market, Boston. [Boston, 1788?]

12°: [A]⁶; 6 leaves, pp. [1] 2–12. [1]: title (caption); on [1]: catalogue; on 11: list of stationery.

Bookseller's catalogue: 250 short to full author entries, most of them in one alphabetical list, with two separate, brief subject lists at the end (small books for children; plays, comedies. &c.). Date: dated [1790?] by MH; Folsom was at 30 Union Street from 1787 through the end of the century; the catalogue could be no earlier than 1788 since the latest novels listed in it are several first published in 1788, making 1788 or 1789 more likely then 1790.

MH* (18 × 11 cm. — bound).

124 GUILD, BENJAMIN, 1749–1792
Select catalogue of Benjamin Guild's Circulating Library, containing principally novels, voyages, travels, poetry, periodical publications, and books of entertainment, at the Boston Book-Store, no. 59, Cornhill. Boston: Printed by Edmund Freeman. 1788.

Small 4°: [A]⁴B⁴C²; 10 leaves, pp. [1–2] 3–7 [8] 9–20. [1]: title; [2]: conditions; 3: catalogue; 20: list of stationery, and note about supplying gentlemen's libraries and country traders.

Circulating library and bookseller's catalogue: 525 short author entries, arranged in full alphabetical order. Note on p. 19: 'The foregoing is a selection from the [gener]al assortment intended for the convenience of subscr[ibers an]d others who do not wish for a complete catalogue: and they are not only for loan but for sale, together with a very numerous collection of Authors in the various branches of science, such as Law, Physick, Divinity, Agriculture, Navigation, &c. Catalogues of which may be seen at the above place.'

Shera, pp. 149, 261.

MH* (18 × 11.5 cm. — unbound).

[Prichard, William, fl. 1782–1809

Catalogue of a large and valuable collection of books, moral, scientific, and amusing, to be sold by William Prichard, October 24th, 1788. Philadelphia: Printed by Eleazer Oswald? 1788.]

Advertised in the *Pennsylvania Packet*, Oct. 24–25, 1788. Evans 21406; McKay 128; *STE*, p. 702.

125   RUSSELL, JOSEPH, 1734–1795, AND SAMUEL CLAP, 1745–1809

Catalogue of books, belonging to the estate of the late Benjamin Lincoln, Esq; Attorney at Law, to be sold at public vendue, at Russell and Clap's Auction-Room, Court-Street, on Wednesday, May, 7, 1788, precisely at ten in the morning. [Boston: Printed by Adams and Nourse, 1788.]

Broadside. 39 × 31 cm. 3 cols.

Auction catalogue: 120 consecutively numbered, short author entries, mostly law books, arranged in no apparent order. MH calls its unique copy a variant of Evans 21204, but it probably is the only real item, since Evans's description was not based on an actual copy. This catalogue is not reproduced on Microprint in *EAI*. Attribution of printer is from Evans.

Evans 21204; McKay 127; *STE*, p. 753.

MH*.

126   UNION LIBRARY COMPANY OF HATBOROUGH, Pennsylvania

The charter, laws, and catalogue of books, of the Union Library Company of Hatborough. With a short account of the first establishment thereof prefixed. Philadelphia: Printed by Zachariah Poulson, Jun.r on the west side of Fourth-Street, between Market and Arch-Streets. M DCC LXXXVIII.

8°: [A]⁴B–D⁴E²; 18 leaves, pp. [1–4] 5–7 [8] 9–17 [18–19] 20–36. [1]: title; [2]: blank; [3]: 'A Short Account of the Establishment of the Library'; [4]: charter; [8]: 'An Act . . .' [laws]; [18]: list of members; [19]: catalogue.

Social library catalogue: 382 mostly short and medium author entries, with a smattering of quasi-subject entries [i.e., 'Halton's Arithmetick' is also listed as 'Arithmetick (Halton's entire system of),' a feature not unique to this catalogue], numbered non-consecutively with accession/shelf numbers, and arranged alphabetically; donors of books named. See Chester T. Hallenbeck, 'A Colonial Reading List from the Union Library of Hatboro, Pennsylvania,' *PMHB* 56 (1932): 289–340, for a reprint of some of the borrowing records from this library.

Evans 21138; Sabin 30831; Cutter 17; *STE*, p. 347.

PPL* (19.5 × 12 cm. — bound).

See also McKay 126A (Smith), 126B (Prichard), 126C (Prichard), 126D (Prichard), 126E (Prichard), 126F (Prichard), 126G (Prichard), 126H (Prichard), 126I (Prichard), 127A (Dellap), 127B (Jay), 127C (Smith), 128A (Prichard), 128B (Barclay), 128C (Smith), 128D (Jones), 128E (Procter)

—————— 1789 ——————

127 CAMPBELL, SAMUEL, 1763?–1836

Samuel Campbell's catalogue of books, for 1789. Comprehending above twenty thousand volumes, in arts, sciences and miscellaneous literature, forming a general assortment of the principal authors ancient and modern; among which will be found, the following scarce and valuable books, [list of 38 books]. The books are in general good editions and well bound, except otherwise expressed in the catalogue, and will be sold for cash, at the most reasonable prices. Country merchants and teachers will particularly find it their interest in applying for books and stationary, at Samuel Campbell's book and stationary store, no. 44, Hanover-Square, corner of the Old-Slip, New York, where catalogues are delivered (gratis) to gentlemen who please to call or send for them. [New York: Printed by Samuel Campbell, 1789.]

8°: π1[=G4] [A]⁴B–F⁴[G]⁴(–G4); 28 leaves, pp. [1–2] [5] 6–48 [49] 50–53 [54] 55–58 [=56]. [1]: title; [2]: index; [5]: catalogue; [49]: appendix; on 52: stationery; [54]: 'Books printed for and sold by Samuel Campbell'; on 57: second part of appendix.

Bookseller's catalogue (including appendices): 1532 consecutively numbered (except for the 24 entries in the second appendix), short and medium author entries, with place and date of publication, arranged by format and within format by subject. Subject headings are the same as in Campbell's 1787 catalogue (item 114 above), except 'natural and moral philosophy' has been added to the 'arts and sciences . . .' heading, 'music, vocal and instrumental' is an added heading, and the order of appearance of the headings has been changed. Publisher's catalogue of books printed for and sold by Samuel Campbell: 13 full author and title entries, with prices, and descriptive and laudatory comments. Note on p. [2]: 'The various impositions to which the public are daily subjected in purchasing incorrect and spurious editions, has induced S.C. to print at the name of each book, the place where, and the time when printed, that purchasers may at one view observe that the books in this collection are in general the best editions, and many of them scarce and valuable.' The statement in *EAI* that the 'unique copy is mislaid' is now doubly incorrect.

Bristol 6910; m.p. 45447 (not reproduced); Brigham, p. 46; *STE*, p. 131.
MWA* (lacks pp. 53–56), RPB* (21.5×14 cm. — unbound; lacks most of the t.p.).

128 CRUKSHANK, JOSEPH, 1746?–1836

A catalogue of books to be sold by Joseph Crukshank, printer and stationer, in Market-Street, between Second and Third-Streets, Philadelphia. [Philadelphia: Printed by Joseph Crukshank,] MDCC-LXXXIX.

12°: A⁶; 6 leaves, pp. [1–3] 4–12. [1]: title; [2]: blank; [3]: catalogue; on 12: list of stationery.

Bookseller's catalogue: 250 short and medium author entries, arranged alphabetically.

Bristol 6929; m.p. 45461; *STE*, p. 196.
PPL* (17.5×11 cm. — bound).

129 GUILD, BENJAMIN, 1749–1792

New select catalogue of Benjamin Guild's Circulating Library, containing principally novels, voyages, travels, poetry, periodical publications, and books of entertainment, at the Boston Book-Store, no. 59, Cornhill. Boston: Printed for Benjamin Guild. MDCCLXXXIX.

8°: [A]⁴B–D⁴E²; 18 leaves, pp. [1–2] 3–36. [1]: title; [2]: conditions; 3: catalogue; 36: list of stationery articles and advertisement about supplying libraries and country traders.

Circulating library and bookseller's catalogue: 1075 short author entries, arranged in full alphabetical order. Note on p. [2]: 'The following Catalogue contains only a selection from the numerous volumes on hand; the remaining part of the Library is also for circulation, and consists of a very general assortment in the various branches of Science, History and polite Literature, and in various languages.' On p. 35 is a note, the same as appeared on p. 19 of Guild's 1788 Catalogue (see item 124 above), indicating that the books are also for sale.

Evans 21868; Brigham, p. 47; Shera, pp. 149, 261; *STE*, p. 331.

CSt, MBAt*, MH* (pp. 17–18 mutilated), MHi*, MWA* (19.5×11 cm. — bound), MdBP, PPL*, RPJCB* (pp. [1]–4 slightly mutilated).

130 HOPPIN AND SNOW, Providence, Rhode Island

To-morrow, (being the 12th of May) at nine in the morning, will be sold by public vendue, at Hoppin and Snow's Auction-Office, opposite the Market, in Providence, the following catalogue of books. [Providence, 1789.]

Broadside. 40.5×24.5 cm. 3 cols.

Auction catalogue: 173 consecutively numbered, short author entries, arranged in no apparent order. Date: dated from contemporary ms. note on back: 'Auction May 12, 1789.'

Bristol 6966; m.p. 45497; *STE*, p. 367.

RPJCB*.

131 LIBRARY COMPANY OF PHILADELPHIA

A catalogue of the books, belonging to the Library Company of Philadelphia; to which is prefixed, a short account of the institution, with the charter, laws and regulations. Communiter bona profundere deorum est. Philadelphia: Printed by Zachariah Poulson, Junior, in Fourth-Street, between Market-Street and Arch-Street. M DCC LXXXIX.

8°: [a]⁴b–e⁴, A–Eee⁴; 224 leaves, pp. [i–iii] iv–v [vi–vii] viii–xi [xii–xiii] xiv–xxvi [xxvii] xxviii–xxix [xxx–xxxi] xxxii–xxxvii [xxxviii–xxxix] xl, [1] 2–369 [370–71] 372–84 [385] 386–406 [407–8] (variants—a: 214–15 misnumbered '114–115'; b: 213–14 misnumbered '113–114'). [i]: title; [ii]: blank; [iii]: account of library; [vi]: blank; [vii]: charter; [xii]: blank; [xiii]: laws; [xxvii]: rules; [xxx]: blank; [xxxi]: list of members; [xxxviii]: advertisement (see below); [xxxix]: 'Arrangement' (see below); [1]: catalogue; [370]: blank; [371]: addenda; [385]: index of authors' names; [407]: errata; [408]: blank.

Social library catalogue: 4000 full author entries, with place and date of publication, numbered with accession/shelf numbers, and arranged by subject, and then by format within each subject (subject headings are given in the arrangement, below); donors of books are identified. Advertisement on p. [xxxviii]: 'The inconvenient arrangement of the former Catalogues having been much complained of, as tending to prolong and perplex the enquiry after particular authors, and affording no general view of the different subjects contained in the library, the following plan was suggested, and it is hoped will be more satisfactory. In conformity to the general delineation of human science, laid down by Bacon, and afterwards illustrated and enlarged by D'Alembert, the books have been divided into three classes, corresponding with the three great divisions of the mental faculties—Memory, Reason and Imagination. It has been attempted to render the subdivisions of the several classes sufficiently ample, to combine only those which proceeded from a common source, and could not be separated without difficulty, and to adapt the arrangement rather to the science than the subject. The arrangement will not, perhaps, escape censure, nor the books appear to have been always classed with propriety; but, it should be remembered, that little less than an universal acquaintance with them was competent to a task of the kind . . . [which was done as extra work by weary workers; some names of donors omitted in error].'

Arrangement, pp. [xxxix]–xl: Memory: sacred history; ecclesiastical history; civil history (including biography, antiquities, military and naval history . . .); natural history; voyages and travels; geography and topography. Reason: theology; mythology; ethics, or the moral system in general; grammars, dictionaries, and treatises on education; logic, rhetoric and criticism; general and local politics; trade and commerce; law; metaphysics; geometry; arithmetic and algebra; mechanics; astronomy, astrology and chronology; optics, pneumatics, hydrostatics, hydraulics, phonics, and gnomonics; navigation and naval architecture; civil architecture; the military art; heraldry; anatomy, medicine and chemistry; agriculture and gardening; arts and manufactures; experimental and natural philosophy, and elementary treatises on the arts and sciences. Imagination: poetry and the drama; works of fiction, wit and humor; the fine arts. Miscellanies.

Sabin indicates that this catalogue was reprinted in 1793, but I can find no evidence of this.

Evans 22066; Sabin 61785; Cutter 18; Ranz, p. 119; STE, p. 676.

BL, CtY* (3 copies; 1: has 1st, 2nd, and 4th supplements supplied in ms., with the note, 'Out of Print'; 2: variant a), DLC* (variant a), MB* (2 copies, one John Adams'), MBAt*, MH, MHi* (George Washington autograph copy), MWA* (21.5×14 cm. — bound), MdHi, MiU-C*, NN*, PPAmP* (variant a, largely uncut), PPL* (4 copies; 1, variant a), RPJCB* (variant b).

132 LIBRARY COMPANY OF WILMINGTON, Delaware

A catalogue of the books belonging to the Library Company of Wilmington. Wilmington: Printed by Brynberg and Andrews, at the Post-Office, Market-Street, 1789.

12°: A⁶B⁴; 10 leaves, pp. [1–3] 4–14 [15] 16–19 [20]. [1]: title; [2]: blank; [3]: act of incorporation and laws; on 13: directions for librarian; [15]: catalogue; [20]: blank.

Social library catalogue: 100 short author entries, arranged alphabetically.

Bristol 6973; m.p. 45750; Sabin 104582; Waters 574; *STE*, p. 1007.

CSmH (19×11 cm. — bound).

133 NEW YORK SOCIETY LIBRARY

The charter, bye-laws, and names of the members of the New-York Society Library. With a catalogue of the books belonging to the said Library. New-York: Printed by Hugh Gaine, at his book-store and printing-office, at the Bible, in Hanover-Square. M,DCC,LXXXIX.

8°: [A]⁴B–K⁴; 40 leaves, pp. [1–3] 4–11 [12] 13–16 [17] 18–80. [1]: title; [2]: blank; [3]: charter; [12]: act to remove doubts respecting the charter; on 13: bye-laws; [17]: catalogue; on 77: list of members.

Social library catalogue: 1450 short to full author (mostly) and title entries (with much duplication; many books listed both ways), arranged alphabetically, and by format within each letter.

Evans 22018; *STE*, p. 610.

CtY* (with NNS bookplate), MWA* (20×12 cm. — bound), NN*, NNS.

[Prichard, William, fl. 1782–1809

Catalogue of a gentleman's library, consisting of a well-chosen collection of moral, sciencial, historical, mathematical, classical, and entertaining modern and ancient authors, will be sold, April 3d, 1789, at William Prichard's Auction-room, in Second-street, next door to Christ's-Church yard. Philadelphia: Printed by Eleazer Oswald? 1789.]

Advertised in the *Pennsylvania Packet*, Apr. 2–4, 1789. Evans 22081; McKay 129; *STE*, p. 702.

134 PRICHARD, WILLIAM, fl. 1782–1809

William Prichard's catalogue of books, &c. &c. [Philadelphia, 1789.]

12°: A–B⁶; 12 leaves, pp. [1] 2–22 [23–24]. [1]: title (caption); on [1]: catalogue; on 20: lists of maps, charts, and prints; stationery; jewelry; plated ware; japanned ware; music and musical instruments; and genuine patent medicines; [23]: blank. Bookseller's catalogue: 600 short author entries, most of them in one alphabetical list, with two subject lists at the end (sentimental treats for the ladies [mostly novels]; French). Date: dated [1788] by Evans and *STE*, but could be no earlier than 1789, since the latest novel listed in the catalogue is one first published in that year.

Evans 21405; *STE*, p. 702.

RPJCB* (18.5×11.5 cm. — unbound).

135 RICE, HENRY, d. 1804, AND COMPANY, Philadelphia

Rice and Co. book-sellers and stationers, south side of Market-street, next door but one to Second-street, Philadelphia; have imported in the last vessels from London, Dublin, and Glasgow, a large and general assortment of books, and stationary ware, which they will dispose of by wholesale and retail on very moderate terms; among which are, . . . [Philadelphia, 1789?]

Broadside. 42×33 cm. 5 cols.

Bookseller's catalogue: 300 short (mostly) to full author (mostly) and title entries, arranged in no apparent order; plus a list of stationery, and an advertisement for musical instruments. Date: dated 1789 because the latest novel listed in the catalogue is one first published in that year, while the majority of the entries date from 1786 to 1788.

Bristol 7051; m.p. 45579; *STE*, p. 738.

MiU–C* (bound with *American Museum* 7 (Jan.–June 1790), and therefore dated [1790]), PHi*.

See also McKay 128F (Hunter), 128G (Prichard), 128H (Prichard), 129A, 129B (Patton), 129C (Patton), 129D (Patton), 129E (Patton), 129F (Hubley), 129G (Patton), 129H (Patton), 129I (Patton), 129J (Hayt), 129K (Barclay), 129L (Patton)

——————————— 179? ———————————

[Larkin, Ebenezer, 1767–1813, and Samuel, 1773–1849
Catalogue of books, for sale by E. and S. Larkin, no. 47, Cornhill,
Boston. . . . Boston. 12°: 92 pp.]

Origin of entry unknown. Sabin 39039.

——————————— 1790 ———————————

[Bayley, Samuel
Catalogue of a valuable collection of books, in divinity, history,
physic, novels, miscellanies, philosophy, navigation, geography, dictionaries, &c. &c. Will be sold by public auction, on Friday, the 30th
of April instant, at the shop of Mr. Samuel Bayley near the Ferry-
way in Newburyport. Newburyport: Printed by John Mycall. 1790.]

Advertised in the *Essex Journal*, Apr. 21, 1790. Evans 22394; *STE*, p. 67.

136 CAMPBELL, ROBERT, d. 1800

A [ca]talo[g]u[e] of [b]oo[k]s, sold by Robert Campbell, at his
new book & stationary store, on the west side of Second-street, below
the Market, and five doors above Chesnut-street.————[Philadel-
phia, 1790?]

Broadside. 40×33.5 cm. 4 cols.

Bookseller's catalogue: 225 short author entries, most of them in one unordered
list, with two subject lists at the end (school books; small histories); plus a list of
stationery. Date: according to Brown's *Directory*, p. 27, Campbell gave his address in the form above only in 1790. The missing letters in the title have been
cut out of the DLC copy.

Evans 22388; *STE*, p. 131.

DLC* (bottom right corner torn).

[Catalogue of a choice and valuable collection of modern books;
among which are, elegant folio family Bibles, several valuable medical
publications, divinity, history, voyages, travels, &c. and a curious assortment of beautiful maps and prints, to be sold on the 2d day of

December, 1790, at a large and commodious room in Mr. Daniel Peters's tavern, at the sign of the Emperor of Germany, in Gay-street, five doors from Market-street. Baltimore: Printed by W. Goddard and J. Angell. 1790.]

The origin of Evans's entry is unknown; probably from some as yet undiscovered advertisement. Evans 22393; Wheeler 522; McKay 131; *STE*, p. 138.

137 CHANDLER, JANE (EMOTT), 1732?–1801

Catalogue of books, for sale by Mrs. Chandler, in Elizabeth-Town, New Jersey, being the library of the late Rev. Dr. Chandler, deceased. The prices affixed are in specie. Elizabeth-Town: Printed by Shepard Kollock. M,DCC,XC.

12°: [A]⁶B–C⁶D⁶(–D6); 23 leaves, pp. [1–3] 4–42 [43–46]. [1]: title; [2]: blank; [3]: catalogue; [43]: blank.

Private library sale catalogue: 1450 short author entries, with prices, most of them in one alphabetical list, with a separate brief list of tracts at the end. The library belonged to Rev. Thomas Bradbury Chandler (1726–90).

Evans 22399; Morsch 110; McKay 132; Brigham, p. 47; *STE*, p. 141.

MWA* (18.5×12 cm. — bound), NjEli.

[Charleston Library Society
Catalogue. Charleston, 1790.]

Cutter is the only authority for this entry; he specifies that the catalogue lists 742 volumes, in author entries. Cutter 21.

138 HARVARD COLLEGE. LIBRARY

Catalogus Bibliothecae Harvardianae Cantabrigiae Nov-Anglorum. Bostoniae: Typis Thomae et Johannis Fleet. MDCCXC.

8°: [A]⁴B–Zz⁴(U and W but no Y in both alphabets); 184 leaves, pp. [π1–4], i–iii [iv], 1–205 [206] 207–358 [359–60] (232 misnumbered '322', corrected by hand in all copies, except DLC's. Variants—a: 221 offset, '22¹'; b: 110 misnumbered '101'; c: 221 misnumbered '212'). [π1]: title; [π2]: blank; [π3]: preface; [π4]: blank; i: 'Ordo Capitum' (contents); [iv]: blank; 1: catalogue (1: 'Pars I'; [206]: blank; 207: 'Pars Secunda'); [359]: blank.

College library catalogue: 9800 medium (mostly) and full author entries, with place and date of publication, arranged by subject and in full alphabetical order within each subject. Subject headings: Pars I. Agricultura; algebra; anatomia; antiquitates; architectura; artes; astronomia; auctores et Graeci et Latini; Biblia sacra; biographia; botanice; catalogi; chartae tabulaequae aeneae; chronologia; chymia et metallurgia; commercium et mercatura; concordantiae sacrarum scripturarum; critica sacra; ecclesiastici scriptores antiqui; ethica; geographia; geometria; grammaticè; heraldica; historia; historia antiquitatesque ecclesiae; historia antiquitatesque judaeorum; historia naturalis; itineraria; jus civile; jus ecclesiasticum; jus municipale; jus naturale et politicum; libri periodici; logica; manuscripti; materia medica; mathematica; metaphysica; medicina et chirurgia; miscellanea; musica; mythologia; numismata et pondera; opera dramatica; orientalis et rabbinica literatura; philologia; philosophia naturalis et experimentalis; poetica; res politicae; rhetorica; societates literariae; theologia (by far the largest category); vocabularia. Pars secunda complectitur varios tractatus plerumque in distinctis voluminibus colligatos. Tractatus biographici; tractatus de antiquitatibus tam sacris, quam profanis; tractatus de commercio; tractatus ecclesiastici scriptoresque antiqui; tractatus historici; tractatus mathematici et physici; tractatus medici et chymici; tractatus miscellanei; tractatus morales et metaphysici; tractatus nummarii; tractatus philologici; tractatus poetici; tractatus politici et juridici; tractatus theologici; addenda. This catalogue was compiled by Isaac Smith, according to Evans.

Evans 22559; Sabin 30728; Cutter 19; Shores, p. 283; Ranz, p. 119; *STE*, p. 342. BL, CLCo, CU, CtY* (2 copies; one lacks leaf Zz4), DLC* (variants a and b), MB* (variant c; lacks leaf Zz4), MBAt* (2 copies; 1: 22.5 × 14 cm. — bound; 2: sig. Dd, pp. 201–8, repeated, lacks leaf Zz4), MH* (4 copies; only Houghton copy seen: variant c, lacks leaf Zz4), MHi* (variant b), MWA* (variant c), MiU-C* (variant a, lacks leaf Zz4), OO, PPAmP* (2 copies; 1: variant a, lacks leaf Zz4; 2: lacks pp. 102–10), PPL* (variant b), RPJCB* (variants a and b, sig. P folded incorrectly, resulting in jumbled pagination between pp. 104 and 113).

139 HAYT, LEWIS, fl. 1787–1793
Catalogue of books. On Monday next, the 1st day of March, will be sold by publick vendue, at Lewis Hayt's Office, in State-Street, the following books, most of which are in elegant bindings: . . . [Boston, 1790.]

Broadside. 52 × 20 cm. 2 cols.

Auction catalogue: 186 consecutively numbered short author entries, arranged in no apparent order. Each entry has a ms. notation by it of uncertain import. Dated 'Boston, Feb. 27, 1790' at the bottom of the right column.
MHi*.

140 MILTON AND DORCHESTER LIBRARY,
Massachusetts

A catalogue of books belonging to the subscribers at Milton and Dorchester. [Boston?, 1790?]

8°: [A]⁴; 4 leaves, pp. 1–4 [5–8]. 1: title (caption); on 1: catalogue; [5]: list of subscribers.

Social library catalogue: 50 short author entries, arranged in no apparent order, numbered consecutively by volumes. Date: dated 'ca. 1790' by MHi, though it could be earlier since none of the books listed in the catalogue was first published anywhere near 1790. The latest the catalogue could have been published is 1795; in that year one of the members included in the list of subscribers, Rev. Nathaniel Robins, died (*Sibley's Harvard Graduates*, 12: 203). The only record of this item is two sets of photographs, one at MHi and another at MH. The MHi photographs are noted as having been 'Given by N. T. Kidder, June 16, 1931,' who, according to the *Mass. Hist. Soc. Proceedings*, 64 (June 1931): 285, is Nathaniel T. Kidder of Milton, Mass.

MH* (photographs only), MHi* (photographs only; 15 ×9.5 cm. — unbound).

141 PAYNE, JONAS, AND PHILIP HEARN,

A catalogue of books, to be sold, at Payne and Hearn's book store on the bay, Savannah, for cash or produce. [Savannah: Printed by James and Nicholas Johnston, 1790.]

Broadside. 41.5 ×36 cm. 4 cols.

Bookseller's catalogue: 325 short author entries, listed by format and then alphabetically within each format (except folio and quarto); plus a brief list of stationery and other wares. Date: the DLC copy has the date '10 May 1790' written in, in an eighteenth-century hand, after 'Savannah' in the title, which may indicate that this is really an auction catalogue. Payne and Hearn advertised in the *Georgia Gazette*, Apr. 22, 1790, that 'In a few days catalogues will be published and given gratis.' The latest novels listed in the catalogue are several first printed in 1789. Attribution of printer from Evans.

Evans 22755; *STE*, p. 641.

DLC*.

142 PENNSYLVANIA HOSPITAL, Philadelphia

A catalogue of the books belonging to the Medical Library in the Pennsylvania Hospital; to which are prefixed, the rules to be observed in the use of them. Philadelphia: Printed by Zachariah Poulson, Junior, on the west side of Fourth-Street, between Market-Street and Arch-Street. MDCCXC.

8°: [A]⁴B–D⁴E²; 18 leaves, pp. [1–3] 4–5 [6–7] 8–35 [36]. [1]: title; [2]: blank; [3]: rules; [6]: blank; [7]: catalogue; [36]: blank.

Medical library catalogue: 365 medium and full title entries, with place and date of publication, and, for donated books, names of donors; arranged by format, and numbered consecutively within each format. A supplement to this catalogue was published in 1794; see item 192 below. Evans contends that this 1790 catalogue was 'reprinted, with additions, in 1794,' and therefore includes both the original catalogue and the supplement under no. 27510. However, it is more likely that only the supplement was printed in 1794.

Evans 22795 and 27510; Cutter 20; STE, p. 677.

CtY-M, DLC*, DNLM, MiU-C*, NHi* (18.5×11.5 cm. — unbound; interleaved with blanks), NNNAM* (interleaved with blanks), OkU, PHi*, PPC, PPL* (3 copies), RPJCB* (interleaved with blanks).

[Prichard, William, fl. 1782–1809
Catalogue of a sale of books, by auction, will commence tomorrow evening, the 18th [March] instant, at the store where the Post-Office was lately kept, in Chesnut-street, a few doors above Front-street. Philadelphia: Printed for William Prichard. 1790.]

Advertised in the *Pennsylvania Packet*, Mar. 17–19, 1790. Evans 22815; McKay 130; STE, p. 702.

143 RAGUET, CLAUDIUS PAUL

Catalogue of French, and other books, for sale by Claudius P. Raguet, in Front-street, between Chesnut and Walnut-streets, and nearly opposite to the City Vendue, Philadelphia. [Philadelphia: Printed by Carey, Stewart, and Co., 1790.]

8°: [A]⁴; 4 leaves, pp. [1] 2–8. [1]: title (caption); on [1]: catalogue.

Bookseller's catalogue: 390 French (short title), and 50 English (short author), entries, arranged in full alphabetical order within each language group. This catalogue was printed in the advertising pages of the Mar. 1790 issue of the *American Museum*; MWA notes that it was 'perhaps also issued separately.' There is no specific evidence of this, since it has not been found separate from the magazine, but it is included in this checklist because both Bristol and Brigham also list it as a separate. Attribution of printer from MWA.

Bristol 7483; m.p. 45984; Brigham, p. 48; *STE*, p. 713.

MWA*(22×12.5 cm. — bound), MiU-C* (bound with *American Museum*, 7 [1790], following p. 344), N.

144 RICE, HENRY, d. 1804, AND COMPANY, Philadelphia
Rice and Co's catalogue of books. [Philadelphia, 1790?]

12°: A–E⁶ (although E6 is signed 'F'); 30 leaves, pp. [1–3] 4–18 [19] 20–34 [35] 36–60. [1]: title (lacking in unique copy); [2] blank? (lacking); [3]: caption title, as given above; on [3]: catalogue. Except for the first three lines, pp. 24 and 42 are the same; the catchword indicates that the text of this page belongs at p. 42 and not at p. 24.

Bookseller's catalogue: 1150 short to full author (mostly) and title entries, some with descriptive or laudatory comments, arranged by subject, with some subject groups in alphabetical order and some not. Subject headings: philosophy; history and general policy; philology; livres Francois; elements of history for schools; mythology; geography; chronology; polite literature; polite arts; manners of nations; works of entertainment and fancy; optics, perspective, astronomy, &c.; navigation; life, morals, and manners; memoirs and characters; domestic œconomy; rural recreations; husbandry and gardening; farriery; law; physic, surgery, and chemistry; mathematics; artillery, fortification, &c.; architecture; trade and commerce; moral philosophy; church of England; church of Rome; youth's museum; books designed for the instruction and entertainment of young persons; libri classici; the stage. Date: dated [1791] by MWA, Bristol, *STE*, and Brigham, but 1790 seems more likely since the latest novels listed in the catalogue are several first published in 1790, and a spot check of other entries shows none any later than that.

Bristol 7812; m.p. 46274; Brigham, p. 50; *STE*, p. 738.

MWA*(17×10 cm. — bound; lacks pp. [1–2]).

145 THOMAS, ISAIAH, 1749–1831
The friends of literature, who wish to encourage the art of printing in America, are respectfully informed that American editions of the following books, (all of which were printed in the United States) are now selling by Isaiah Thomas, in Worcester, and by said Thomas & Company, in Boston, viz. [Worcester: Printed by Isaiah Thomas, 1790?]

8°: [A]²; 2 leaves, pp. [1–4]. [1]: title (caption); on [1]: catalogue; on [4]: advertisement (English, Scotch, and Irish editions, and stationery also available).

Bookseller's catalogue: 200 full title and short author entries, American editions only, arranged by subject. Subject headings: miscellaneous; divinity; law; physick; classical and school books; plays; children's books. Date: dated [1789] by Sabin, and [1791] by Bristol, Brigham, *STE*, and MWA; Bristol and MWA state that the catalogue was dated 1791 'in Thomas's hand.' The internal evidence is not totally consistent, but points more to 1790. The catalogue states that 'Cullen's Materia Medica will be ready for sale in a few days'; the American edition of this book has an imprint date of 1789. The latest books listed in the catalogue are three first published in American editions in 1790, while 30 of the books listed date from 1789 and 40 date from 1788.

Bristol 7839; m.p. 46296; Sabin 95401; Brigham, p. 50; *STE*, p. 829.

MWA*(2 copies, one 22.5×13.5 cm. — bound).

See also McKay 129M (Patton), 129N (Barclay), 129O (Smith), 129P (Barclay), 129Q (Patton), 129R (Smith), 129S (Prichard?), 130A (Prichard? [Duffield]), 130B (Prichard?), 130C (Smith), 130D (Smith), 130E (Smith), 130F, 130G, 130H ([Byles])

———————————— **1791** ————————————

146 BEERS, ISAAC, 1742?–1813

A catalogue of books, sold by Isaac Beers, at his bookstore in New-Haven. [New Haven:] Printed by Thomas and Samuel Green. MDCCXCI.

12°: [A]⁴B²C⁴D²; 12 leaves, pp. [1–3] 4–24. [1]: title; [2]: blank; [3]: catalogue. Bookseller's catalogue: 950 short author entries, arranged by subject and alphabetically within subjects. Subject headings: divinity and ecclesiastical history; history, voyages and travels; law; second hand law; physick, surgery and chemistry; poetry; novels and romances; miscellanies; arts and sciences, mathematics, astronomy, navigation, commerce, English dictionaries, &c.; classics and books for learning French; husbandry, gardening, &c. The CtHi copy may be incomplete because the last subject list has only three entries, stopping with the letter 'D'.

Bristol 7645; m.p. 46123; *STE*, p. 70.

CtHi*(19.5×13 cm. — unbound).

147 CAMPBELL, ROBERT, d. 1800

Robert Campbell's sale catalogue of books. To be sold on the most reasonable terms, at no. 54, south Second-street, second door, below the corner of Chesnut-street, on the west side, Philadelphia. Catalogues are delivered at the place of sale to gentlemen who please to call or send for them: and orders from the country, executed with the utmost care and dispatch. [Philadelphia, 1791.]

12°: [A]1B–D⁶E⁴F²(–F2); 24 leaves, pp. [1–3] 4–45 [46] 47–48. [1]: title; [2]: index; [3]: catalogue; on 44: stationery articles; [46]: list of 23 'Books printed for Robert Campbell.' The only presently known copy of this catalogue may be lacking pp. 49+; the index on p. [2] indicates that an 'Appendix' should begin on p. 49.

Bookseller's catalogue: 875 short to full author entries, arranged by subject and alphabetically within subjects. Subject headings are essentially the same as in Samuel Campbell's 1787 catalogue (item 114 above), but with the categories of 'history . . . ,' 'poems . . . ,' and 'novels . . .' combined. Date: could be no earlier than 1791, and probably no later than 1792, since the latest books listed in the catalogue are several first published in 1791, including at least ten of the 23 'Books printed for Robert Campbell.'

Evans 23244; Brigham, p. 48; *STE*, p. 131.

MWA* (18×11 cm. — bound).

[Carey, John, 1756–1826
A catalogue of scarce and valuable books. Philadelphia: Printed for John Carey, no. 112, Union-Street. 1791.]

Evans's entry was probably based on a newspaper advertisement. Evans 23245; *STE*, p. 133.

148 CAREY, MATHEW, 1760–1839, JAMES H.
      STEWART, fl. 1790–1806, AND COMPANY,
      Philadelphia
      Catalogue of books, stationary, cutlery, &c. for sale at Carey, Stewart, & Co.'s store, no. 22, North Front-street, Philadelphia. [Philadelphia: Printed by Carey, Stewart, & Co., 1791.]

12°: A⁶; 6 leaves, pp. [1] 2–12. [1]: title (caption); on [1]: catalogue; 12: lists of blanks, stationery, cutlery, and medicines.

Bookseller's catalogue: 350 short author entries, most of them in one alphabetical list, with several separate, brief subject lists at the end (pamphlets; dramatic pieces; children's books; spelling books). Date: according to Brown, *Directory*, p. 28, Carey and Stewart were in business together in 1790 and 1791. 1791 is the most likely date for this catalogue because it lists the 'American Museum 8 vols.'

and vol. 8 was for July to December of 1790, so the catalogue must have been printed after that, probably early in 1791. This item may have been a back-of-the-book catalogue as well as being issued separately; it is bound at the end of the PHi copy of Necker, *Of the Importance of Religious Opinions* (Philadelphia: Carey, Stewart, & Co., 1791) (Evans 23588), though other copies, such as that at MWA, do not include the catalogue.

Evans 23247; Brigham, p. 49; *STE*, p. 134.

MiU-C* (2 copies, bound with, but not part of, *American Museum*, 9 [Jan.–June 1791], and 10 [July–Dec. 1791]), MWA* (19.5×11.5 cm. — bound), NN*, PHi*.

149 DABNEY, JOHN, 1752–1819

Catalogue of books, for sale or circulation, in town or country, by John Dabney, at his book and stationary store, and circulating library, in Salem: consisting of the most approved authors in history, lives, memoirs, novels, antiquities, geography, poetry, voyages, travels, divinity, husbandry, navigation[,] miscellanies, arts, sciences, &c. Including many of the latest and most celebrated volumes in Europe and America. Here you may range the world from pole to pole, / Increase your knowledge, and delight your soul; / Travel all nations, and inform your sense, / With ease and safety, at a small expense. ———Anon. / All new books, on every useful and entertaining subject, with all such as appear advertised, from time to time, relating either to schools, amusement, navigation, or the general business of life, are obtained as soon as published, for sale or loan, at the lowest prices. Handsome assortment of stationary, of every article in general use, constantly for sale, to the satisfaction of the purchaser. [Salem:] Printed [by Thomas Cushing] for J. Dabney. MDCCXCI.

12°: A–B⁶C⁶(–C⁶); 17 leaves, pp. [1–3] 4–33 [34]. [1]: title; [2]: advertisement (see below); [3]: catalogue; 32: stationery; [34]: conditions of the circulating library, and advertisements for binding, and books bought or exchanged.

Circulating library and bookseller's catalogue: 625 short (mostly) to full author entries, most of them in one alphabetical list, with two separate, brief subject categories at the end (Bibles, dictionaries, school-books, navigation books, &c.; tragedies, comedies, farces, operas, essays, and other entertainments). Attribution of printer from Evans and MHi.

From advertisement, p. [2]: 'A Circulating Library, like the volume of Nature, is found to be an interesting Miscellany, but composed of an assemblage of productions extremely opposite in their nature and tendency. Many of those productions are known to be highly beneficial, others very agreeable and engaging; and some, it will be added, are injurious to Society. If as many of the latter are excluded as possible, and an arrangement be formed of the most eligible, it may be considered not only as a Repository of Rational Amusement, but as a Museum, from whence may be derived materials capable of forming the minds of individuals to solid virtue, true politeness, the noblest actions, and the purest benevolence.' This passage seems to be an attempt to combat the frequent charge that circulating libraries consisted primarily of morally dangerous books, i.e., novels.

Evans 23304; Tapley, p. 350; Shera, pp. 141–42, 149, 151, 261; Brigham, p. 49; STE, p. 201.

MHi*, MWA* (20×12 cm. — bound), PPL*, RPJCB*.

150 NEW YORK SOCIETY LIBRARY
Continuation of the catalogue of the New-York Society Library. [New York: Printed by Hugh Gaine, 1791.]

8°: L–N⁴O²; 14 leaves, pp. [81] 82–106 [107] 108 [=28]. [81]: title (caption); on [81]: catalogue; [107]: list of additional members.

Social library catalogue: 400 short to full author entries, arranged alphabetically and by format within each letter. Usually bound with the 1789 New York Society Library catalogue, item 133 above. Date: NNS dates the catalogue [1791] from their own contemporary records.

Evans 23618; STE, p. 610.

MWA* (18.5×12 cm. — unbound), NN*, NNS.

151 PLAN of the book auction to be the first of July next. [Savannah: Printed by James and Nicholas Johnston, 1791.]

Broadside. 38×24.5 cm. Partly 1 col., partly 3 cols.

Auction catalogue: 70 short author entries arranged in irregular lots, with prices per lot. Note at bottom: 'The Books laid out for the smaller Lots may be seen at Hearn's Book Store, where Numbers at One Dollar each are now selling, also at the Printing Office.' Philip Hearn, therefore, may be the 'author' of this catalogue. Date: dated 'Savannah, May 19, 1791,' at bottom right. Attribution of printer from Evans.

Evans 23702; STE, p. 685.

DLC*.

152 YALE COLLEGE. LIBRARY
Catalogue of books in the library of Yale-College, New-Haven. [New-Haven:] Printed by T. & S. Green. MDCCXCI.

8°: [A]²B–G⁴; 26 leaves, pp. [1–5] 6–50 [51–52]. [1]: half-title: 'Catalogue of Yale-College Library.'; [2]: blank; [3]: title; [4]: blank; [5]: catalogue; [51]: index.

College library catalogue: 1800 short author entries (2700 volumes according to a note on p. 50), numbered with location numbers, arranged by subject and in full alphabetical order within subjects. Subject headings (some with subheadings): languages; geography; logic; rhetoric and belles lettres; mathematics; natural philosophy and astronomy; moral philosophy; ancient philosophy; anatomy, physic and surgery; law; divinity (by far the largest category, with many subdivisions); history; biography; antiquities, voyages and travels; miscellanies). The catalogue was compiled by Ebenezer Fitch and Amos Bassett, according to CtY.

Evans 24015; Sabin 105896; Bates 2809; Shores, p. 28; Cutter 22; Ranz, p. 119; *STE*, p. 1020.

CtHi* (2 extra blank leaves at end), CtY* (6 copies, some with imperfections), DLC*, MH*, MWA* (4 extra blank leaves at end, with several ms. additions), PPL* (20.5×13.5 cm. — bound), PU.

See also McKay 132A (Jay), 132B (Jay), 132C (Barclay), 132D (Jay), 132E (Sutton), 132F (Pintard), 132G, 132H, 132I (Jay), 132J (Jay), 132K (Barclay)

————————— 1792 —————————

153 ALLEN, THOMAS, fl. 1785–1799

– – –New-York– – –1792.– – –Thomas Allen's sale catalogue of books, consisting of a very extensive collection of valuable books in every branch of science and polite literature, ancient and modern, which will be disposed of, wholesale and retail, on reasonable terms, at his book and stationary store, no. 12, Queen-Street, New-York. T. Allen presents his sincere thanks to his friends and customers, and to the public in general, for their former favours, and begs leave to inform them, that he has removed from no. 16, to no. 12, Queen-street; and is constantly enlarging his assortment by fresh importations of books from various parts of Europe. He flatters himself that at his store will be found as elegant a collection, and at as low prices, as at any place in this city. Catalogues delivered at the place of sale, gratis. New-York: Printed for Thomas Allen, bookseller and stationer, no. 12, Queen-Street.—1792.

8°: π1[=G4] [A]⁴B–F⁴G⁴(–G4); 28 leaves, pp. [1–3] 4–55 [56]. [1]: title; [2]: index, and advertisement for quantity buyers; [3]: catalogue; 53: stationery, &c.; on 54: list of 18 books 'printed for Thomas Allen'; on 55: advertisement for bookbinding; [56]: blank.

Bookseller's catalogue: 1328 consecutively numbered, short to full author (mostly) and title entries, arranged by subject and alphabetically within subjects. Subject headings: divinity and ecclesiastical history; law, physic, surgery, chemistry, anatomy and midwifery; history, biography and voyages; arts and sciences, philosophy, mathematics, mechanics, perspective geography, gazetteers, &c.; novels and romances; miscellanies; poetry, poetical translations, and dramatic works; books for the Greek and Latin classics; dictionaries, grammars, &c. for the Spanish, Italian, French and English classics; pamphlets, plays and tracts.

Evans 24033; Brigham, p. 51; *STE*, p. 15.

MHi* (19.5×12.5 cm. — unbound), MWA*, PPL*.

[Carey, John, 1756–1826

Catalogue of part of a private library, consisting of a number of scarce and valuable books, particularly the Greek and Latin classics. Philadelphia: Printed [by Mathew Carey] for John Carey, no. 26, Pear street. 1792.]

Evans's entry was probably based on newspaper advertisements. Evans 24172; *STE*, p. 133.

154 CAREY, MATHEW, 1760–1839

Mathew Carey's catalogue of books, for August, 1792. [Philadelphia: Printed by Mathew Carey, 1792.]

12°: A⁶; 6 leaves, pp. [1] 2–4 [5] 6–7 [8] 9–12. [1]: title (caption); on [1]: catalogue; 12: stationery and blanks, plus a list of 18 books 'printed by Mathew Carey,' with prices.

Bookseller's catalogue: 775 short author entries, arranged by subject. Subject headings: law; medical, surgical, and chemical books; religious books; history, voyages, and travels; miscellanies; poetry and drama; novels; school books; French books; German books; navigation; pamphlets; dramatic pieces. Despite the monthly intervals and lack of true title-pages, this and the following four catalogues do not appear to have been printed as part of Carey's *American Museum*.

Evans 24173; Brigham, p. 51; *STE*, p. 134.

MHi*, MWA* (20×12.5 cm. — bound).

155 CAREY, MATHEW, 1760–1839
Mathew Carey's catalogue of books, for September, 1792. [Philadelphia: Printed by Mathew Carey, 1792.]

12°: A⁶; 6 leaves, pp. [1] 2–12. [1]: title (caption); on [1]: catalogue; 12: stationery, and a list of 19 books 'printed by Mathew Carey,' with prices.

Bookseller's catalogue: 775 short author entries, arranged by subject (as in his August 1792 catalogue). As Brigham notes, 'much of the text seems set from the same type' as the August catalogue. Although the MiU-C copy is bound with the *American Museum*, it does not seem to have been printed as part of that magazine because it is of both different size and different format.

Bristol 7950; m.p. 46403; Brigham, p. 51; *STE*, p. 134.

MWA* (19.5 × 12.5 cm. — bound; lacks bottom of leaf A1), MdHi*, MiU-C* (bound with *American Museum*, 11 [Jan.–June 1792]), N (2 copies).

156 CAREY, MATHEW, 1760–1839
Mathew Carey, no. 118, Market-street, Philadelphia, has imported from London, Dublin, and Glasgow, an extensive assortment of books, among which are the following: [Philadelphia: Printed by Mathew Carey, 1792.]

12°: [A]⁶; 6 leaves, pp. [1] 2–12. [1]: title (caption); on [1]: catalogue. Running title: 'M. Carey's catalogue for October, 1792.'

Bookseller's catalogue: 925 short author entries, arranged by subject (as in the August catalogue, omitting all after 'school books'; the only presently known copy of this catalogue could, therefore, be incomplete).

Evans 24174; Brigham, p. 52; *STE*, p. 134.

MWA* (18.5 × 11 cm. — unbound).

157 CAREY, MATHEW, 1760–1839
Mathew Carey, no. 118, Market-street, Philadelphia, has imported from London, Dublin, and Glasgow, an extensive assortment of books, among which are the following: [Philadelphia: Printed by Mathew Carey, 1792.]

12°: A–B⁶; 12 leaves, pp. [1] 2–24. [1]: title (caption); on [1]: catalogue. Running title: 'M. Carey's catalogue for November, 1792.'

Bookseller's catalogue: 1050 short and medium author entries, arranged by subject and alphabetically within subjects. Subject headings: law; medical, surgical, chemical and farriers' books; religious books; history, voyages, and travels; miscellanies; poetry and drama; novels and romances; books for schools, colleges,

&c.; agricultural books; books of navigation; French books. The list of French books which begins on p. 24 appears to terminate abruptly one third of the way through an alphabetical listing, suggesting that both known copies of this catalogue may be incomplete.

Evans 24175; Brigham, pp. 51–52; *STE*, p. 134.

MWA* (19.5 × 12 cm. — bound), MiU-C* (lacks pp. 13–24; bound with, but not part of [different size and format], the *American Museum*, 11 [Jan.–June 1792]).

158 CAREY, MATHEW, 1760–1839

Mathew Carey, no. 118, Market-street, Philadelphia, has imported from London, Dublin, and Glasgow, an extensive assortment of books, among which are the following: [Philadelphia: Printed by Mathew Carey, 1792.]

12°: A–B⁶; 12 leaves, pp. [1] 2–7 [8] 9–24. [1]: title (caption); on [1]: catalogue; on 24: advertisement (thanks public; constant supply of new books). Running title: 'M. Carey's catalogue for December 1792.'

Bookseller's catalogue: 1075 short and medium author entries, arranged by subject and alphabetically within subjects. Subject headings are as in the November catalogue, with one addition, Italian books. This catalogue is very similar to, but not a duplicate of, the November catalogue; some entries are added and some are deleted. The *EAI* comment that the MWA copy (pp. 13–24 only) is bound continuous with its copy of the October catalogue was once true, but MWA has since separated the two.

Evans 24176; *STE*, p. 134.

MWA* (18.5 × 11.5 cm. — unbound; lacks pp. [1]–12), MiU-C* (bound with, but not a part of [different size and format], the *American Museum*, 11 [Jan.–June 1792]).

[Catalogue of about two thousand volumes of books, on various subjects, many of which are very scarce, to be sold at Mr. Starck's tavern. Baltimore: Printed by David Graham. 1792.]

Advertised in the *Baltimore Daily Repository*, Feb. 10, 1792, according to Minick.
Evans 24182; Minick 57; McKay 132L; *STE*, p. 138.

159 DAVIS, GEORGE

Law Books. George Davis, in the Prothonotary's Office of the Supreme Court, Philadelphia, respectfully acquaints the gentlemen of the bar and their students, in this and the other states, that by the late arrivals from Dublin, he has received the following collection of books, which he is encouraged to hope, from a confidence in the moderation of his prices, as from the patronage he has hitherto experienced, will claim their particular attention. Immediate respect shall be paid to any order by letter addressed to him; and gentlemen at any time favoring him with a list of such books as they may have occasion for, he will, if he has them not, write for them from Ireland, if they direct him so to do, so that they may be had in a few months after the order sent. G.D. expects shortly a further very general and valuable collection from the same place, in which will be included Term Reports complete, 4 vols. and several third and fourth vols. of the same Reports. No. 313, High-street, Philadelphia, September 25, 1792. [Philadelphia, 1792.]

Broadside. 33.5×21 cm. 2 cols.

Bookseller's catalogue: 75 short author entries, all law books, arranged by format.

Bristol 7971; m.p. 46420; *STE*, p. 206.

PHi*.

160 GAINE, HUGH, 1726–1807

Hugh Gaine's catalogue of books, lately imported from England, Ireland, and Scotland, and to be sold at his book-store and printing-office, at the Bible in Hanover-Square. New-York: Printed by Hugh Gaine, ——1792.——

8°: [A]⁴B–C⁴[D]⁴; 16 leaves, pp. [1–3] 4–24 [25–32]. [1]: title; [2]: blank; [3]: catalogue; 23: stationery; on 24: drugs and medicines; [25]: 'New books, just published by H. Gaine' (reproduces full title-pages for 6 books); [31]: advertisement for 'Dr. Ryan's Incomparable Worm-destroying Suger Plums' (variant: [25–28] blank, [29–32] omitted).

Bookseller's catalogue: 725 short and medium author and title entries, arranged by subject. Subject headings: law; physic and surgery; divinity; history, &c.; novels; miscellany; philosophy, mathematics, &c.; grammars, dictionaries, &c.; Greek and Latin classics; chap books, plays, farces, &c. The NN variant is the copy reproduced on *EAI*.

Evans 24336; *STE*, p. 297.

MiU-C* (23.5×13.5 cm. — bound), NN* (variant).

161 HALL, SAMUEL, 1740–1807

Catalogue of books, to be sold by Samuel Hall, at no. 53, Cornhill, Boston. [Boston: Printed by Samuel Hall, 1792.]

Broadside. 46.5 × 29 cm. 3 cols.

Bookseller's catalogue: 125 short to full author and title entries, some with prices and some with comments of praise or description, arranged in three groups: miscellaneous (unlabeled); for the instruction of children and youth; schoolbooks. Dated 'April, 1792' at bottom of sheet. Attribution of printer from Evans.

Evans 24375; Ford 2648; *STE*, p. 335.

MB*.

162 LIBRARY COMPANY OF BURLINGTON, New Jersey

A catalogue of books, belonging to the Library Company of Burlington; taken on the 20th March, 1792: to which is prefixed, a brief account of the rise and progress of the institution, a list of the names of the present members, and a summary of the laws and regulations of the Company. Burlington, printed by Isaac Neale. M,DCC,XCII.

8°: [A]⁴B–D⁴E²; 18 leaves, pp. [1–3] 4–35 [36] (?—some page numbers trimmed off in binding). [1]: title; [2]: blank; [3]: account of library; on 4: list of 65 members; on 5: summary of laws; on 7: rules; 9: catalogue; [36]: blank.

Social library catalogue: 850 short author entries, arranged by subject and by format within subjects, and numbered non-consecutively with shelf/accession numbers within each format. Subject headings: history and chronology; husbandry and gardening; biography; voyages and travels; physic, surgery, chemistry, anatomy; novels, romances, tales, fables; law; poetry; philosophy; philology; school books; commerce and navigation; geography; natural history; farriery; letters; polite literature or belles lettres; politics; morals and manners; arts and sciences; drama; miscellanies; sermons; divinity.

Evans 24159; Morsch 161; *STE*, p. 125.

NjHi (could not be located, 1974, though this copy was photographed for *EAI* in 1960).

163 NEW YORK SOCIETY LIBRARY

A farther continuation of the catalogue of books belonging to the New-York Society Library, with the names of the additional members of the said Society. [printer's monogram.] New-York: Printed by Thomas & James Swords, at their printing-office, no. 27, William-Street; where printing in general is executed with neatness, accuracy and dispatch, and on reasonable terms. —1792.—

8°: π1 P–R⁴; 13 leaves, pp. π[i–ii], [109] 110–27 [128–29] 130–31 [132] [=26]. π[i]: title; π[ii]: blank; [109]: catalogue; [128]: blank; [129]: list of members; [132]: blank.

Social library catalogue: 375 short to full author entries, arranged alphabetically. Evans 24610; Keep, p. 240; *STE*, p. 610.

NHi (not located, 1974), NN* (19×11.5 cm. — bound; lacks t.p.), NNS.

[New York Society Library

A farther continuation of the catalogue of books belonging to the New-York Society Library, with the names of the additional members of the said society. New York: Printed by Thomas and James Swords. . . . 1792. 8°; 100 pp.]

Publication announcements apparently lead Evans to postulate two editions of this catalogue, this one and the preceding item; the preceding edition, however, is the only one actually printed. Evans 24611; *STE*, p. 610.

[Prichard, William, fl. 1782–1809

Literature, William Prichard's sale of books by auction will commence on Monday evening, February 13, 1792, at Mr. A. Hubley's Vendue-store, in Front-street, a few doors below Chesnut-street. When will be sold a valuable collection of ancient and modern authors. Philadelphia: Printed for William Prichard. 1792.]

Evans's entry was probably based on a newspaper advertisement. Evans 24712; McKay 133; *STE*, p. 702.

164 RUSSELL, JOSEPH, 1734–1795, AND SAMUEL CLAP, 1745–1809

On Tuesday morning, 16th October, at ten o'clock, will be sold by public vendue, at Russell and Clap's Auction-Room, the following collection of books, viz. [Boston, 1792.]

Broadside. 45×35 cm. 3 cols.

Auction catalogue: 246 consecutively numbered, short author entries, arranged by format. Date: the books listed in an auction catalogue typically are older editions, and therefore not too useful for dating; in this case, none of them was first published more recently than around 1780. But of the several years after 1780 when October 16 fell on a Tuesday, 1792 seems the most likely.

Bristol 8133; m.p. 46568; Ford 2672; McKay 133D; *STE*, p. 753. MHi*.

165 THOMAS, ISAIAH, 1749–1831

Catalogue of books to be sold by Isaiah Thomas, at his bookstore in Worcester, Massachusetts. Consisting of history, voyages, travels, geography, antiquities, philosophy, novels, miscellanies, divinity, physick, surgery, anatomy, arts, sciences, husbandry, architecture, navigation, mathematicks, law, periodical publications, poetry, plays, musick, &c. &c. November, MDCCXCII. Printed at Worcester, Massachusetts, by Isaiah Thomas and Leonard Worcester.

12°: A–C⁶D⁴; 22 leaves, pp. [i–ii] iii [iv] [5] 6–42 [43–44]. [i]: title; [ii]: blank; iii: contents; [iv]: blank; [5]: catalogue; 40: stationery; 42: advertisement (Thomas will supply gentlemen with libraries on the best terms; books bought and exchanged); [43]: blank.

Bookseller's catalogue: 1175 short and medium author entries, arranged by subject and in full alphabetical order within subjects. Subject headings: divinity and ecclesiastical history; law; physick, surgery, & chymistry; history, chronology, biography, antiquities, voyages, & travels; miscellanies; poetical works; novels and sentimental works, &c.; dramatick works, &c.; algebra, arithmetick, architecture, surveying, &c.; magazines and reviews; cookery; jests; dictionaries and classical and school books, &c.; sacred musick; children's books; chapman's books, &c. Note on p. 41: 'Most of the Books in this Catalogue, and many others, are to be sold also by said Thomas, and Andrews, at Faust's Statue, no. 45, Newbury Street, Boston.'

Evans 24845; Sabin 95402; Nichols 206; Brigham, p. 52; *STE*, p. 829. MHi* (16.5 × 10 cm. — unbound), MWA* (lacks leaf D4).

166 YOUNG, WILLIAM, 1755–1829

Books for sale, at William Young's book and stationary store, no. 52, Second-street, the corner of Chesnut-street, 1792. [Philadelphia: Printed by William Young, 1792.]

12°: A⁶; 6 leaves, pp. [1] 2–12. [1]: title (caption); on [1]: catalogue.

Bookseller's catalogue: 400 short author entries, arranged alphabetically. This catalogue looks like it might also have served as a back-of-the-book catalogue, although such catalogues are rarely as long as 12 pages; in addition, a survey of the books printed in 1792 by Young (in the copies reproduced on m.p.) failed to turn up this catalogue at the back of any.

Evans 25062; Sabin 106122; *STE*, p. 1023.

DLC, NN* (20.5 × 13 cm. — bound).

See also McKay 133A (Hayt), 133B (Prichard [Reiche]), 133C (Hayt)

—————————— 1793 ——————————

167 ALBANY LIBRARY, Albany, New York

A catalogue of the books belonging to the Albany Library: with the law of the legislature of New-York, to incorporate the trustees; the bye-laws of the corporation; &c. &c. &c. Albany: Printed by Barber and Southwick: M,DCC,XCIII.

8°: [A]⁴B⁴[C]⁴D⁴E⁴(–E4); 19 leaves, pp. [1–2] 3–38. [1]: title; [2]: list of trustees; [3]: act of incorporation, including list of members; 11: laws; 17: catalogue. Variant—8°: [A]⁴B⁴[C]⁴D⁴; 16 leaves, pp. [1–2] 3–32. [1]: title (as above); [2]: list of trustees; [3]: act of incorporation, including list of members; 11: laws; 17: catalogue.

Social library catalogue. The catalogue portion of the volume exists in two forms. In the longer, and perhaps therefore later, form (N copy, the one reproduced on Microprint), it occupies pp. 17–38 and contains 675 short author entries, numbered with what appear to be location numbers, arranged alphabetically and by format within each letter. In the shorter variant (MB and MH copies), the catalogue occupies pp. 17–32 and contains 500 entries, having the same form and arrangement as those in the longer variant. The alphabetical sequence of the catalogue is complete in the shorter variant, and p. 32 also has what seem to be a few supplementary entries, for letters B–J.

Bristol 8256; m.p. 46680; McMurtrie, *Albany*, 80; Thompson, p. 253; *STE*, p. 12.

MB* (17.5 × 11.5 cm. — bound; variant), MH* (variant), MiD (could not be located, 1974), N.

[Baltimore Circulating Library, Baltimore, Maryland
Catalogue of the books in the Baltimore Circulating Library, Frederick-street, one door north of Market-street. Baltimore: Printed by Philip Edwards. 1793.]

Evans's entry was probably based on advertisements in *Baltimore Evening Post*.
Evans 25133; Minick 102; *STE*, p. 46.

168   BLAKE, WILLIAM PYNSON, 1769–1820

A catalogue of books, for sale or circulation, by William P.
Blake, at the Boston Book-Store, no. 59, Cornhill. Consisting of the
most approved authors, in history, voyages, travels, lives, memoirs,
antiquities, philosophy, novels, divinity, law, physic, surgery, chemistry, geography, husbandry, navigation, arts, sciences, architecture,
miscellanies, poetry, plays, &c. &c. Boston: Printed for William P.
Blake, at the Boston Book-Store, no. 59, Cornhill. MDCCXCIII.

12°: A–D⁶; 24 leaves, pp. [1–3] 4–47 [48] (variant: p. 7 not numbered). [1]:
title; [2]: conditions of circulating library; [3]: catalogue; on 45: stationery; on
46: 'Fancy Articles'; 47: advertisement (perfumery; libraries, country traders
supplied; books bought or exchanged); [48]: blank.

Circulating library and bookseller's catalogue: 1450 short author entries, most
of them in one fully alphabetical list, with one brief subject list at the end (Bibles,
dictionaries, classical and school books, navigation books, &c.).

Evans 25206; Brigham, p. 52; Shera, pp. 138, 141, 149, 261; *STE*, p. 96.
MB*, MWA* (19×12 cm. — bound), MiU-C* (t.p. mutilated, leaf D1 torn,
leaf D6 lacking), RPJCB* (variant).

169   CAREY, MATHEW, 1760–1839

Carey's [   ] a n[ew] sys[tem] of modern ge[ography] . . .
by William G[uthrie]. . . . [Philadelphia: Printed by Mathew Carey,
1793.]

4°: [A]²; 2 leaves, pp. [1–4]. [1]: advertisement for subscription edition of Guthrie's *New System of Modern Geography* to be published by Carey; [2]: list of 150
French books, short author entries, arranged alphabetically, and 5 Italian books,
short author entries; [3]: list of 33 consecutively numbered, medium and full
title entries, with prices, and some with excerpts from reviews, for books and
pamphlets 'lately published by Mathew Carey'; on [3]: list of 48 full author entries, arranged in no apparent order, for books 'for sale at said Carey's.' Date:
Carey began publishing his edition of Guthrie in 1793; see Evans 25574. This
may have originally been printed as a back-of-book catalogue, but I have not yet
found it in any Carey-printed book of the period. The NjR copy is a photograph
of a copy that was in the possession of Mrs. C. F. Borden of Shrewsbury, N.J., in
1969; the bottom half of pp. [1–2] of this copy is torn away.

Bristol 8299.

NjR* (27.5×22.5 cm. — unbound; photograph only).

170 CAREY, MATHEW, 1760–1839

Mathew Carey, no. 118, Market-street, Philadelphia, has imported from London, Dublin, and Glasgow, an extensive assortment of books, among which are the following: . . . [Philadelphia: Printed by Mathew Carey, 1793.]

12°: A–B⁶; 12 leaves, pp. [1] 2–24. [1]: title (caption); on [1]: catalogue; on 24: advertisement (as in Dec. 1792 Carey catalogue). Running title: 'M. Carey's catalogue for January, 1793.'

Bookseller's catalogue: 1075 short and medium author entries, arranged by subject and alphabetically within subjects (subject headings as in Carey's Dec. 1792 catalogue, item 158 above). This catalogue is only slightly different from the Dec. 1792 catalogue.

Evans 25253; Brigham, p. 53; STE, p. 134.

MWA* (19.5×11.5 cm. — bound).

[Catalogue of a great variety of valuable books, and two book-cases, to be sold at Mr. Starck's tavern, May 4, 1793. Baltimore: Printed by D. Graham. 1793.]

Evans's entry was probably based on an advertisement. Evans 25266; Minick 112; McKay 134; STE, p. 138.

171 CHILDS, FRANCIS, 1763–1830, AND COMPANY, New York

New-York, Nov. 1793. Francis Childs & Co's. sale catalogue of books, which will be sold wholesale and retail, on reasonable terms, at their book and stationary store, Water-Steet, corner of King-Street. Book-binding performed with elegance and dispatch. New-York: Printed by Childs and Swaine. MDCCXCIII.

8°: [A]⁴B–D⁴E²; 18 leaves, pp. [1–3] 4–36. [1]: title; [2]: blank; [3]: catalogue; 35: stationery; on 36: advertisement for John Moore's *Journal During a Residence in France*, 'just published, and for sale by Francis Childs & Co.'

Bookseller's catalogue: 700 medium title and short author entries, arranged by subject. Subject headings: divinity; law; physic, chemistry, and botany; history, voyages, and travels; mathematics, philosophy, and miscellanies; plays and farces; dictionaries, classics, schoolbooks, &c.

Evans 25295; Brigham, p. 53; STE, p. 148.

MWA* (18.5×12.5 cm. — bound).

172 HACKER, ISAAC, 1750?–1818

A catalogue of books sold by James Phillips, George Yard, Lombard Street, London: and sold also by Isaac Hacker, Salem: of whom may be had Bibles, testaments, and stationary wares in general. [Salem,] 1793.

8°: A⁸; 8 leaves, pp. [1–2] 3–15 [16]. [1]: title; [2]: catalogue; on 15: advertisement for several books 'In the Press.'

Bookseller's catalogue: 140 full title entries, arranged alphabetically by author, even though the title precedes the author's name in each entry, with prices ('in Sterling Money, at London'). The books in this catalogue are all religious books, most specifically by, about, or for Quakers; it has one special category, beginning on p. 13, for books 'on the slave-trade.'

Bristol 8356; m.p. 46770; Tapley, p. 354; *STE*, p. 333.

MSaE* (17×11 cm. — unbound).

173 HARRIS, THADDEUS MASON, 1768–1842

A seleced catalogue of some of the most esteemed publications in the English language. Proper to form a social library: with an introduction upon the choice of books. By Thaddeus M. Harris, A. M. Librarian of Harvard University, and author of "The Natural History of the Bible," and "A Short and Practical System of Punctuation." Catalogues given gratis by the publishers. Printed at Boston, by I. Thomas and E. T. Andrews, Faust's Statue, no. 45. Newbury Street. 1793.

12°: A–B⁶; 12 leaves, pp. [i–iii] iv–v [vi] [7] 8–23 [24]. [i]: title; [ii]: 'Observations upon Books and Reading'; [iii]: 'Introduction'; [vi]: 'Arrangement'; [7]: catalogue; [24]: list of 13 books 'Lately Published . . . and to be Sold by Thomas and Andrews.'

Model social library catalogue: 250 short to full author entries, many with place and date of publication, arranged by subject and in full alphabetical order within subjects. The subject headings are given in the 'Arrangement', p. [vi], which is modeled on that of the 1789 Philadelphia Library Company catalogue (item 131 above), with its three major divisions of memory, reason, and imagination, but with the following headings omitted: trade and commerce; mechanics; astrology and chronology; optics . . . ; navigation . . . ; civil architecture; military art; heraldry; anatomy. . . .

Evans 25587; Sabin 30521; Brigham, p. 53; Thompson, p. 59; *STE*, p. 339.

CtY*, MHi*, MWA* (17×10.5 cm. — unbound).

174 HAYT, LEWIS, fl. 1787–1793

Catalogue of books to be sold by public auction, at Lewis Hayt's office in State-Street, on Monday, the 8th day of July, viz. . . . [Boston, 1793.]

Broadside. 39.5 × 40 cm. 5 cols.

Auction catalogue: 383 consecutively numbered, short and medium author entries, arranged in no apparent order. Dated at bottom left: 'Boston, July 3, 1793.'
Evans 25267; Ford 2677; McKay 135; *STE*, p. 138 (under title).
MHi*.

175 HUNTER, GEORGE, AND COMPANY, New York

Catalogue of books, to be sold by George Hunter, and Co. at their store in Queen-Street, on Monday afternoon, the twenty seventh day of May, instant, being the property of a gentleman deceased. Sales to begin precisely at five o'clock. [New York, 1793.]

Broadside. 32 × 27 cm. 4 cols.

Auction catalogue: 266 consecutively numbered, short author entries; nearly half are law books, the rest a miscellaneous collection. Date: according to McKay, Hunter was active as a book auctioneer in New York in 1793–94; of those two years, May 27 fell on a Monday in 1793.
Bristol 8375; m.p. 46788; McKay 134B; *STE*, p. 372.
MWA*, NHi*.

176 LARKIN, EBENEZER, 1767–1813

Ebenezer Larkin's catalogue of books, for sale, wholesale and retail, at his book and stationarystore no. 50, Cornhill, Boston. Consisting of a very extensive collection of the latest and most approved authors, in divinity, law, physick, surgery, chemistry, history, biography, voyages, travels, miscellanies, novels, poetry, musick, arts and sciences, philosophy, navigation, astronomy, geography, architecture[,] trade and commerce[,] mathematicks, bookkeeping, &c. &c. To all which large additions are constantly making. Publick and private libraries will be supplied on as reasonable terms as at any other bookstore whatever. Catalogues delivered gratis. Printed at Boston, [by Thomas and Andrews] for Ebenezer Larkin. MDCCXCIII.

12°: A–E⁶; 30 leaves, pp. [1–3] 4–14 [15] 16–60 (30 misnumbered '22'; variant: p. 15 numbered). [1]: title (variant: 'Larkins's' for 'Larkin's', 'no. 40' for 'no.

50', and 'MDCCLXCIII' for 'MDCCXCIII'); [2]: blank; [3]: catalogue; 60: stationery.

Bookseller's catalogue: 1400 short and medium author entries, arranged by subject and alphabetically within subjects. The subject headings are essentially those given in the title, combined into groups of two, three, or more (i.e., the second heading is: law, physic, surgery, and chemistry), plus: English dictionaries, gazetteers, cookery, farriery, &c.; Latin & Greek classics, school books, &c.; pamphlets, plays and tracts. Except for portions of the title (most of which is the same), p. [2], the running heads (in Thomas & Andrews they correspond to the subject heading of the entries on the page; in Larkin they are 'E. Larkin's Catalogue of Books' throughout), and the lack of a page number on p. 15 (in some issues), this catalogue is an exact duplicate of Thomas and Andrews's 1793 catalogue (item 181 below), even including all of the stationery articles. Apparently Larkin's whole stock (and also David West's—see item 182) was supplied by Thomas and Andrews. No copy of this catalogue was reproduced on Microprint because none could be located in 1968.

Bristol 8391; m.p. 46803 (but no copy reproduced); *STE*, p. 408.

MBAt*, MH* (20×12 cm. — unbound), MiU-C* (variant), N, NN* (lacks t.p.; variant), Nh.

177 LIBRARY COMPANY OF PHILADELPHIA

Supplement to the catalogue of books, belonging to the Library Company of Philadelphia. Communiter bona profundere deorum est. Philadelphia: Printed by Zachariah Poulson, Junr. Librarian, no. 30, north Fourth-Street, near the University. M DCC XCIII.

8°: [A]⁴B–E⁴; 20 leaves, pp. [1–3] 4–38 [39–40]. [1]: title; [2]: 'Arrangement' (as in 1789 catalogue, item 131 above); [3]: catalogue of books 'added to the Library since August, 1789'; [39]: blank.

Social library catalogue: 350 full title entries, with place and date of publication, and, for donated books, name of donor; arranged by subject and by format within subjects, and numbered with shelf/accession numbers, a separate sequence for each format. Subject headings: as in the 1789 catalogue (item 131 above).

Evans 25995; Sabin 61785; Cutter 25; *STE*, p. 676.

DLC* (lacks pp. [39–40]), MB* (bound with 1789 catalogue), MWA* (22.5×14 cm. — unbound), MdHi, NN*, PPL* (2 copies), RPJCB*.

178 MECHANIC LIBRARY SOCIETY, New Haven, Connecticut

The constitution and bye-laws of the Mechanic Library Society of New-Haven, with a catalogue of books and list of the proprietors. New-Haven [:] Printed by Abel Morse, M,DCC,XCIII.

8°: [A]⁸(–A5ᵛ,6,7,8) [B]⁸(–B1ʳ,6,7,8) (A5ᵛ and B1ʳ cancelled by being pasted to one another); 9 leaves, pp. [i–ii], [1] 2–7 (8 cancelled) ([8] cancelled) [9–10] 11–17 [=18]. [i]: title; [ii]: blank; [1]: constitution; 5: bye-laws; (8 cancelled: beginning of catalogue); ([8] cancelled: blank); [9]: report of meeting of Society, dated '7th of January 1794'; [10]: catalogue.

Social library catalogue: 210 short author entries, arranged in full alphabetical order. As explained by the card catalog at the Beinecke Library at Yale, the 'page numbered 8, printed on verso of p. 7, has been cancelled by pasting it to the next leaf. The cancelled page contains the beginning of the catalogue which has been revised and printed on p. 10.' Apparently the constitution, bye-laws, catalogue, and list of proprietors were printed in 1793 in what was probably an 8 leaf octavo pamphlet. Then in 1794, a revised catalogue was printed, leaves 6–8 of the original octavo were removed, the page numbered 8 in the original (verso of p. 7), on which began the catalogue, was cancelled by having the blank recto of the first leaf of the new catalogue pasted to it. The original part is clearly dated 1793 in the imprint; the new part can be dated from the meeting report on p. [9]. The two parts use different paper and are set in different type.

Bristol 8410; m.p. 46831; Sabin 52974; Bates II, 2831; Thompson, p. 257; *STE*, p. 568.

CtY* (2 copies; 19.5 × 12 cm. — unbound).

179 NEW YORK SOCIETY LIBRARY

The charter, bye-laws, and names of the members of the New-York Society Library: with a catalogue of the books belonging to the said Library. New-York: Printed by T. & J. Swords, no. 27, William-Street. —1793.—

8°: [A]⁴B–M⁴N² (variant: N not signed); 50 leaves, pp. [1–5] 6–14 [15] 16–21 [22–23] 24–99 [100]. [1]: title; [2]: blank; [3]: advertisement (see below); [4]: blank; [5]: charter; [15]: 'An Act To remove Doubts respecting the Charter'; on 16: bye-laws; on 19: an ordinance; on 21: list of trustees; [22]: blank; [23]: catalogue; 89: list of members; [100]: blank.

Social library catalogue: 2100 short author entries, numbered with accession/shelf numbers, arranged alphabetically and by format within each letter, with a brief, separate list of German books at the end. The advertisement on p. [3] apologizes for the fact that the catalogue is not, as originally intended, arranged by subject, a task that is delayed due to its immensity. One glimpses here, perhaps, a sense of competition with the Library Company of Philadelphia, which moved to a subject listing in its 1789 catalogue. Fourteen photostat facsimiles of this catalogue were prepared in 1942 as no. 166 in the Massachusetts Historical Society Photostat Americana, Second Series.

Evans 25915; Sabin 54543; Cutter 23; Ranz, p. 119; *STE*, p. 610.

DLC*, MH* (2 copies—B copy: pp. [5]–6 mutilated), MWA* (20×12.5 cm. — unbound), MiU-C*, NHi*, NN*, NNS, PPL* (variant), RPJCB*, ViW.

180 RHODE ISLAND COLLEGE [BROWN UNIVERSITY]. LIBRARY

Catalogue of books belonging to the Library of Rhode-Island College. Providence: Printed by J. Carter. M,DCC,XCIII.

4°: [A]⁴B–E⁴; 20 leaves, pp. [1–3] 4–38 [39–40]. [1]: title; [2]: blank; [3]: catalogue; [39]: blank.

College library catalogue: 1200 short author entries, arranged by format and in full alphabetical order within each format.

Evans 26077; Sabin 8604; Cutter 26; Alden 1334; Ranz, p. 119; *STE*, p. 118.

MB* (lacks leaf E4), MWA* (lacks leaf E4), PU, RHi*, RPB, RPJCB* (18.5×12 cm. — bound).

181 THOMAS, ISAIAH, 1749–1831, AND EBENEZER TURRELL ANDREWS, 1766–1851

Thomas and Andrews's catalogue of books, for sale, wholesale and retail, at their book and stationary store, Faust's Statue, no. 45, Newbury Street. Boston. Consisting of a very extensive collection of the latest and most approved authors, in divinity, law, physick, surgery, chemistry, history, biography, voyages, travels, miscellanies, novels, poetry, musick, arts and sciences, philosophy, navigation, astronomy, geography, architecture, trade and commerce, mathematicks, bookkeeping, &c. &c. To all which large additions are constantly making. Publick and private libraries will be supplied on as reasonable terms as at any other bookstore whatever. Catalogues delivered gratis. Printed at Boston, by Thomas and Andrews, Faust's Statue, no. 45, Newbury Street. MDCCXCIII.

12°: A–E⁶; 30 leaves, pp. [1–3] 4–60 (variant: p. 5 not numbered). [1]: title; [2]: cut of Faust's statue and advertisement for Thaddeus Harris's *A Selected Catalogue*, 'Just published'; [3]: catalogue; 60: stationery.

Bookseller's catalogue: 1400 short and medium author entries, arranged by subject and alphabetically within subjects (subject headings closely approximate the list in the title). This catalogue was reprinted, with minor changes, as the 1793 Ebenezer Larkin catalogue and the 1793 David West catalogue, which see.

Evans 26252; Sabin 95449; Brigham, p. 54; *STE*, p. 829.

MHi* (17×11 cm. — unbound), MWA* (variant; has prices penned in by I. Thomas).

182 WEST, DAVID, 1765–1810

David West's catalogue of books, for sale, wholesale and retail, at his book and stationary store, no. 36, Marlborough Street, Boston. Consisting of a very extensive collection of the latest and most approved authors, in divinity, law, physick, surgery, chemistry, history, biography, voyages, travels, miscellanies, novels, poetry, musick, arts and sciences, philosophy, navigation, astronomy, geography, architecture, trade and commerce, mathematicks, bookkeeping, &c. &c. To all which large additions are constantly making. Publick and private libraries will be supplied on as reasonable terms as at any other bookstore whatever. Catalogues delivered gratis. Printed at Boston [by Thomas and Andrews], for David West. MDCCLXCIII [i.e., 1793].

12°: A–E⁶; 30 leaves, pp. [1–3] 4–60 (variant: p. 40 not numbered). [1]: title; [2]: blank; [3]: catalogue; 60: stationery.

Bookseller's catalogue: 1400 entries, as in the 1793 Thomas and Andrews catalogue, the preceding item. Except for portions of the title (most of which is the same), p. [2], and the running heads (in Thomas and Andrews they correspond to the subject heading of the entries on the page; in West they are 'West's Catalogue of Books' throughout), this catalogue is an exact duplicate of the 1793 Thomas and Andrews catalogue. Thomas and Andrews must have been supplying West's stock as well as Ebenezer Larkin's (see item 176 above).

Evans 26468; Sabin 102718; Brigham, p. 54; *STE*, p. 987.

MHi* (variant; lacks t.p.), MWA* (19 × 12 cm. — bound).

See also McKay 133E (Jay), 133F (Hayt), 133G (Barclay), 133H (Barclay), 133I (Barclay), 134A (Dellap), 134C, 135A (Hayt), 135B (Hayt), 135C (Jay), 135D (Jay), 135E (Hart), 135F (Jay)

———————————————— 1794 ————————————————

183 CAMPBELL, ROBERT, d. 1800

Robert Campbell's catalogue of books; now selling on the lowest terms, at no. 54. south Second Street, second door below the corner of Chesnut Street, on the west side. Philadelphia: Printed [by Robert Campbell] September 13th, 1794.

12°: π1[=G2]A–F⁶[G]²(–G2); 38 leaves, pp. [1–3] 4–69 [70] 71–74 [75–76] (63 misprinted ℰ9; variant: 7 of p. 72 not struck). [1]: title; [2]: contents; [3]: catalogue; on 66: stationery (including maps and charts); on 69: list of prints; [70]: list of 42 'books printed for Robert Campbell,' full title entries, with prices; [75]: blank.

Bookseller's catalogue: 1500 short and medium author entries, arranged by subject and alphabetically within subjects. Subject headings: law; divinity, sermons, and ecclesiastical history; history, travels, voyages, miscellanies, moral philosophy, biography, poetry, dramatic works, novels, &c. (the largest category, very miscellaneous); physic, surgery, chemistry, natural history, botany, &c.; arts, sciences, natural philosophy, architecture, arithmetic, book-keeping, mathematics, navigation, geography and tactics; French and Italian books; spelling books, grammars, dictionaries, &c., for the English classes; dictionaries, grammars, and other books for the Latin classes; books for the Greek classes; tragedies, commedies [sic], farces, &c.; pamphlets, &c.; small histories and chap books; odd volumes, magazines, reviews, &c. Attribution of printer from MWA.

Evans 26727; Brigham, p. 54; *STE*, p. 131.

MH* (variant), MWA* (variant; and lacks leaf [G]1), MiU-C* (16.5×10.5 cm. — unbound; a few ms. additions), PHi* (variant; lacks leaf [G]1).

184 CAMPBELL, SAMUEL, 1763?–1836

Samuel Campbell's sale catalogue of books, for 1794. Comprehending above fifty thousand volumes, in arts, sciences, and miscellaneous literature; forming a general assortment of the principal authors, ancient and modern. Among which will be found, many scarce and valuable books in divinity, physic, surgery, midwifery, philosophy, novels, architecture, anatomy, voyages, travels, poetry, dramatic works, geography, miscellanies, history, biography, arts, sciences, law, dictionaries and grammars, for English, Latin, Greek, and French classes, &c. The books in general are good editions and well bound, except otherwise expressed in the catalogue; and will be sold for cash, at the most reasonable prices. Country booksellers, merchants, traders, and teachers, will particularly find it their interest in applying for books and stationary, at Samuel Campbell's book and stationary store, no. 124, Pearl Street, (formerly no. 37, Hanover Square) directly opposite the Bank of New-York, where catalogues will be delivered gratis to gentlemen who please to call or send for them. N.B. Orders from the country executed with the utmost care and attention; and a large discount made to those who purchase quantities. [New York: Printed by Samuel Campbell, 1794.]

8°: π^2 A–I⁴K² (π^2 probably = K3–4); 40 leaves, pp. [i–iv], [1] 2–57 [58] 59–76. [1]: title; [ii]: blank; [iii]: index of subject headings; [iv]: advertisements (paper made; bring in rags; books imported; rationale of catalogue [see below]); [1]: catalogue; [58]: stationery; on 59: appendix to catalogue; on 63: catalogue of 'American Editions' which are 'printed and sold by Samuel Campbell'; on 76: advertisements (bookbinding; printing).

Bookseller's catalogue. Main catalogue: 1550 consecutively numbered, short and medium author entries, with place and date of publication, arranged by subject, by format within subjects, and alphabetically within format. The subject headings are essentially those of Samuel Campbell's 1787 catalogue, item 114 above, with slight rearrangements and omitting 'Newbery's books. . . ,' and adding 'maps and charts' and 'livres François.' Appendix: another 114 short and medium author entries, with place and date of publication, arranged by format and alphabetically within format. Catalogue of American editions: 323 consecutively numbered, short and medium author entries, arranged alphabetically, with prices but without place and date of publication, though each of these books also appears in the main catalogue with this information. Although the editions in this last list are not all, as claimed, printed by Samuel Campbell, the list is otherwise accurate in that the editions *are* American ones of about the date of the catalogue. The note on p. [iv] regarding the need for including place and date of publication in the main catalogue is essentially the same as that which appeared on p. [2] of Samuel Campbell's 1789 catalogue (item 127 above). *STE* incorrectly gives [Philadelphia] as the place of publication.

Evans 26728; Brigham, pp. 54–55; *STE*, p. 131.

MWA* (22×14 cm. — bound).

185   CAREY, MATHEW, 1760–1839

Mathew Carey's catalogue of books, &c. for sale, on the most reasonable terms at no. 118, Market-Street, near Fourth-Street, Philadelphia. Philadelphia: Printed [by Mathew Carey] March 12, 1794.

8°: [A]²B–H⁴I²; 32 leaves, pp. [1–2] 3–4 [5] 6–64. [1]: title; [2]: advertisement (thanks public for encouragement, which he hopes to continue to merit); 3: contents; on 3: list of plays; [5]: main catalogue.

Bookseller's catalogue. List of plays, pp. 3–4: 200 short title entries, arranged in full alphabetical order, in 3 columns. Main catalogue: 1900 short and medium author entries, arranged by subject and in full alphabetical order within subjects. Subject headings: law; religion; physic, surgery, chemistry; history, voyages, travels, &c.; miscellanies (largest category); novels and romances; mathematics,

&c.; agriculture; poetry, the drama, &c.; song-books; Latin and Greek school-books; English school-books; architecture; French books.

Evans 26730; Brigham, p. 55; *STE*, p. 134.

MH*, MWA* (23 ×14.5 cm. — bound), MiU–C*, RPJCB*.

[Connelly, John, fl. 1792–1800

Catalogue of a choice collection of books in various branches of literature. To be sold at John Connelly's Auction Store, no. 78 South Front-Street. Philadelphia: Printed by John Fenno. 1794.]

Origin of entry unknown. Evans 26816; McKay 137; *STE*, p. 183.

186 DABNEY, JOHN, 1752–1819

Additional catalogue of books, for sale or circulation, in town or country, at the Salem Bookstore; comprising, among other subjects of universal literature and entertainment, theology, history, antiquities, biography, geography, philosophy, metaphysics, astronomy, politics, &c. Together with a numerous collection of modern novels and histories. Also, an extensive and elegant assortment of books & stationary. A constant supply from Europe and various parts of the Union, of all the new, curious, and interesting publications, in every branch of polite literature: variety of magazines, reviews, other periodical works, and dramatic entertainments; including every performance of literary merit, at any time advertised in the public papers, for sale or loan. Publications and classics of every kind—English, French, Latin, and Greek, for the use of academies, schools, and individuals, in large or small quantities. Books exchanged for books: or the full value in cash paid for second-hand libraries or parcels of books. [Catalogues received gratis.] [Newburyport:] At Osborne's Office, printed for J. Dabney, at Salem. MDCCXCIV.

12°: A–C⁶; 18 leaves, pp. [1–3] 4–34 [35–36]. [1]: title (brackets around 'Catalogues received gratis' in original); [2]: advertisement (maintains pleasing variety; orders books from abroad; sells second-hand books; supplies libraries); [3]: catalogue; 34: stationery; [35]: blank.

Circulating library and bookseller's catalogue: 775 short author entries, arranged in nearly full alphabetical order, with several brief subject lists at the end (dictionaries, classics, school books, &c.; navigation; Bibles, testaments, &c.). The place of publication is given as Newburyport because the only Osborne who could have printed this catalogue in 1794 was George J. Osborne, whose office was in Newburyport in that year, according to the MWA Printers File. Bristol 8636 (m.p. 47020) is a red herring; the MSaE copy corresponds exactly to all other copies.

Evans 26840; Tapley, p. 355; Shera, pp. 149, 153, 261; Brigham, p. 55; *STE*, p. 201.

MHi* (lacks leaf C6), MSaE* (lacks leaf C6), MWA* (lacks leaf C6), NN* (20.5×12.5 cm. — bound), PPL* (lacks leaf C6), RPJCB* (lacks sig. C, pp. 25–[36]; bound with 1791 Dabney catalogue).

187 DORCHESTER LIBRARY, Dorchester, Massachusetts

Rules and orders of the Dorchester Library, with a catalogue of the books, August, MDCCXCIV. Printed at Boston, by I. Thomas and E. T. Andrews, Faust's Statue, no. 45, Newbury Street. MDCCXCIV.

12°: A⁶; 6 leaves, pp. [1–3] 4–6 [7] 8–12. [1]: title; [2]: blank; [3]: rules and orders; [7]: catalogue.

Social library catalogue: 135 short author entries, with prices, arranged alphabetically.

Bristol 8652; m.p. 47035; *STE*, p. 231.

CtY*, MHi*, MWA* (17.5×11 cm. — unbound; with 6 pp. of ms. additions), RPJCB*.

188 FELLOWS, JOHN, 1759–1844

Supplement to John Fellows's Circulating Library. [New York, 1794?]

12°: A–B⁶ (A⁵ signed 'A2', B5 signed 'B2'); 12 leaves, pp. [1] 2 [3] 4–24. [1]: title (caption); on [1]: conditions; [3]: catalogue (apparently incomplete—it stops in the middle of the R's on p. 24).

Circulating library catalogue: 232 consecutively numbered short and medium author and title entries, arranged alphabetically. Date: dated [1796?] by Bristol, but [1794?] by NHi, which seems more likely, because of this comment on p. [1]: 'He expects from England, this Spring, all the novels published in 1793.' Several other dates in the catalogue also lend credence to 1794.

Bristol 9541; m.p. 47778 (not reproduced); *STE*, p. 263.

NHi* (18 cm.).

189 FOLSOM, JOHN WEST, 1758–1825

John W. Folsom's catalogue of books for sale and circulation, consisting of a large assortment of all the principal authors in divinity physic surgery philosophy novels architecture anatomy voyages travels antiquities poetry navigation geography miscellanies history biography arts sciences dictionaries plays, &c. The books in general are good editions, and well bound, and will be sold at the most reasonable prices, at John W. Folsom's book and stationary-store, no. 30, Union-Street, Boston, where catalogues will be delivered gratis, to gentlemen who will please to call or send for them. Orders from the country executed with the utmost care and attention, and a large discount made to those who purchase quantities. Printing in its various branches executed on moderate terms. [Boston: Printed by John Folsom, 1794.]

12°: A⁶B–G⁴/²; 24 leaves, pp. [1–48]. A1ʳ: title; A1ᵛ: advertisement, and conditions of the circulating library; A2ʳ: circulating library catalogue; on F3ʳ: sale catalogue; G2ʳ: stationery; G2ᵛ: advertisements for several newly published books.

Circulating library and bookseller's catalogue. Circulating catalogue: 1086 consecutively numbered, medium to full author and title entries, arranged by format and alphabetically within format, with separate brief listings of plays, and 'Additions to the Circulating Library' at the end. All volumes of multivolumed sets are numbered separately, so the actual number of titles in the catalogue is much fewer than 1086; frequently, entries for vol. 2+ of a multivolumed work indicate the separate contents of each volume. A symbol by some of the entries in this section is used to indicate that they are for sale as well as loan. Sale catalogue: 240 short author entries, most of them in one alphabetical list, with a brief list of 'Small Histories' at the end. Date: the advertisement on G2ᵛ is dated, 'Boston, December 24, 1794.' This catalogue is not reproduced on Microprint because no copy could be located in 1968.

Bristol 8665; m.p. 47046 (not reproduced); *STE*, p. 273.

MB* (20×12 cm. — bound), MBAt*, MH*.

190 FRANKLIN LIBRARY COMPANY, Franklin, Connecticut

The constitution of the Franklin Library Company. Also, subscribers names, and catalogue of books. Norwich: Printed by John Trumbull. M,DCC,XC,IV.

8°: [A]⁴; 4 leaves, pp. [1–2] 3–8. [1]: title; [2]: rules of agreement; on 4: subscribers' names; on 5: catalogue.

Social library catalogue: 110 short author entries, arranged by subject. Subject headings: divinity; history; poetry; law; metaphysics; geography; travels; biography; novels; physic; philosophy; 'chritisism' [*sic*]; various subjects.

Evans 27430; Trumbull 731; Thompson, p. 255; Shera, p. 291; *STE*, p. 621 (under Norwich).

CtHi* (uncut), CtY* (uncut), MWA* (23×15 cm. — unbound).

[Hoppin, Benjamin, 1747–1809
Catalogue of a great variety of new books, to be sold on Friday, 23d of May, instant, at nine o'clock, in the morning, at Benjamin Hoppin's auction room. Providence: Printed by Bennett Wheeler. 1794.]

Origin of entry unknown. Evans gives the auctioneer's name as 'Hopkins.' Evans 27137; McKay 136, *STE*, p. 367.

[Keatinge, George, d. 1811?
Catalogue of books. Baltimore, 1794.]

Advertised in the *Maryland Journal*, May 23, 1794. Minick 179; Bristol 8712; m.p. 47088; *STE*, p. 396.

191 LIBRARY COMPANY OF PHILADELPHIA

Second supplement to the catalogue of books, belonging to the Library Company of Philadelphia. Communiter bona profundere deorum est. Philadelphia: Printed by Zachariah Poulson, Jun. Librarian, number eighty, Chesnut-Street. December 1, M DCC XCIV.

8°: [A]⁴B–D⁴E1; 17 leaves, pp. [1–3] 4–34. [1]: title; [2]: blank; [3]: catalogue of books 'added to the Library since the thirty-first of December, 1792.'

Social library catalogue: 440 full author entries, (counting individual titles in bound pamphlet collections separately), with place and date of publication, and, for donated books, name of donor; arranged by format and in full alphabetical order within format, and numbered with shelf/accession numbers, a separate sequence for each format.

Evans 27509; Cutter 28; *STE*, p. 676.

DLC*, MB* (bound with 1789 catalogue), MWA* (22×13.5 cm. — unbound), MdHi, NN*, PPL* (2 copies), RPJCB*.

192 PENNSYLVANIA HOSPITAL, Philadelphia

Catalogue of the books which have been added to the Medical Library in the Pennsylvania Hospital, since the year M DCC XC. [colophon:] [Philadelphia:] Printed by Zachariah Poulson, Junior. [1794.]

8°: [F]⁴G–L⁴; 24 leaves, pp. [37] 38–62 [63] 64–66 [67] 68–72 [73] 74–78 [79–84] [=48] (variant: 77 not numbered). [37]: title (caption); on 37: catalogue; [63]: rules for preservation of paintings, castings, and anatomical preparations, dated '27th. of the First month, 1794' on 66; [67]: description of the anatomical museum; [73]: index of authors and editors 'in the Catalogues of Books, Printed in 1790 and 1794'; on 78: colophon; [79]: blank.

Medical library catalogue: 300 entries, as in the 1790 catalogue, item 142 above. Usually bound with, and not distinguished from, the 1790 catalogue of the Pennsylvania Hospital Library. See the discussion under the earlier catalogue.

Evans 27510 (with 1790 catalogue); Cutter 24 (dated 1793); *STE*, p. 677.

CtY-M, DLC* (variant; and lacks leaves L2–4), DNLM, MiU-C* (lacks leaves L3–4), NHi* (18.5×11.3 cm. — unbound; lacks leaves L2–4; interleaved with blanks), NNNAM, OkU, PHi* (lacks leaves L2–4), PPC, PPL* (3 copies; lack leaves L2–4), RPJCB* (has ms. additions on leaves L2–4).

193 PHILADELPHIA COMPANY OF PRINTERS AND BOOKSELLERS

A catalogue of books, published by the different members of the Philadelphia Company of Printers and Booksellers, and now for sale, at Mathew Carey's Book-store, no. 118, Market-street. Philadelphia: Printed by D. Humphreys, no. 48, Spruce-street. M.DCC.XCIV.

12°: [A]1[=D2]B⁶C⁴D²(–D2); 12 leaves, pp. [1–3] 4–24. [1]: title (variant: 'Wm. Spotswood's Book-store,' for 'Mathew Carey's Book-store, no. 118, Market-street.'); [2]: blank; [3]: catalogue.

Publishers' catalogue: 400 short to full author entries, American editions, with prices, most of them in one fully alphabetical list, with several brief additional lists at the end (additional books; pamphlets; plays and farces; small histories, & chap books; maps and charts; prints). The Spotswood variant is the one reproduced on Microprint.

Bristol 8823; Sabin 61521 and 89650.

MH* (19×11.5 cm. — unbound), PHi*. Variant: Evans 27506; Sabin 89650; *STE*, p. 165. MHi* (listed in card catalog under Phila. Co. of Printers, but shelved under Wm. Spotswood).

194 STEPHENS, THOMAS, fl. 1793–1797

A catalogue of books now offered for sale by Thomas Stephens, at his book-store, no. 77, south Second Street. Philadelphia: Printed by Wrigley & Berriman, no. 149, Chesnut Street.—1794.

8°: [A]⁴B²; 6 leaves, pp. [1–3] 4–11 [12]. [1]: title; [2]: blank; [3]: catalogue; [12]: blank.

Bookseller's catalogue: 200 short to full author entries; the first 3 pages contain an alphabetical list of law books, and the rest of the catalogue is a general list arranged in no apparent order. Stephens also published a catalogue of prints and paintings in 1794; see Bristol 8876.

Evans 27741; Sabin 91310; Brigham, p. 56; *STE*, p. 804.

MWA* (21.5 × 14 cm. — bound).

195 WILLIAMS COLLEGE. LIBRARY

A catalogue of books, in the Library of Williams College, Wil—liamstown. Bennington: Printed by Anthony Haswell. M,DCC,-XCIV.

8°: [A]⁸; 8 leaves, pp. [1–3] 4–16. [1]: title; [2]: blank; [3]: catalogue.

College library catalogue: 180 short author entries, arranged by subject and in full alphabetical order within subjects. Subject headings: divinity and ecclesiastical history; history, voyages and travels; arts and sciences; languages; poetry; miscellanies.

Evans 28101; Sabin 104426; Cutter 27; McCorison 323; Ranz, p. 119; *STE*, p. 1006.

MHi* (lacks pp. 13–16), MWiW* (23 × 14.5 cm. — bound; top of leaf [A]8 torn away).

See also McKay 135G (Pole [Barclay]), 135H (Morris), 136A (Hunter), 136B (Smith), 136C (Jay), 136D (Walker)

———————————— 1795 ————————————

196 BLAKE, WILLIAM PYNSON, 1769–1820, AND
LEMUEL, 1775–1861

Catalogue of American editions of books for sale by Wm. P. and Lemuel Blake, no. 1, Cornhill, Boston. [Boston, 1795?]

Broadside. 5 cols. Entries include prices. Title and description from Anderson Auction Co., *A Collection of Early American Books and Pamphlets* [Auction Catalog No. 413, Nov. 13, 1905] (New York: Douglas Taylor and Co., 1905), p. 12, where it is described in enough detail to convince one that it existed in 1905; present location unknown. Probably very similar to the Thomas, Andrews, and

Penniman 1796 broadside catalogue of American publications, item 226 below.
Evans 31835 (dated 1797)?; *STE*, p. 96 (dated 1797).

197 BOSTON LIBRARY SOCIETY
Catalogue of books in the Boston Library. January 1, 1795.
[Boston, 1795.]

8°: [A]⁴B–C⁴; 12 leaves, pp. [1] 2–23 [24]. [1]: title (caption); on [1]: catalogue;
21: rules and regulations; on 23: list of officers, and note about location of library;
[24]: blank.

Social library catalogue: 425 short author entries, arranged in full alphabetical
order.

Evans 28317; Sabin 6730; Cutter 29; Ranz, p. 119; *STE*, p. 106.
MWA* (21 × 13 cm. — unbound).

198 CAREY, MATHEW, 1760–1839
Catalogue of books, pamphlets, maps, and prints, published
by Mathew Carey, 118, Market Street, Philadelphia. [Philadelphia:]
Printed by Wrigley and Berriman, no. 149, Chesnut Street. M.DCC.-
XCV.

12°: A–B⁶; 12 leaves, pp. [1–3] 4–24. [1]: title; [2]: blank; [3]: catalogue of
books; on 22: list of 43 maps; on 23: list of 13 prints; on 23: list of 16 pamphlets
'for sale by M. Carey,' with prices.

Publisher's catalogue: 76 consecutively numbered, medium and full title entries,
all with prices, and many with either a comment about the book or its table of
contents, arranged in no apparent order, in one large, unlabeled general list,
plus three shorter lists for chap books, pamphlets, plays and farces.

Evans 28388; Brigham, p. 56; *STE*, p. 133.
DLC* (lacks sig. B), MWA* (18 × 10.5 cm. — bound), MiU-C* (lacks pp.
13–24), PPL*, RPJCB*.

199 CARTER, JOHN, 1745–1814, AND WILLIAM
WILKINSON, 1760–1852
Catalogue of books, for sale by Carter and Wilkinson, at the
Providence Book-Store, opposite the market. [Providence: Printed
by Carter and Wilkinson, 1795.]

Broadside. 46 × 28.5 cm. 3 cols.

Bookseller's catalogue: 325 short author entries, most of them in one alphabetical list, with three brief subject lists at the end (pamphlets; plays; maps [set in 2 columns within the third column]). Variant: maps are set in one column only, and the main list has two additional titles. Date: both variants dated 1795 by Alden on the basis of the publication dates of the books listed.

Evans 28396; Alden 1411; Brigham, p. 56; *STE*, p. 137.

MWA*. Variant: Alden 1410. RHi* (46.5×28 cm.).

200 DAVIS, GEORGE

Law books— — —latest Irish editions. George Davis respectfully informs his friends and the gentlemen of the profession generally through the United States, that the following books, being his late extensive importation, are ready for sale, at the same moderate prices as have, for several years last past, so universally recommended them. Orders from any distance, addressed to him in writing, for a single book or an entire library, will be received with thanks, and meet with the most prompt attention. No. 313, High-street, Philadelphia, November 16, 1795. [Philadelphia, 1795.]

Broadside. 33.5×20 cm. 2 cols.

Bookseller's catalogue: 140 short author entries, all law books, with prices, arranged by format.

Bristol 9071; m.p. 47395; *STE*, p. 206.

RPJCB* (ms. letter on verso from Davis to James Hamilton of Carlisle, Pa.).

[Dover Social Library, Dover, New Hampshire

Catalogue of books in the Social Library. Dover: Printed by Samuel Bragg, Jun., 1795. Broadside.]

Origin of entry unknown. Evans 28585; *STE*, p. 232.

[Hoppin, Benjamin, 1747–1809

A catalogue of a most valuable collection of books, among which are a variety of useful and elegant sermons, and several celebrated treatises on divinity. To be sold at auction at the office of Benjamin Hoppin, beginning the morning after commencement at nine o'clock. Providence, 1795.]

Advertised in the *Providence Gazette*, Aug. 22, 29, 1795. McKay 138E; Alden 1418; Bristol 9143; m.p. 47458; *STE*, p. 367.

[Hoppin, Benjamin, 1747–1809

Food for sentimentalists. A catalogue of a variety of books for sale Wednesday, April 29, 1795 at B. Hoppin's Auction Office. Providence: Printed by Bennett Wheeler. 1795.]

Advertised in the *Providence Gazette*, Apr. 18, 1795. Evans 28856; McKay 138; Alden 1419; *STE*, p. 367.

201 JAY, FREDERICK

Catalogue of books, for sale by Frederick Jay, on Friday the 8th of May, at ten o'clock, at his auction-room, no. 167 Pearl-street, opposite the National Bank. [colophon:] New-York, May 7, 1795.— Printed by T. & J. Swords, no. 99 Pearl-street, four doors west of the Old-Slip.

Broadside. 44×27 cm. 4 cols.

Auction catalogue: 182 consecutively numbered, short author (mostly) and title entries, arranged in no apparent order.

Bristol 9149; m.p. 47467; *STE*, p. 385.

CtHi*.

[Keddie, James, fl. 1794–1795

Catalogue of books, the remaining stock of James Keddie, at his store, no. 144, Market street, consisting of divinity, law, physic, history, romance, agriculture, classics, school books, &c. and are generally of the best European editions. Baltimore: Printed by P. Edwards and J. W. Allen. 1795.]

Advertised in the *Maryland Journal*, Nov. 3, 1795. Evans 28915 and Minick 238 (both under 'Kedzie'); *STE*, p. 396.

202 LARKIN, EBENEZER, 1767–1813

Eben. Larkin's exchange catalogue, Boston. [Boston, 1795.]

4°: [A]²; 2 leaves, pp. [1–4]. [1]: title and catalogue; [2]: blank.

Publisher's catalogue: 36 short author entries, arranged alphabetically, with prices. Date: a ms. note from Larkin to Mathew Carey on p. [3] is dated 'Oct. 20, 1795.'

Bristol 9165.

PHi* (22.5×18.5 cm. — unbound).

203 LOGANIAN LIBRARY, Philadelphia

Catalogue of the books belonging to the Loganian Library; to which is prefixed, a short account of the institution, with the law for annexing the said library to that belonging to "The Library Company of Philadelphia," and the rules regulating the manner of conducting the same. Philadelphia: Printed by Zachariah Poulson, Junior, number eighty, Chesnut-Street. M DCC XCV.

8°: [A]⁴B–Dd⁴Ee²; 110 leaves, pp. [i–iii] iv–x [xi] xii–xiii 14–64 [65] 66–72 [73] 74–205 [206–7] 208–20 (variants—a: 205 misnumbered '502'; b: 199 not numbered; c: 1 and 4 of 154 not struck; d: 1 of 104 not struck; e: 1 of 194 not struck; f: 1 of 196 not struck). [i]: title; [ii]: blank; [iii]: short account of library; v: act for annexing the Loganian Library to the Lib. Co. of Phila.; [xi]: rules; xiii: catalogue of English books; [65]: author index to English books; [73]: part II: catalogue of Hebrew, Greek, Latin, French, Italian, &c. books; [206]: blank; [207]: author index to Hebrew . . . books.

Social library catalogue. Catalogue of English books: 700 full author and title (mostly) entries, with place and date of publication, arranged by format, and numbered (nearly consecutively) with shelf/accession numbers within each format. Catalogue of Hebrew, Greek, Latin, French, Italian, &c. books: 2200 full author entries, with place and date of publication, arranged by format, and numbered (nearly consecutively) with shelf/accession numbers within each format.

Evans 29314; Sabin 61798; Cutter 30; Ranz, p. 119; *STE*, p. 677 (under Philadelphia).

CtY* (2 copies—1 [Franklin collection]: variants a, b, d; 2 [Beinecke]: variant a), DLC*, MB*, MBAt*, MH* (variant a), MHi* (variant a), MWA* (variants a, c), NN* (22.5×13.5 cm. — bound), PHi* (variants a, e, f), PPAmP* (2 copies—1: half uncut; 2: variant a), PPL* (5 copies—1: interleaved with blanks with ms. notations of damage to, and rebinding of, the books; 2: lacks pp. 209–16, has ms. additions and notations; 3: variant b; 4: variant b, lacks pp. 209–20; 5: a perfect copy).

204 MELCHER, JOHN, 1759–1850

Catalogue of books, &c. for sale by John Melcher, printer and book-seller, at his printing-office and book-store, corner of Market-Street, near the Court-House, Portsmouth, where the printing business is prosecuted with neatness and dispatch, on very moderate terms. [Portsmouth, 1795.]

Broadside. 53×41 cm. 6 cols.

Bookseller's catalogue: 450 short (mostly) to full author entries, arranged alphabetically, plus lists of stationery and blanks. Dated 'June, 1795' at the bottom of column six.

RPJCB*.

205 MOREAU DE SAINT-MÉRY, MÉDÉRIC LOUIS ÉLIE, 1750–1819, AND COMPANY

Catalogue of books, stationary, engravings, mathematical instruments, maps, charts, and other goods of Moreau de St. Mery, & Co's. store, no. 84, south Front-Street, corner of Walnut. Index [in 6 lines, 2 cols.]. Philadelphia [: Printed by Moreau de Saint-Mery], 1795.

8°: [A]1[=L2?] B–K⁴[L]²(–L2) (variant: sig. K unsigned); 38 leaves, pp. [1–3] 4–76. [1]: title; [2]: advertisement, in French and English (sell books, stationery, engravings; do printing and book-binding; fulfill special orders); [3]: catalogue ([3]: English books; on 22: libri Latini; 26: libri Italiani & Spagnuoli; on 26: Deutsche bucher; 30: Hollandsche bockken; on 30: livres Français; 62: copy books.—livres d'ecriture; 63: maps.—cartes geographiques; 69: plans divers; 70: first supplement); 75: stationery. Papeterie, & objets qui en dépendent (in French and English).

Bookseller's catalogue: 1150 medium (mostly) and full author entries (for English, Latin, and German books) and title entries (for Italian & Spanish, Dutch, and French), arranged, as indicated above, by language and then in full alphabetical order within language groups. Attribution of printer from Evans.

Evans 29107; Brigham, p. 56; *STE*, p. 541.

MB* (lacks t.p., pp. 5–6, 75–76), MWA* (15.5 × 10 cm. — bound), PPAmP* (variant).

[Muirhead, James

Catalogue of books and stationary, received by the Romulus and other late vessels from London. To be had at the store of James Muirhead, no. 7, Elliot-street. Charleston: Printed by W. P. Harrison & Co., no. 38, Bay. 1795.]

Origin of entry unknown. Evans 29128; *STE*, p. 546.

[New York Society Library

Catalogue. New York: T. & J. Swords. 1795. 8°: 99 pp.]

Origin of entry unknown; probably refers to the 1793 New York Society Library catalogue. Sabin 54545.

206 POWER, NICHOLAS

Books and stationary, a handsome collection, just received and for sale by N. Power, at his printing-office near the Court-House in Poughkeepsie, among which are. . . . [Poughkeepsie, 1795.]

Broadside. 43 × 26 cm. 3 cols.

Bookseller's catalogue: 225 short author entries, arranged by subject; plus a list of stationery and an advertisement for 'Hutchin's Almanacks for 1796' and 'Gaine's Pocket Almanacks.' Subjects (not actually labeled): religion; entertainment (novels, essays, poetry, etc.); law; medicine; school books; classics; pamphlets. Date: the advertisement for a 1796 almanac, and the fact that the latest novels listed in the catalogue are several first published in 1795, make 1795 the most likely date. This item is not reproduced on Microprint because the NN copy could not be located in 1968.

Bristol 9253; m.p. 47563 (not reproduced); Stark 1150; *STE*, p. 695.
NN*.

207 RICE, HENRY, d. 1804, AND PATRICK,
fl. 1792–1804

Henry & Patrick Rice's catalogue of a large and valuable collection of books, in the several branches of ancient and modern literature, for 1795. To be sold, wholesale and retail, at their book and stationary-store, no. 50, Market-street, Philadelphia; where wholesale purchasers will meet the greatest encouragement, and libraries be furnished on very reasonable terms. To their present very extensive stock will be added every new work of merit, which will be printed in any part of the United States. They will at all times have a general assortment of imported goods in the line of their business. Philadelphia: Printed for H. & P. Rice, no. 50, Market-Street. [1795.]

12°: [A]1[=H2]B–G⁶[H]²(–H2); 38 leaves, pp. [i–ii], [1] 2–72 [73–74]. [i]: title; [ii]: table of contents; [1]: catalogue; on 72: stationery; [73]: list of plays.

Bookseller's catalogue: 1870 short to full author entries, arranged by subject and in full alphabetical order within subjects, numbered consecutively (to #1783), exclusive of pamphlets. Subject headings: religion; law; physic, surgery, &c.; history, biography, &c.; miscellanies; novels and romances; poetry; arts, sciences, philosophy, &c.; natural history; schoolbooks; pamphlets. The list of plays has an additional 200 short title entries, arranged in full alphabetical order.

Bristol 9273; m.p. 47580; *STE*, p. 738.
PHi* (17 × 11 cm. — unbound).

208 SPOTSWOOD, WILLIAM, 1753?–1805

William Spotswood's catalogue of books, &c. for sale on the most reasonable terms at no. 55 Marlborough-street, the fifth house below Mr. Salisbury's hardware-store. Also, a variety of the best stationary ware. To country booksellers and shop-keepers, purchasers for social libraries, and others who buy in quantity, a considerable abatement will be made from the usual retail prices. Boston: [Printed by William Spotswood,] 1795.

12°: [A]1[=G4?]B–F6[G]4(–G4); 34 leaves, pp. [1–3] 4–68. [1]: title; [2]: table of contents; [3]: catalogue.

Bookseller's catalogue: 1000 medium and full author (mostly) and title entries, arranged by subject, by format within subject, and alphabetically within format. Subject headings: law; religion; medicine, surgery, and chemistry; history, biography, voyages, travels, philosophy, mathematics, miscellanies, &c. (by far the largest category); livres François; novels and romances; architecture, maps, charts, &c.; books in common binding; books in blue boards, or sewed and in paper covers; plays and farces; school books. Attribution of printer from Evans.

Evans 29558; Sabin 89651; *STE*, p. 800.

MHi* (19.5×12 cm. — unbound).

209 STEPHENS, THOMAS, fl. 1793–1797

Stephens's catalogue of books, &c. for 1795. The whole contained in the list will be sold on the most reasonable terms, at Thomas Stephens's book and stationary store, no. 57, south Second street; where every encouragement is offered to wholesale purchasers, and the highest value immediately given for libraries or parcels of books. Philadelphia: no. 57, south Second Street. [colophon:] W. W. Woodward, printer, south side of Chesnut Street, Franklin's Head, no. 36. [1795.]

12°: [A]2B–H6; 44 leaves, pp. [1–5] 6–48 [49] 50–64 [65] 66–74 [75] 76–84 [85–88]. [1]: title; [2]: blank; [3]: advertisement (grateful for support, which he hopes will continue); [4]: blank; [5]: catalogue of books; [49]: catalogue of music; [65]: supplement; 73: stationery; [75]: catalogue of prints and paintings; [85]: table of contents and colophon; [86]: blank.

Bookseller's catalogue. Catalogue of books: 889 consecutively numbered, short to full author and title entries, arranged by subject. Subject headings: law; second hand law; divinity; physic, surgery, and chemistry; natural history, gardening, &c.; mathematics, &c.; history, voyages, and travels; biography, novels, &c.;

French books; Latin; Italian books; miscellanies; school books; second hand books. Catalogue of music: 505 consecutively numbered song title entries, in no apparent order. Supplement: 209 consecutively numbered short author and title entries (books), arranged in no apparent order. Catalogue of prints and paintings: 273 consecutively numbered titles, in several groups (prints; views; sea views; 51 sketches and drawings of Cipriani; framed prints; paintings).

Bristol 9307; m.p. 47610; Brigham, p. 57; *STE*, p. 804.

MWA* (18.5×10.5 cm. — bound).

See also McKay 137A (Jay), 137B (Jay), 137C (Jay), 137D (Jay), 137E (Morris), 137F (Jay), 137G (Jay), 137H (Jay), 137I (Morris), 137J (Jay), 137K (Morris), 137L (Jay), 137M (Morris), 137N (Morris), 137O (Morris), 137P (Bleecker), 137Q (Jay), 138A (Jay), 138B (Hoffman), 138C (Baylis), 138D (Shannon [M'Kenzie?]), 138F (Legge), 138G (Legge), 138H (Legge), 138I (Hart), 138J (Footman [Barron]), 138K (Hart), 138L (Jay [Wayland]), 139

————————————— 1796 —————————————

210 BAILEY AND WALLER, Charleston, South Carolina

A new catalogue of books, of the latest publications, newest editions, & in elegant bindings, just imported from Europe, by Bailey and Waller, no. 27, Elliott Street, opposite Bedon's Alley, Charleston. [Charleston, 1796?]

12°: A–C⁶(A2 signed 'A'); 18 leaves, pp. [1–3] 4–33 [34–36]. [1]: title; [2]: blank; [3]: catalogue; 31: notice of large assortment of plays, blank books, ledgers, etc., and advertisement for bookbinding; on 31: stationery; [34]: blank.

Bookseller's catalogue: 875 short author entries, arranged by subject, by format within subjects, and alphabetically within format. Subject headings: law; physic, surgery, &c.; history, voyages, travels, &c.; novels, &c.; divinity; school books; common prayers; Bibles; spelling books; miscellaneous books. Date: dated [1795?] by Bristol, but could be no earlier, and probably not much later, than 1796 since the latest novels listed in the catalogue were first published in that year.

Bristol 9016.

ScU (17.3×10.5 cm. — unbound).

211 BLAKE, WILLIAM PYNSON, 1769–1820

Catalogue of books, for sale or circulation, by William P. Blake, at the Boston Book-Store, no. 59, Cornhill. Consisting of the most celebrated authors in history, voyages, travels, lives, memoirs, antiquities, philosophy, novels, divinity, law, physic, surgery, chemistry, geography, husbandry, navigation, arts, sciences, architecture, miscellanies, poetry, plays, &c. &c. Boston: Printed for William P. Blake. 1796.

12°: A–D⁶E⁴(–E4); 27 leaves, pp. [1–3] 4–51 [52] 53 [54]. [1]: title; [2]: conditions of circulating library; [3]: catalogue; [54]: stationery and other articles. Pp. 48–[54] set in larger type than pp. [1]–47.

Circulating library and bookseller's catalogue: 1900 short author entries, most of them in one fully alphabetical list, with several brief subject lists at the end (livres Francois; law books; Bibles, dictionaries, classical and school books, navigation, mathematics, &c.; tragedies, comedies, and farces).

Evans 30098; *STE*, p. 96.
NN* (19.5 × 12 cm. — bound).

212 BRADFORD, THOMAS, 1745–1838

Bradford's catalogue of books and stationary, wholesale & retail, for 1796. Country store-keepers supplied with all kinds of books & stationary at his wholesale and retail book & stationary store, south Front Street, no. 8. Philadelphia: Printed by Thomas Bradford, no. 8, south Front Street, 1796.

8°: A–I⁴; 36 leaves, pp. [i–ii], [1] 2–68 [69–70]. [i]: title; [ii]: blank; [1] catalogue of books; on 60: stationery; on 63: list of 26 maps and charts; on 65: list of blank forms; on 66: supplement; [69]: advertisements for two books, being published.

Bookseller's catalogue: 925 medium and short author entries (including 20 in the supplement), arranged by subject and then in two separate alphabetical sequences plus a brief unalphabetized group within each subject. Subject headings: law; physic, surgery & chemistry; religion; history, voyages, travels, &c.; miscellanies (largest category); novels and romances; mathematics; agriculture; dramatic works, poetry, &c.; school books, translations of the classics, dictionaries of languages, &c.; French and English books; architecture; plays and farces. See the next item also.

Evans 30121; Brigham, p. 57; *STE*, p. 109.
MWA* (16 × 10 cm. — bound).

213 BRADFORD, THOMAS, 1745–1838

Bradford's catalogue of books and stationary, wholesale & retail, for 1796. Country store-keepers supplied with all kinds of books

& stationary at his wholesale and retail book & stationary store, south Front Street, no. 8. Philadelphia: Printed by Thomas Bradford, no. 8, south Front Street, 1796.

8°: A–I⁴[K]⁴; 40 leaves, pp. [i–ii], [1] 2–66 [67] 68–73 [74–78]. [i]: title; [ii]: blank; [1]: catalogue of books; on 60: stationery; on 63: list of maps and charts; on 65: list of blank forms; [67]: supplement; [74]: list of 'Books Published by Thomas Bradford'; [78]: blank. The only difference in the titles of this and the preceding item is in the type used to print 'Bradford's'; it is in lower case italic (with capital B) in this catalogue, and all in capitals in the preceding; otherwise the typesetting of the two titles is the same.

Bookseller's catalogue. Catalogue of books: 950 entries (including 120 in the supplement), as in the previous item. List of books 'Published by Thomas Bradford': 20 short author entries, with prices, arranged in no apparent order. Most, but not all of the books in this last list were published by Bradford; those that were not, however, were American editions.

Bristol 9497.

PHi* (16.5 ×10.5 cm. — bound).

214 CAMPBELL, ROBERT, d. 1800

Robert Campbell's catalogue for 1796: containing a very extensive and valuable collection of books in the different departments of literature and science; now selling at very reduced prices, at no. 40, south Second-street: where country store-keepers, public and private libraries, are supplied on very low terms. N.B. A liberal price will be given for libraries or parcels of books. Philadelphia: January 1st, 1796.

8°: [A]1[=M2]B–L⁴M²(–M2); 42 leaves, pp. [1–3] 4–83 [84]. [1]: title; [2]: index; [3]: catalogue; on 81: stationery; [84]: blank.

Bookseller's catalogue: 2100 consecutively numbered, short to full author (mostly) and title entries, arranged by subject and alphabetically within subjects. Subject headings as in Robert Campbell's 1794 catalogue, item 183 above, except that the order has been changed, and novels are put in a separate category, and a list of 'American Publications' has been added, pp. 66–79, containing nearly 400 entries, with prices, and arranged alphabetically, most of which are apparently also listed elsewhere in the catalogue.

Evans 30153; Brigham, p. 57; *STE*, p. 131.

CtHi*, MWA* (21.5 ×14 cm. — bound).

[Carter, John, 1745–1814, and William Wilkinson, 1760–1852 Catalogue of the books in the circulating library. Providence: Printed by Carter & Wilkinson. 1796. Broadside?]

Advertised in the *Providence Gazette*, June 11, July 2, 1796. Alden 1463; Bristol 9505; m.p. 47750; *STE*, p. 137.

215 GLOUCESTER UNITED LIBRARY, Gloucester, Rhode Island

Catalogue of books, belonging to the Gloucester United Library: with rules and laws for rendering the same useful, and for governing said Library Company. This Library was established in October, 1795, and a charter of incorporation granted by the honourable General Assembly. Printed at Providence, by Carter and Wilkinson, opposite the Market. 1796.

12°: A⁶; 6 leaves, pp. [1–4] 5 [6] 7–9 [10] 11–12. [1]: title; [2]: blank; [3]: introduction (a plea for more members); [4]: catalogue; [6]: rules and laws; on 8: list of members; [10]: charter.

Social library catalogue: 115 short author entries, arranged in full alphabetical order.

Evans 30492; Alden 1469; Thompson, p. 255; *STE*, p. 312.

RHi (unavailable summer 1975).

216 HAVERHILL LIBRARY, Haverhill, Massachusetts

Haverhill Library. Printed at Newburyport by Blunt and March. [1796.]

8°: [A]⁴B–C⁴; 12 leaves, pp. [1–5] 6–10 [11] 12–22 [23–24]. [1]: blank; [3]: title; [4]: blank; [5]: rules and regulations 'made and accepted April 12, 1796'; [11]: catalogue; [23]: blank.

Social library catalogue: 175 short author entries, arranged alphabetically. Date: the rules and regulations are dated 1796, and none of the books listed in the catalogue were published later than that; Blunt and March were in business together as printers in Newburyport only during 1794–96, according to the MWA Printers File.

Bristol 9568; m.p. 47800; *STE*, p. 348.

MH* (18.5 × 12 cm. — bound; with ms. additions), MWA* (lacks pp. 17–[24]).

[Keatinge, George, d. 1811?

Sale catalogue of books, for 1796. Part first. Containing a general assortment of English books, in every department of polite literature. Part second. Contains a collection of French and German books.—

Now selling wholesale and retail on the most reasonable terms. Baltimore: Printed for George Keatinge, no. 149, Market-Street. 1796.]

Advertised in the *Maryland Journal and Baltimore Advertiser*, May 6, 1796. Evans 30652; Minick 290; *STE*, p. 396.

217 LARKIN, SAMUEL, 1773–1849

A catalogue of books, for sale or circulation, by Samuel Larkin, at the Portsmouth Book Store, opposite the Post-Office, Market-Street, Portsmouth. Consisting of the most approved authors, in history, voyages, travels, lives, memoirs, philosophy, novels, divinity, law, physic, surgery, chemistry, geography, husbandry, navigation, arts, sciences, architecture, miscellanies, poetry, plays, &c. &c. Portsmouth: Printed for Samuel Larkin, at the Portsmouth Book-Store, Market-Street: 1796.

12°: A–B⁶C²; 14 leaves, pp. [1–5] 6–26 [27–28]. [1]: title; [2]: blank; [3]: conditions of the circulating library; [4]: blank; [5]: catalogue; 25: stationery; [27]: blank.

Circulating library and bookseller's catalogue: 650 short author entries, most of them in one alphabetical list, with one separate, brief list of chap books, pamphlets, plays, &c., at the end.

Evans 30672; *STE*, p. 408.

MWA* (17×9.5 cm. — unbound), NN*.

218 LIBRARY COMPANY OF PHILADELPHIA

Third supplement to the catalogue of books, belonging to the Library Company of Philadelphia. To which is prefixed, a continuation of the bye laws and regulations of the Company. Communiter bona profundere deorum est. Philadelphia: Printed by Zachariah Poulson, Junior, Librarian, number eighty, Chesnut-Street. June 30, 1796.

8°: [A]⁴B–E⁴; 20 leaves, pp. [i–iii] iv–vi [7] 8–38 [39–40] (variant: 32 misprinted ᴢƐ). [i]: title; [ii]: blank; [iii]: continuation of bye-laws and regulations; [7]: catalogue of books 'added to the Library since the first day of December, 1794'; [39]: blank.

Social library catalogue: 400 full author entries, counting separate titles in bound pamphlet collections individually, with place and date of publication, and, for donated books, name of donor; arranged by format and in full alphabetical order within format, and numbered with shelf/accession numbers, a separate sequence for each format.

Evans 31001; Cutter 32; *STE*, p. 676.

CtY* (lacks leaf E4; bound with 1789 catalogue), DLC* (lacks pp. [39–40]; bound with 1793 supplement), MB* (bound with 1789 catalogue), MWA* (22.5×14.5 cm. — unbound), MdHi, NN*, PPL* (3 copies—1: lacks pp. 31–[40], bound with 1789 catalogue; 2: variant, bound with 1793 supplement; 3: separate), RPJCB*.

219 MASSACHUSETTS HISTORICAL LIBRARY, Boston

Catalogue of books in the Massachusetts Historical Library. Printed by S. Hall, no. 53, Cornhill, Boston. 1796.

8°: [A]⁴B–E⁴; 20 leaves, pp. [1–3] 4–40. [1]: title; [2]: blank; [3]: catalogue.

Historical society library catalogue: 1050 short (mostly) and medium author entries, with place and date of publication (mostly American editions), arranged in full alphabetical order. Note on p. 40: 'This catalogue does not include unbound books and pamphlets—nor European publications, except these have some connexion with American history—nor a large collection of news-papers. . . .' Most of the books are historical in nature. This library belonged to the Massachusetts Historical Society, founded in 1791 and incorporated in 1794.

Evans 30770; Sabin 45851; Cutter 31; Ranz, p. 119; *STE*, p. 507.

CLU, DLC* (4 copies), ICN, ICU, InU, MB* (2 copies), MBAt*, MWA* (23×14.5 cm. — unbound), N, NN* (2 copies), Nh, PBL, PMA, PPAmP* (largely uncut), PPL*, RPJCB*.

220 NANCREDE, PAUL JOSEPH GUÉRARD DE, 1760–1841

Joseph Nancrede's catalogue of books in the various branches of literature; lately imported from London, Dublin, Paris, and other capitals of Europe; for sale, wholesale and retail, at his bookstore, no. 49 Marlbro' Street, Boston: consisting principally of a variety of publications in divinity, law, physic, chemistry, biography, voyages, miscellanies, novels, arts and sciences, geography, universal history, navigation, astronomy, mathematicks, trade and manufactures, book keeping, &c. In order to extend his business, J. N. intends keeping a general assortment of old books, scarce tracts, and new publications: and, from the correspondence he has established in Europe as well as in the continent, he expects he shall be able to give general satisfaction, both in regard to cheapness and accuracy of the editions. Gentlemen who have duplicates, may excha[nge] them for books or cash. To country-booksellers and shop-keepers, [pur]chasers for social libraries, and others who buy [in quan]tities, a considerable abatement will be made fro[m the usu]al retail prices. [Boston, 1796.]

12°: [A]1[=E6?]B–D⁶E⁶(–E6); 24 leaves, pp. [i–ii], [1] 2–46. [i]: title; [ii]: advertisement for a 'New Pronouncing Dictionary, French and English'; [1]: catalogue of English books; 34: catalogue of French books; 44: supplement of French books; 45: appendix of English books; 46: stationery ware (including mathematical instruments).

Bookseller's catalogue. Catalogue of English books: 1250 short author (mostly) and title entries (including 25 in the appendix), most in one fully alphabetical list, with two separate, brief lists at the end for pocket-size books and pamphlets, and plays. Catalogue of French books: 370 short title entries (including 37 in the supplement), arranged in full alphabetical order. Date: an advertisement on p. 33 notes that Nancrede's edition of *Paul and Virginia* is 'This Day (September 30) Published'; it was published in 1796. An advertisement appears on p. 43 for Nancrede's edition of *Les Aventures de Telemaque*, 'Maintenant sous presse et se publiera'; this was published in 1797. The latest novels listed in the catalogue are two first published in 1796. Therefore, 1796 seems the most likely date for the catalogue.

Evans 30833; Brigham, p. 58; *STE*, p. 549.

MWA* (17.5×10 cm. — bound; t.p. slightly mutilated), MHi (listed in card catalog, but lost for some time).

221 NORWICH LIBRARY COMPANY, Norwich, Connecticut

A catalogue of books belonging to Norwich Library Company. To which are annexed, extracts from the bye-laws of said Company. Norwich: Printed at the press of J. Trumbull, for the Company. [1796?]

12°: [A]⁴B²; 6 leaves, pp. [1–3] 4–12. [1]: title; [2]: blank; [3]: catalogue; on 9: extracts from bye-laws.

Social library catalogue: 100 short author entries arranged alphabetically. Date: dated 1796 by Bristol and CtHi; the latest books listed in the catalogue are several first printed in 1794, so it could be no earlier than that. The CtHi copy has prices and additional entries handwritten in.

Bristol 9647; Sabin 55919.

CtHi* (18.5×12 cm. — unbound).

222 PELHAM, WILLIAM, 1759–1827

William Pelham respectfully solicits the attention of the public to the following conditions of his circulating library, no. 59, Cornhill, Boston. [Boston, 1796.]

Broadside. 44×27 cm. Partly 2 cols., partly 3 cols.

Circulating library and bookseller's catalogue: 200 short author entries, arranged in alphabetical order. Date: dated 1796 because Pelham began his bookstore and circulating library in that year (see broadside announcement of the opening, Evans 30971), and the latest books listed in the catalogue are several first published in 1796, while many of the entries date from 1795.

MWA*.

223 PORTSMOUTH LIBRARY, Portsmouth, New Hampshire

Rules and catalogue of the Portsmouth Library. [Portsmouth:] Printed by John Melcher. [1796?]

8°: [A]⁴B–C⁴; 12 leaves, pp. [1–3] 4–6 [7–8] 9–23 [24]. [1]: title (half-title); [2]: blank; [3]: rules; [7]: names of proprietors; [8]: catalogue; [24]: blank.

Social library catalogue: 220 short author entries, with shelf numbers, arranged alphabetically. Date: the rules are dated Aug. 1, 1796, and the latest books listed in the catalogue are several first published in 1792; therefore, 1796 is a logical guess.

Thompson, p. 257.

MB* (15.5×9.5 cm. — unbound).

[Rainbow, Thomas, and Robert Hannah

Catalogue of the books in the Norfolk Circulating Library. Norfolk: Printed by Willett & O'Connor, for Rainbow & Hannah, at the Norfolk Circulating Library. 1796.]

Advertised in the *Norfolk Herald*, Dec. 5, 1795, and Jan. 9, 1796. Evans 31068; *STE*, p. 616 (under Norfolk).

224 RICE, HENRY, d. 1804, AND PATRICK, fl. 1792–1804

Henry & Patrick Rice's catalogue of a large and valuable collection of books, in the several branches of ancient and modern literature. For 1796. To be sold, wholesale and retail, at their book and

stationary-store, no. 16, S. Second-Street, Philadelphia; where wholesale purchasers will meet the greatest encouragement, and libraries be
furnished on very reasonable terms. To their present very extensive
stock will be added every new work of merit, which will be printed
in any part of the United States. They will at all times have a general
assortment of imported goods in the line of their business. Philadelphia, Printed for H. & P. Rice, no. 16, south Second-street. [1796.]

12°: [A]1[=H6?]B–G⁶[H]⁶(–H6) (F2 signed 'E2'); 42 leaves, pp. [i–ii], [1] 2–72
[73] 74–82. [i]: title; [ii]: table of contents; [1]: catalogue; on 72: stationery;
[73]: appendix, listing 'New Publications and New Editions.'

Bookseller's catalogue: the main catalogue, pp. [1]–72, is identical to pp. [1]–72
of the Rices' 1795 catalogue (item 207 above); the appendix contains 140 short
to full title and author entries, most of them in one general list, with some attempt to group like books together, plus special lists of new novels and new
plays at the end.

Bristol 9683; m.p. 47900; Brigham, p. 58; *STE*, p. 738.

MWA* (17.5×10.5 cm. — bound; pp. 81–82 mutilated).

225 SPRINGFIELD LIBRARY COMPANY, Springfield, Massachusetts

Catalogue of books, belonging to the Springfield Library Company, April, 1796. [Springfield: Printed by Francis Stebbins, 1796.]

4°: [A]⁴; 4 leaves, pp. [1–3] 4–7 [8]. [1]: title (half-title); [2]: blank; [3]: catalogue; 7: regulations; [8]: blank.

Social library catalogue: 160 short author entries, arranged by subject and by format within subjects. Subject headings: divinity and ethics; history, biography,
travels and voyages; miscellanies; poetry; novels. Attribution of printer from
Evans.

Evans 31227; Sabin 89881; *STE*, p. 800.

MSCV* (2 copies, one 21.5×16.5 cm. — bound).

226 THOMAS, ISAIAH, 1749–1831, EBENEZER T. ANDREWS, 1766–1851, AND OBADIAH PENNIMAN, 1776–1820

American publications. Catalogue of books, for sale, wholesale
or retail, at the bookstore of Thomas, Andrews & Penniman, Albany.
[Albany: Printed by Barber and Southwick, 1796.]

Broadside. 59×47 cm. 5 cols.

Bookseller's catalogue: 475 short author entries, American editions, with prices, most of them arranged in one alphabetical list, with two separate, brief lists at the end for music and small histories. Date: could be no earlier than 1795, since the latest novels listed in the catalogue are several first published in that year. According to Thomas's *History of Printing*, I: 403, Thomas, Andrews and Penniman started business in Albany in 1796; therefore, 1796 is the most likely date. Attribution of printer from Evans.

Evans 31293; Sabin 95450; McMurtrie, *Albany*, 135; *STE*, p. 830. NHi*.

227 THOMAS, ISAIAH, 1749–1831, EBENEZER T. ANDREWS, 1766–1851, AND OBADIAH PENNIMAN, 1776–1820

Thomas, Andrews & Penniman's list of books for exchange. [Albany: Printed by Thomas, Andrews & Penniman, 1796.]

4°: [A]²; 2 leaves, pp. [1–4]. [1]: blank; [3]: catalogue; [4]: blank.

Publisher's catalogue: 65 short author entries, with prices, arranged in no apparent order. Date: ms. note on [1] reads, 'To Mathew Carey from Thomas, Andrews & Penniman, Albany, September 25, 1796. . . .'

Bristol 9725a.

PHi* (22.3 × 17 cm. — unbound).

228 THOMAS, ROBERT BAILEY, 1766–1846

Robert B. Thomas, has for sale at his book & stationary store, in Sterling, the following books & stationary,—to which additions are constantly making—[colophon:] Leominster: Printed by Charles Prentiss—1796.

12°: [A]²; 2 leaves, pp. [1–4]. [1]: title (caption); on [1]: catalogue; on [4]: stationery; on [4]: colophon.

Bookseller's catalogue: 175 short author entries, most of them in one alphabetical list, with brief lists at the end of school books; books 'Just Printed for said Thomas, and sold as above'; small histories, chapmen's books. Although both the DLC and the MWA copies of this catalogue are bound at the end of Thomas's *Farmer's Almanack . . . for 1797* (Evans 31294), it was separately printed (and perhaps also separately distributed), since the printers of the almanac were Manning and Loring in Boston, while Charles Prentiss printed the catalogue in Leominster.

Evans 31295; Brigham, p. 58; *STE*, p. 830.

DLC*, MWA* (18.5 × 12 cm. — bound).

229 THOMAS, SON AND THOMAS, Worcester, Massachusetts

Catalogue of books to be sold by Thomas, Son & Thomas, at their bookstore, in Worcester, Massachusetts: consisting of history, voyages, travels, geography, antiquities, philosophy, novels, miscellanies, divinity, physic, surgery, anatomy, arts, sciences, husbandry, architecture, navigation, mathematicks, law, periodical publications, poetry, plays, music, &c. &c. &c. October, MDCCXCVI. Printed at Worcester, Massachusetts, by Thomas, Son & Thomas.

12°: A–D⁶; 24 leaves, pp. [1–5] 6–47 [48]. [1]: title; [2]: blank; [3]: advertisement (libraries supplied, books bought and exchanged, printing done); [4]: blank; [5]: catalogue; on 47: stationery; [48]: blank.

Bookseller's catalogue: 950 short author entries, arranged by subject and alphabetically within subjects. Subject headings: divinity and ecclesiastical history; law; physic, surgery and chemistry; history, chronology, biography, antiquities, voyages and travels; miscellanies; poetical works; novels & sentimental works, &c.; dramatic works, &c.; algebra, arithmetic, architecture, surveying, &c.; classical and school books; sacred music; chapmen's books and small histories; pamphlets; children's books. Thomas, Son and Thomas were: Isaiah Thomas (1749–1831), Isaiah Thomas, Jr. (1773–1819), and Alexander Thomas (1775–1809?).

Evans 31290; Sabin 95452; Nichols 325; Brigham, p. 58; *STE*, p. 829.

CtY* (lacks pp. 37–[48]; leaves A1–2 slightly mutilated), MHi*, MWA* (18.5×11 cm. — bound), PPL* (lacks t.p. and pp. 37–[48]).

230 TRANSYLVANIA LIBRARY, Lexington, Kentucky

[Catalogue of books in Transylvania Library Lexington containing upwards of four hundred volumes. For the year one thousand seven hundred ninety-six. Lexington, Ky.: Printed by John Bradford. . . .] [1796.] 13 × 21 cm. [8] pp.

McMurtrie apparently found a copy of this item in the Lexington Public Library, but as *STE* notes, 'The unique copy reported by McMurtrie is not now to be found.' The title above is from McMurtrie, who comments, 'Two-thirds of title page missing in the only copy located. Title reconstructed as above from the remaining fragment and from a notice in the *Kentucky Gazette* of April 16, 1796: "This day published and may be had at the Library Room at 9 pense, a catalogue of the books in Transylvania Library containing upwards of 400 volumes."' Evans 30694; McMurtrie, *Kentucky*, 56; *STE*, p. 424 (under Lexington).

[A valuable collection of books in different departments of literature and science. Philadelphia, 1796. 8°; 2100 lots.]

Origin of entry unknown. Evans 31482; *STE*, p. 931.

[Young, William P.

Catalogue of books, containing besides his former collection, a considerable importation, per the Carolina, from London, just opened, the best editions. In superb bindings, including, also, his assortment of stationary. Charleston: Printed by W. P. Young, at Franklin's Head, no. 43, Broad-Street. 1796.]

Evans's entry may refer to Young's catalogue found at the back of *Palladium of Knowledge: or, the Carolina and Georgia Almanac, for . . . 1797* (Evans 31682), although the title of that catalogue is quite different from the one above, which was taken from an advertisement in the *City Gazette*, Apr. 27, 1796. Evans 31681; *STE*, p. 1023.

See also McKay 139A (Baylis) 139B (Hoffman), 139C (Folsom), 139D (Nathan)

———————————— 1797 ————————————

231 ALBANY LIBRARY, Albany, New York

Albany Library. Additional catalogue. 1797. [Albany:] Printed by Charles R. and George Webster. [1797.]

8°: [A]⁴; 4 leaves, pp. [1–3] 4–7 [8]. [1]: title (half-title); [2]: blank; [3]: catalogue; [8]: blank.

Social library catalogue: 110 short author entries, numbered with shelf/accession numbers, and arranged alphabetically.

Bristol 9831; m.p. 48036; McMurtrie, *Albany*, 142; *STE*, p. 12.

MiD (could not locate, 1974), N (17×9.5 cm. — bound; uncut).

[Blake, William P., and Lemuel

Catalogue of American editions. . . . 1797.]

Evans 31835; *STE*, p. 96: *see* Blake 1795 entry, item 196 above.

232 BLUNT, EDMUND MARCH, 1770–1862

New catalogue of books, for sale by Edmund M. Blunt, at the Newburyport Book-Store, sign of the Bible, State-Street, (five doors below Mr. Davenport's Tavern,). . . . [Newburyport,] October 1797.

Broadside. 56×43 cm. 6 cols.

Bookseller's catalogue: 325 short to full author (mostly) and title entries, arranged alphabetically. Advertisement at bottom for writing-paper, stationery, printing, and book-binding.

Bristol 9868; m.p. 48063; Brigham, p. 59; *STE*, p. 98.

MWA*.

233 BOSTON LIBRARY SOCIETY

Catalogue of books in the Boston Library. May 1, 1797. [Boston, 1797.]

8°: [A]⁴B–C⁴D²; 14 leaves, pp. [1] 2–27 [28]. [1]: title (caption); on [1]: catalogue; 23: act of incorporation; 25: rules and regulations; on 27: list of officers; [28]: blank.

Social library catalogue: 500 short author entries, arranged in full alphabetical order.

Bristol 9872; m.p. 48065; Cutter 34; *STE*, p. 106.

MBAt (could not be located, 1975), MH*, MWA* (23.5×14 cm. — unbound).

234 CAMPBELL, ROBERT, d. 1800

Robert Campbell and Co's. catalogue for 1797: containing a very extensive and valuable collection of books in the different departments of literature and science; now selling at very reduced prices, at no. 40, south Second-street: where country store-keepers, public and private libraries, are supplied on very low terms. N.B. A liberal price will be given for libraries or parcels of books. Philadelphia: 1797.

8°: π1 A–L⁴M²(G mis-signed 'F'); 47 leaves, pp. [i–ii], [1] 2–89 [90–92] (variant: 1 of 51 not struck). [i]: title (variant: 'depatments' for 'departments'); [ii]: index; [1]: catalogue; on 88: stationery; [91]: advertisement for bill books; [92]: proposals to publish Smollett's Continuation of Hume's History of England by subscription, dated 'January 1st 1797.'

Bookseller's catalogue: 2605 consecutively numbered, short to full author and title entries (much duplication—probably only 2200 separate titles), arranged by subject and alphabetically within subjects. Subject headings as in R. Campbell's 1796 catalogue (item 214 above), minus 'American publications,' plus 'Livres François.'

Evans 31913; Brigham, p. 59; *STE*, p. 131.

MWA* (21.5 × 13.5 cm. — bound; variant), ViU* (lacks pp. 83–[92]).

[Caritat, Louis Alexis Hocquet de, b. 1752
Catalogue of the Circulating Library of H. Caritat. New York: Printed for H. Caritat, Pearl-Street, no. 3. 1797.]

Origin of entry unknown, though Evans's source, whatever it was, may perhaps have actually been a reference to Caritat's 1798 circulating library catalogue (see item 251 below). Evans 31916; *STE*, p. 134.

235 CARLISLE LIBRARY COMPANY, Carlisle, Pennsylvania

Rules of the Carlisle Library Company; with a catalogue of books belonging thereto. Carlisle: Printed by George Kline. [1797.]

8°: A⁸; 8 leaves, pp. [1–2] 3–15 [16]. [1]: title; [2]: blank; 3: rules and regulations; 9: catalogue; [16]: blank.

Social library catalogue: 120 short author entries, arranged by subject. Subject headings: history; voyages; travels; biography; husbandry; miscellaneous (largest category). Date: dated 'Carlisle, March 7, 1797,' at the head of the rules and regulations, p. 3; rule XII, p. 8, specifies that the Treasurer shall have a catalogue and the rules printed 'as soon as can be done conveniently.'

Evans 31917; Thompson, p. 254; *STE*, p. 135.

DLC* (15.5 × 9.5 cm. — bound).

236 FREDERICKTOWN LIBRARY COMPANY, Fredericktown, Pennsylvania

A catalogue of books belonging to the Fredericktown Library Company to which is prefixed, the objects, articles, and conditions on which the said Company is incorporated. Washington [Pa.]: Printed for the Company by John Colerick. 1797.

12°: [A]⁶; 6 leaves, pp. [1–3] 4–12. [1]: title; [2]: blank; [3]: conditions; 7: act of incorporation; 9: catalogue.

Social library catalogue: 130 short author entries, arranged alphabetically.

Evans 32155; Thompson, p. 255; *STE*, p. 284.

MWA* (18 × 11 cm. — unbound).

237 HARTFORD LIBRARY COMPANY, Hartford, Connecticut

The constitution of the Hartford Library Company; extracts from the by-laws, and a catalogue of the books. [monogram initials of printer.] Hartford: Printed by Hudson & Goodwin. M,DCC,-XCVII.

8°: [A]⁴B⁴C²; 10 leaves, pp. [1–3] 4–20. [1]: title; [2]: blank; [3]: constitution; 8: extract from by-laws; 10: catalogue.

Social library catalogue: 250 short author entries, arranged by subject and alphabetically within subjects. Subject headings: history and travels; divinity; philosophy; poems; miscellanies; novels.

Evans 32232; Cutter 33; Trumbull 820; Thompson, p. 256; *STE*, p. 340.

CtHi* (has some ms. additional entries), DLC*, MWA* (19.5×12.5 cm. — unbound).

[Homes, John
Catalogue of books for sale at John Homes's book and stationary store, opposite the north door of the State House, State Street, Boston. Boston: Printed for John Homes. 1797. 12°; 21 pp.]

Origin of entry unknown. Evans 32268; *STE*, p. 363.

238 HUDSON, BARZILLAI, 1741–1823, AND GEORGE GOODWIN, 1757–1844

Hudson & Goodwin, have for sale at their store opposite the North Meeting-House, Hartford, the following books, which they have lately received from London, Dublin, and elsewhere. [Hartford: Printed by Hudson and Goodwin, 1797.]

Broadside. 42.5×33.5 cm. 6 cols.

Bookseller's catalogue: 625 short author entries, arranged by subject and in full alphabetical order within subjects; plus a list of stationery. Subject headings: divinity and ecclesiastical history; law; medicine; history, biography, voyages, and travels; novels; poetry; miscellanies; arts and sciences; languages and school books. Date: could be no earlier, and probably is no later, than 1797, since the latest novel listed in the catalogue is one which was first published in that year, while many of the novels date from the several years immediately prior to 1797.

Bristol 9975; m.p. 48154; *STE*, p. 370.

CtHi*, CtY* (dated [18—], with ms. list of books on verso), NHi*.

239 LIBRARY COMPANY OF BALTIMORE,
Maryland

A catalogue of the books, &c. belonging to the Library Company of Baltimore; to which are prefixed, the bye-laws of the Company, and an alphabetical list of the members. [7 line quotation, from *Telemachus.*] Baltimore: Printed by John Hayes, in Public-Alley. 1797.

12°: π⁶ A–B⁶C⁴(–C4) (π3 signed 'B3'); 21 leaves, pp. [i–iii] iv–xii, [1] 2–30. [i]: title; [ii]: blank; [iii]: bye-laws; x: list of members; [1]: catalogue.

Social library catalogue: 800 short (mostly) and medium author (mostly) and title entries, arranged by subject and in full alphabetical order within subjects; donors of books identified. Subject headings: divinity and ecclesiastical history; ethics, moral philosophy, and metaphysics; natural philosophy, arts and sciences; physic and surgery; natural history, husbandry, agriculture, &c.; law and politics; history, antiquities, chronology, and biography; voyages, travels and geography; belles lettres and classics; poetry and plays; novels, tales, fables and romances; miscellanies; postscript (late entries).

Evans 31769; Minick 336; *STE*, p. 46.

MWA* (17.5×10.5 cm. — bound), MdHi.

240 LIBRARY COMPANY OF BURLINGTON,
New Jersey

Additional catalogue of Burlington Library. [Burlington: Printed by Isaac Neale, 1797.]

8°: A⁴; 4 leaves, pp. 37–42 [43–44] [=8] (continuous·with the 1792 catalogue, item 162 above). 37: title (caption); on 37: catalogue; 41: additional laws and rules; on 41: list of 68 members; [43]: blank.

Social library catalogue: 120 short title entries, arranged by subject and by format within subjects, and numbered with shelf/accession numbers within each format. Subject headings: agriculture; biography; divinity, chymistry & physic; geography; history; novels, romances & tales; philosophy; polite literature, morals and manners; law & politics; travels, tours, journals & voyages. Date: a note on p. 42 states that the catalogue is 'Published by order of the directors. . . . Attest, John Griscom, Secretary. September 10, 1797.'

Evans 31896 (but reproduced in *EAI* with Evans 24159, the 1792 catalogue); Morsch 338; *STE*, p. 125.

NjHi (bound with 1792 catalogue; could not be located, 1974).

241 NANCREDE, PAUL JOSEPH GUÉRARD DE, 1760–1841

Books published by Joseph Nancrede, no. 49, Marlborough Street, Boston. [Worcester: Printed by Thomas, Son & Thomas, 1797.]

4°: Y⁴(–Y1 and 2); 2 leaves, pp. [181–84] [=4], the last leaves at the end of Jacques Henri Bernardin de Saint-Pierre, *Botanical Harmony Delineated* (Worcester: Printed [by Thomas, Son & Thomas] for J. Nancrede, 1797) (at MWA— Evans 32795). [181]: title (caption); on [181]: catalogue.

Publisher's and bookseller's catalogue: 110 entries, in two unlabeled divisions; the first seven entries are full title entries, with laudatory advertising comments, for books published by Nancrede; the second section consists of 100 or so short author and title entries, arranged in no apparent order, for books Nancrede was selling but did not publish himself. This catalogue seems to have been printed as an integral part of the Saint-Pierre volume, with little likelihood that it was also intended for separate distribution; it is listed here because Bristol and DLC treat it as a separate catalogue. In several other books published by Nancrede in 1797 there are catalogues at the end that are all similar, yet different, each one designed to use up the remaining pages in the last signature after all the text had been set; none of these seem to have been separately printed or intended for separate distribution.

Bristol 10010; m.p. 48186; *STE*, p. 549.
DLC* (21 × 13 cm. — bound).

[New York Society Library
Additional catalogue of books belonging to the New-York Society Library. New York: Printed by T. & J. Swords?, 1797.]

Origin of entry unknown. Evans 32569; *STE*, p. 586.

242 SIMOND, L., AND COMPANY, New York

Catalogue of a well chosen collection of books, mostly French: of the finest editions; and richly bound. They are to be sold at auction the 20th day of August 1797, at L. Simond and Co's store, Steven's-wharf. Printed at no. 81, Beekman-street, New-York. 1797.

12°: A–C⁶; 18 leaves, pp. [1–3] 4–33 [34–36]. [1]: title; [2]: advertisement (see below); [3]: catalogue; [34]: blank.

Auction catalogue: 750 short title entries, mostly French books, arranged by subject. Subject headings: physic, anatomy, &c.; literature, poetry, &c.; natural philosophy, sciences, oeconomy; translations; history, geography, travels (largest category); moral philosophy; religious works. An unusual feature of this catalogue is that included in some entries, on an irregular basis, is an indication of the number of copies of that book to be sold. The printed date of the auction in the title has been crossed out and '10 October' handwritten in. In 1797, 81 Beekman Street was the office of the *Gazette Francais*. From the advertisement on p. [2]: 'This Collection of books, selected by a man of learning, versed in French and European Litterature [*sic*], had been intended to form the basis of a French Library to be established at New-York . . . a compleat assortment in every branch . . . now offered . . . to the public.'

McKay 140.

NHi* (18.5×11.5 cm. — unbound; uncut).

243 SOCIAL LIBRARY IN SALEM, Massachusetts

Bylaws and regulations of the incorporated proprietors of the Social Library in Salem. [Salem: Printed by Thomas C. Cushing, 1797?]

8°: [A–D]⁴; 16 leaves, pp. [1] 2–6 [7] 8–32. [1]: title (caption); on [1]: bylaws and regulations; [7]: catalogue; on 32: note encouraging the donation of books to the library.

Social library catalogue: 400 short author entries, arranged in full alphabetical order. Date: according to Tapley, p. 244, the library was incorporated in 1797, so that is the earliest the catalogue could have been published; and since the latest books listed in the catalogue are several first published in 1796, the catalogue itself is not likely to be much later than that. Tapley also notes (p. 246) that some of the loan records for this library are located at MSaE. Attribution of printer from Evans.

Evans 32800; Sabin 75745; Cutter 35; Tapley, p. 365; Thompson, p. 258; *STE*, p. 756.

MBAt*, MH, MSaE, MWA* (22.5×14.5 cm. — unbound; many additional entries in ms.).

244 THOMAS, ISAIAH, 1749–1831, EBENEZER T. ANDREWS, 1766–1851, AND OBADIAH PENNIMAN, 1776–1820

Catalogue of books for sale either by wholesale or retail, by Thomas, Andrews & Penniman, at the Albany Bookstore, no. 45, State-Street; where catalogues will be delivered gratis to any person who will call or send for them. Orders from the country executed with the utmost care, and attention; and a large discount made to those who purchase to sell again. Albany: Printed by Loring Andrews & Co. for Thomas, Andrews & Penniman. [1797?]

12°: A–C⁶; 18 leaves, pp. [1–4] 5–35 [36]. [1]: title; [2]: blank; [3]: advertisement (good editions; quantity buyers encouraged; will import special books, supply libraries, and pack books carefully; bookbinding); [4]: catalogue; on 34: stationery; [36]: blank.

Bookseller's catalogue: 825 short author entries, most of them in one alphabetical list, with several brief subject lists at the end, each alphabetical (Bibles, dictionaries, classical and school books; children's books; law; medical; architecture. Date: dated [1798] in all the sources below except Evans, and MWA, but since the latest novels listed in the catalogue are three first published in 1797, and many of the novels listed date from 1795 and 1796, 1797 seems to be the more likely date.

Evans 32918; Sabin 95451; Brigham, p. 60; McMurtrie, *Albany*, 208; *STE*, p. 830. MWA* (20×12 cm. — bound), NN*.

[Todd, Joseph J.
Catalogue of books in the circulating library in Joseph J. Todd's book-store, no. 12 Westminster Street. Providence, 1797.]

Advertised in the *Providence Gazette*, July 15, 1797. Alden 1553; Bristol 10131; m.p. 48275; *STE*, p. 844.

245 UNION LIBRARY, New Milford, Connecticut
        Constitution and bye-laws of Union Library, New-Milford. [Danbury: Printed by Douglas and Nichols. 1797?]

8°: [A]⁸; 8 leaves, pp. [1–3] 4–15 [16]. [1]: title (half-title); [2]: blank; [3]: constitution; on 6: bye-laws; on 8: list of proprietors; on 10: catalogue; 14: numbered lines for expanding the catalogue; [16]: blank.

Social library catalogue: 135 short author entries, numbered consecutively according to the number of volumes, and arranged in no apparent order. Date: CtHi and all of the references below date it [1796?], because that year is mentioned twice in the constitution; but it could be no earlier than 1797 since the latest novels listed in the catalogue are two first published in 1797. Attribution of place of publication and printer from Evans. This catalogue is not reproduced in *EAI* because it had not then been located.

Evans 30868; Bates 2004; Thompson, p. 257; *STE*, p. 579.
CtHi* (20×12.5 cm. — unbound).

246 WEST, JOHN, 1770–1827

A catalogue of books published in America, and for sale at the bookstore of John West, no. 75, Cornhill, Boston. Boston: Printed by Samuel Etheridge. 1797.

12°: A–C⁶; 18 leaves, pp. [1–3] 4–36. [1]: title; [2]: blank; [3]: catalogue; on 36: advertisement noting West's 'Choice Collection' of imported books also.

Bookseller's catalogue: 550 short to full author entries, American editions, with prices, most of them in one alphabetical list, with several brief subject lists at the end (tragedies; comedies; comic operas; farces, &c.; small books and pamphlets). This catalogue is very similar to the Thomas, Andrews and Penniman 1796 catalogue, item 226 above, in content, though not in form.

Evans 33205; Sabin 102734; Brigham, p. 59; *STE*, p. 987.

CSmH, MWA* (18 × 10.5 cm. — bound), MiU-C*, NN*, NhD, RPJCB* (pp. 35–36 slightly mutilated).

247 WHITE, JAMES, 1755?–1824

A catalogue of books, consisting of a large collection of the various branches of literature alphabetically disposed under several heads; to which are added, a great variety of stationary and other articles, for sale, wholesale or retail, at James White's book and stationary-store, Franklin's Head, opposite the prison, Court-Street, Boston. [Boston, 1797?]

8°: [A]⁸B–C⁸; 24 leaves, pp. [1–3] 4–48 (variant: p. 9 not numbered). [1]: title; [2]: blank; [3]: catalogue; on 46: stationery and other articles; on 48: advertisement (writing paper; fresh books imported constantly; quantity buyers encouraged; piano fortes for sale).

Bookseller's catalogue: 1250 short author entries, arranged by subject and alphabetically within subjects. Subject headings: divinity, philosophy, history, voyages, travels, novels, and miscellanies (by far the largest category); anatomy, chemistry, electricity, physic, and surgery; law books, forms of writing, &c.; dictionaries, gazetteers, book-keeping, arithmetic, mathematics, geography, astronomy, school-books, &c.; Bibles; seamen's books, charts, maps, prints, &c.; pamphlets; chap books; penmanship. Date: MWA copy dated, on t.p. in ms., 1798; could be no earlier, and probably is not any later, than 1797 since the latest novel listed in the catalogue is one first published in 1797, while many of the novels date from 1795 and 1796.

Evans 33215; Sabin 103393; Brigham, p. 61 (dated [1798]); *STE*, p. 993 (dated [1798]).

CtY*, MHi* (variant), MWA* (18.5 × 11 cm. — bound).

See also McKay 139E (Clap), 139F (Lang), 139G (Lang)

———————————— 1798 ————————————

248 BLAKE, WILLIAM PYNSON, 1769–1820, AND LEMUEL, 1775–1861

Catalogue of books, for sale or circulation, by W. P. & L. Blake, at the Boston Book-Store, no. 1, Cornhill. Consisting of the most celebrated authors in history, voyages, travels, lives, memoirs, antiquities, philosophy, novels, divinity, law, physic, surgery, chemistry, geography, husbandry, navigation, arts, sciences, architecture, miscellanies, poetry, plays, &c. &c. Boston: Printed for William P. & Lemuel Blake. 1798.

12°: A–E⁶; 30 leaves, pp. [1–3] 4–59 [60]. [1]: title; [2]: conditions; [3]: catalogue; 57; stationery and other articles; [60]: advertisement (supply libraries, country store-keepers, and other quantity buyers).

Circulating library and bookseller's catalogue: 2000 short author entries, most of them arranged in one fully alphabetical list, with several subject lists at the end, each alphabetical (law; Bibles, dictionaries, classical and school books, navigation, mathematics, &c.; maps, charts, &c.; tragedies, comedies, and farces; chap books, pamphlets, &c.).

Evans 33428; Brigham, p. 59; Shera, pp. 149, 262; *STE*, p. 96.

MB*, MH* (19 × 12 cm. — unbound), MWA* (lacks pp. 37–[60], supplied in photostat from MH copy), PPL*.

249 CAMPBELL, SAMUEL, 1763?–1836

Samuel Campbell's sale catalogue of books, for 1798 & 1799. Comprehending, above twenty thousand volumes, in arts, sciences, and miscellaneous literature; forming a general assortment of the principal authors, ancient and modern. Among which will be found, many scarce and valuable books: viz. divinity, physic, surgery, midwifery, philosophy, novels, architecture, voyages, travels, poetry, dramatic works, geography, miscellanies, history, biography, arts, sciences, law, dictionaries and grammars for English, Latin, Greek and French classes, &c. The books in general are good editions and well bound, except otherwise expressed in the catalogue; and will be sold for cash, at the most reasonable prices. Country booksellers, merchants, traders, and teachers, will particularly find it their interest in applying for books or stationary, at Samuel Campbell's book & stationary store, no. 124, Pearl-Street, where catalogues will be delivered gratis, to gentlemen who please to call or send for them. N.B. Orders from the country executed with the utmost care and attention; and a large discount made to those who purchase quantities. [New York: Printed by Samuel Campbell, 1798.]

8°: π1[=G4?] [A]⁴B–F⁴G⁴(–G4); 28 leaves, pp. [i–ii], [1] 2–53 [54]. [i]: title; [ii]: index; [1]: catalogue; on 52: stationery; [54]: list of 38 books 'Printed and Sold by Samuel Campbell,' with prices.

Bookseller's catalogue: 1630 consecutively numbered, short and medium author entries, arranged by subject, by format within subject, and alphabetically within format. Subject headings as in 1794 catalogue, with the addition of medical and surgical pamphlets, and music—vocal and instrumental. Date: dated [1799?] by all sources; could be no earlier than 1798 since the latest novels listed in the catalogue are two first published in that year; and the date in the title indicates that the catalogue could have been published no later than 1798.

Evans 35267; Brigham, p. 61; *STE*, p. 131.

MWA* (22.5 × 14.5 cm. — bound).

250 CAREY, MATHEW, 1760–1839

Philadelphia, June 23, 1798. Mathew Carey's exchange catalogue. [Philadelphia: Printed by Mathew Carey, 1798.]

Broadside. 23 × 19 cm. 2 cols.

Publisher's catalogue: 115 short author entries, with prices, arranged alphabetically; largely American editions (most, though not all, of them published by Carey), along with a few European editions.

Evans 33497; Brigham, p. 60; *STE*, p. 134.

MWA*.

251 CARITAT, LOUIS ALEXIS HOCQUET DE,
b. 1752

Repository of useful and entertaining knowledge: being a catalogue of H. Caritat's Circulating Library. Price one shilling. Look at the end of the catalogue for the late additions made to the library. New York: Printed by William A. Davis & Co. 1798.

12°: π1 A–E⁶F²; 33 leaves, pp. [i–ii], [1] 2–25 [26] 27–30 [31] 32–61 [62–64?] (the incomplete alphabetical list of duodecimo additions on [62] and the stub of a leaf between [62] and [63] indicate that at least one leaf may be lacking). [i]: title; [ii]: blank; [1]: catalogue; [63]: terms of library; [64]: blank.

Circulating library catalogue: 1166 consecutively numbered, and 26 additional, medium and short title (mostly) and author entries, arranged in full alphabetical order within each of two format lists (octavo; duodecimo), one list of livres Francois, and a list of late additions. Evans 31916 and *STE*, p. 134, describe an unlocated Caritat circulating library catalogue dated 1797 (see above), but these may actually be misdated references to the catalogue described here.

NHi* (20.5×12.5 cm. — bound).

252 LARKIN, EBENEZER, 1767–1813

Catalogue of books, for sale by E. Larkin, no 47, Cornhill, Boston. Consisting of a great variety of authors in history, voyages, travels, lives, memoirs, antiquities, philosophy, novels, divinity, law, physic, surgery, chemistry, geography, husbandry, navigation, arts, sciences, architecture, miscellanies, poetry, plays, &c. &c. Boston: Printed for E. Larkin. 1798.

12°: A–D⁶E⁴; 28 leaves, pp. [1–3] 4–54 [55] 56. [1]: title; [2]: blank; [3]: catalogue; [55]: stationery and other articles.

Bookseller's catalogue: 1500 short (mostly) to full author (mostly) and title entries (with much duplication; probably only 1200 separate books listed), most of them in one alphabetical list, with several brief subject lists at the end (maps and charts; pamphlets; plays, operas, farces, &c.; chap books, &c.).

Evans 33982; Brigham, p. 60; *STE*, p. 408.

CSmH, MHi* (lacks pp. 49–56), MWA* (17.5×11 cm. — bound).

253 LIBRARY COMPANY OF BALTIMORE, Maryland

A catalogue of the books, &c. belonging to the Library Company of Baltimore; to which are prefixed, the act for the incorporation of the Company, their constitution, their bye-laws, and, an alphabetical list of the members. [6 lines of quotation from *Telemachus*.] Baltimore: Printed by John Hayes, in Public-Alley. 1798.

8°: [A]⁴B–H⁴[I]⁴K⁴; 40 leaves, pp. [i–iii] iv–xviii, [1] 2–46 [47] 48–62. [i]: title;

[ii]: blank; [iii]: act of incorporation; v: constitution; x: bye-laws; xvi: list of members; [1]: catalogue; [47]: supplementary catalogue; 62: books omitted, and errata.

Social library catalogue: 1600 short and medium author entries, 1200 in the main catalogue and 400 in the supplement, with, for donated books, names of donors; arranged by subject, by format within subject, and in full alphabetical order within format. Subject headings: essentially as in the library's 1797 catalogue, item 239 above.

Bristol 10215; m.p. 48345; Cutter 36; Minick 406; Thompson, p. 253; Ranz, p. 119; *STE*, p. 46.

MdHi*, PHi* (20×12.5 cm. — bound), PPAmP*.

254 LIBRARY COMPANY OF PHILADELPHIA

Fourth supplement to the catalogue of books, belonging to the Library Company of Philadelphia. To which is added, a catalogue of the books that are not to be taken out of the Library, and of those that are to go out under certain restrictions. Communiter bona profundere deorum est. — Philadelphia:—Printed by Zachariah Poulson, Junior, Librarian, no. 106, Chesnut-street. Nearly opposite to the Bank of North America. November 30, 1798.

8°: [A]⁴B–E⁴[F]⁴; 24 leaves, pp. [1–3] 4–40, ²[1] 2–8. [1]: title (variant: lacks the second sentence in the title above ['To which . . . restrictions.']); [2]: blank; [3]: catalogue of books 'which have been added to the Library since the thirtieth of June, 1796'; ²[1]: caption title: 'A catalogue of the books that are not to be taken out of the Library, and of those that are to go out under certain restrictions'; on ²[1]: catalogue of restricted books.

Social library catalogue. Catalogue of books added: 525 full author entries, with place and date of publication, and, for donated books, name of donor; arranged by format and in full alphabetical order within format, and numbered with shelf/accession numbers within each format. Catalogue of restricted books: 85 entries, as above, except not alphabetical within format. The PPL variant copy is reproduced in *EAI*.

Evans 34357; Cutter 37; *STE*, p. 676.

NN* (21×13.5 cm. — bound), PPL* (variant).

255 NANCREDE, PAUL JOSEPH GUÉRARD DE, 1760–1841

Books:—importation of May, 1798. Joseph Nancrede's catalogue of books, just imported from London, for sale, wholesale and retail, at his book-store, no. 49, Marlbro'-street, Boston: consisting principally of a variety of publications in divinity, law, physic, chemistry, biography, voyages, miscellanies, novels, arts and sciences, geography, universal history, navigation, astronomy, mathematics, trade and manufactures, book-keeping, &c. Several of the new works, contained in this catalogue, are analyzed and reviewed in the Monthly Review, Critical Review, Analytical Review, European Magazine, Monthly Magazine, New Annual Register; or in the Medical Review, Annals of Medicine, or in the Evangelical Magazine:—Gentlemen desirous of consulting any of these periodical publications, on particular books, shall, on application at the above store, be furnished with the volume wanted. To country booksellers and shop-keepers, purchasers for social libraries, and others who buy in quantities, a considerable abatement will be made from the usual retail prices. Orders from the country, though never so trifling, executed by the first conveyances, and with as much fidelity as if the persons were present. Boston, June, 1798.

12°: A–G⁶; 42 leaves, pp. [1–3] 4–70 [71] 72–84. [1]: title; [2]: advertisement (for Nancrede's edition of *A History, or, Anecdotes of the Revolution in Russia*, 'This day published'); [3]: catalogue of English books; on 66: stationery; 68: advertisement for several books 'Just Published, by Joseph Nancrede'; [71]: catalogue of French books; 83: 'Burke's Opinion of Murphy's Translation of Tacitus.'

Bookseller's catalogue. Catalogue of English books: 2000 short author (mostly) and title entries (with much duplication; probably only around 1600 separate books are listed), some with descriptive or evaluative comments, arranged by subject and alphabetically within subjects. Subject headings: miscellanies (largest category); divinity; law; physic and surgery; classical authors, Latin and school books; plays; pamphlets. Catalogue of French books: 500 short title entries, most of them in one fully alphabetical list, with a brief list of 'pieces de theatre' at the end. From a note on p. 65: 'In Theology, Law, Politics, Agriculture, History, and Voyages, particular attention has been paid to selecting all that is rare and valuable in the English Language; all new works and scarce tracts, many of which were never seen before in America, are comprised in this assortment.'

Evans 34165; Brigham, p. 60; *STE*, p. 549.

MHi* (lacks pp. 81–84), MWA* (18×11 cm. — bound), NHi*.

256 NORTHINGTON PUBLIC LIBRARY, Farmington, Connecticut

Catalogue of books, belonging to Northington Public Library. [colophon:] Printed at Pittsfield. [1798.]

Broadside. 31 × 19.5 cm. 2 cols.

Social library catalogue: 120 short author entries, arranged by subject and in full alphabetical order within subjects. Subject headings: divinity; history, biography, voyages, and travels; poetry and novels; mathematics, philosophy, & school books; miscellanies. Date: dated 'Northington, November 4, 1798.' at the lower left corner. In addition, a ms. catalogue (undated) is pasted to the facing page (in the ms. scrapbook) containing 60 short author and title entries, most of which also appear in the printed catalogue, but some of which do not. The labeling of this ms. catalogue implies that it lists the first books in the library plus some later additions, all prior to the date of the printed catalogue. The printed catalogue is not separately catalogued at CtY, but is pasted to p. 138, of vol. 1, of the '[Benjamin] Trumbull Manuscript Collections.'

Shera, p. 292; Thompson, p. 255.

CtY*.

257 RUTGERS, HARMON G.

Catalogue of books, for sale by H. G. Rutgers, no. 145, Pearl-Street, on Saturday evening, December 1st, at 6 o'clock. [colophon:] New-York: Printed by Isaac Collins, no. 189, Pearl-Street. [1798.]

Broadside. 40 × 26 cm. 3 cols.

Auction catalogue: 200 consecutively numbered, short author entries, arranged in no apparent order. Date: McKay indicates that Rutgers was active in New York only in 1798 and 1799; Dec. 1 fell on a Saturday in 1798.

Bristol 10505; m.p. 48603; McKay 141; Stark 1249; *STE*, p. 753.

NN*.

258 TRENTON LIBRARY COMPANY, Trenton, New Jersey

Laws and regulations of the Trenton Library Company, agreed to by the said Company on the first Monday in May, 1797. Trenton: Printed by Matthias Day, M,DCC,XCVIII.

8°: [A]⁴B⁴[C]²; 10 leaves, pp. [1–3] 4–18 [19–20]. [1]: title; [2]: blank; [3]: laws and regulations; 8: rules; 10: list of proprietors; 11: catalogue; [19]: blank.

Social library catalogue: 242 short author entries, with prices, and, for donated books, name of donor; arranged by format and numbered consecutively within each format.

Evans 34679; Sabin 96772; Morsch 412; Thompson, p. 258; *STE*, p. 848. NjHi* (21.5×13.5 cm. — bound).

259 WAREHAM SOCIAL LIBRARY, Wareham, Massachusetts

Catalogue of books, belonging to Wareham Social Library, 1798. To be returned the first Tuesday of April, July, October, & January. Printed at Newbedford, by J. Spooner, for the proprietors— 1798.

8°: [A]⁴; 4 leaves, pp. [1–3] 4–7 [8]. [1]: title; [2]: blank; [3]: catalogue; [8]: blank.

Social library catalogue: 125 short author entries, consecutively numbered (according to the number of volumes), but otherwise unordered.

Evans 34955; Sabin 101415; Thompson, p. 258; *STE*, p. 959. MWA* (15.5×9.5 cm. — unbound).

See also McKay 140A (Connelly [Swanwick]), 140B (Clap), 140C (Pole), 141A (Rutgers)

―――――――― 1799 ――――――――

[Baltimore Circulating Library
Catalogue. Baltimore, 1799.]

Advertised in the *American and Daily Advertiser*, Aug. 6, 1799. Minick 469; Bristol 10699; m.p. 48784; *STE*, p. 49.

260 CARITAT, LOUIS ALEXIS HOCQUET DE, b. 1752

Catalogue des livres Francais qui se trouvent chez H. Caritat, libraire et bibliothécaire dans Broad-Way, no. 157, a New-York. [New-York: Imprimé par M. L. & W. A. Davis,] 1799.

12°: π1[=C4?] A–B⁶[C]⁴(–C4) (the only signatures in this item are these somewhat confusing ones: A3 is signed 'A2' [typical of much half-sheet 12° imposition] and B3 is signed 'B'); 16 leaves, pp. [i–ii], [1] 2–29 [30]. [i]: title; [ii]:

blank; [1]: catalogue; [30]: blank (variant—26: blank; text of 29 repeated in place of text of 27).

Circulating library and bookseller's catalogue: 625 short and medium title entries, in French, most of them in one fully alphabetical list, with several, separate brief lists at the end (livres Grecs, Latins, &c.; livres nouveax, imprimés pour le compte de H. Caritat [12 entries, English and French, with prices]; livres reçus au moment de la conclusion du catalogue). A note on p. 29 indicates that the books listed are for both loan and sale. Attribution of printer from Evans.

Evans 35278; Brigham, pp. 61–62; *STE*, p. 134.

DFo* (lacks pp. 27–[30], supplied in photostat; bound with following item), MWA* (19×11 cm. — bound), MnU, NHi*, NN* (2 copies, one a variant).

261 CARITAT, LOUIS ALEXIS HOCQUET DE,
b. 1752

The feast of reason and the flow of soul. A new *explanatory catalogue of H. Caritat's general & increasing circulating library. Intended also to answer the purpose of a sale catalogue, respecting those books marked with a star (*), which H. Caritat has an assortment of for sale, in his book-store, no. 153, Broad-Way. N.B. By the word *explanatory, is to be understood, both the arrangement of the books, the information given of their characters, and the names of their authors: the two last are either taken from the reviewers, or from the works themselves; and the whole has been done, in order to prepare the reader for an easy choice of his books, and a suitable disposition to relish and be pleased with them. Hours of attendance, from half after eight o'clock in the morning till one, and from three o'clock in the afternoon till eight in the evening. New York: Printed by M. L. & W. A. Davis. 1799.

12°: A–S⁶; 108 leaves, pp. [1–5] 6–45 [46] 47–215 [216] (201 misnumbered '261'). [1]: title; [2]: blank; [3]: conditions of the library; [4]: table of contents; [5]: catalogue; [216]: advertisement for six books, 'New Publications, Printed and Sold by H. Caritat.'

Circulating library and bookseller's catalogue: 2400 medium and full author (mostly) and title entries (much duplication; probably only 2000 separate books listed), arranged in three alphabetical lists. The first list (pp. [5]–103) is under the heading 'Arts, Sciences, &c. &c.', and is fully alphabetical by author. Within this list, at appropriate alphabetical locations, are subject headings, each followed by 'See' and a list, again alphabetical, of the authors whose works fit that subject heading. The subject headings treated in this manner are: agriculture, gardening,

&c.; arts and sciences; education; history, antiquities, biography, voyages, travels, &c. (reprinted as part, pp. [46]–53, of this category is the full table of contents to *A Universal History, Antient and Modern*); laws, trials, &c.; medical, surgical, chymical, &c.; military and naval; miscellaneous; natural history; philosophy, natural, experimental and moral, astronomy, &c.; poetry and dramatic; political; theology; trade & commerce. Some of the entries in this list have descriptive or evaluative remarks appended, and some are labeled, 'just published.' The second list (pp. 104–24) is under the heading 'Poetry & Dramatic,' and consists of short title entries in full alphabetical order. The third list (pp. 125–215) is under the heading 'Romances, Novels, Adventures, &c.', and consists of short to full title entries in full alphabetical order; each entry also includes the author's name, and the names of well-known novelists even have a place in the alphabetical list, followed by a short-title list of their works. Most of the entries in this list have descriptive or evaluative remarks appended, and some are labeled, 'just published.'

Evans 35279 (includes an extended comment praising Caritat); Brigham, p. 62; *STE*, p. 134.

DFo*, MWA* (18×11.5 cm. — bound), MnU (lacks t.p.), NN*.

Conrad, Michael and John
[Catalogue of Books. Philadelphia, 1801.]

12°: 76 pp. 2000 entries. Lacks title-page. Although Brigham, Bristol, and *STE* date this item [1799], MWA convincingly dates it [1801]; it is included here only to correct this error in dating.

Bristol 10757; m.p. 48831; Brigham, p. 63; *STE*, p. 183.
MWA.

262 DAVIS, GEORGE
[Philadelphia:] Printed by Zachariah Poulson, junior, no. 106, Chesnut-street, nearly opposite to the Bank of North America. [1799.] Davis's law catalogue, for 1799. Latest London and Irish editions. George Davis respectfully informs his friends and the gentlemen of the profession generally through the United States, that the following books, being his large importation per sundry vessels late from London and Dublin, are now offered for sale, at the same moderate prices as have, for several years past, so universally recommended them. Orders from any distance, addressed to him in writing, for a single book or an entire library, will be received with thanks, and meet with the most prompt attention. No. 319, High-street, Philadelphia, November 5th. 1799.

2°: [A]²; 2 leaves, pp. [1] 2–4. [1]: title (caption); on [1]: catalogue; on 4: advertisement (law book to be published in Dublin by subscription).

Bookseller's catalogue: 190 short author entries, all law books, with prices and some with place of publication, arranged by format.

Bristol 10759; m.p. 48833; *STE*, p. 206.

DLC* (34×20.5 cm. — unbound).

[Dutch, John
Catalogue of a large collection of books, to be sold at auction by John Dutch, at his office, Court Street, Salem, Mass., Apr. 17, 1799. Salem, 1799.]

Advertised in the *Salem Gazette*, Apr. 16, 1799; title based on McKay entry. McKay 142D; Evans 36268; *STE*, p. 235.

263   GORDON, PETER
        Catalogue of books & stationary, for sale, at Peter Gordon's store, in Trenton, near the Market-House. [Philadelphia, 1799.]

Broadside. 29×45 cm. 3 cols.

Bookseller's catalogue: 115 short author and title entries, arranged in no apparent order, plus a list of stationery. Date: dated [Trenton, 1796] by Bristol, but a note on the back of the NjR photocopy says: 'According to a letter from Chester T. Hallenbeck (Charlottesville, Va.) 10/19/1971, he had found a bill from D. Hogan to Mathew Carey "To printing 200 'Books for sale by P. Gordon, Trenton,' " dated June 6, 1799.' NjR has only a photocopy; the original was in the possession of Mrs. C. F. Borden, Shrewsbury, N.J., in 1969.

Bristol 9558.

NjR* (photocopy).

264   HANOVER BOOKSTORE, Hanover, New Hampshire
        Catalogue of books, for sale at the bookstore in Hanover, (a few rods fom Dartmouth College on the road leading to Lebanon.) Consisting of a great variety of authors in divinity, physic, surgery, chemistry, philosophy, history, voyages, travels, geography, husbandry, architecture, novels, poetry, lives, memoirs, plays, &c, [Boston:] Printed for the Hanover Bookstore. 1799.

12°: A–C⁶; 18 leaves, pp. [1–3] 4–35 [36]. [1]: title; [2]: note about sizes of books; [3]: catalogue; 34: stationery; on 35: advertisement for paper hangings;

[36]: advertisement ('constant supply of the newest and most useful publications,' etc.).

Bookseller's catalogue: 675 short to full author entries, most of them in one alphabetical list, with several brief subject lists at the end (classics, school books, arithmetics, &c.; small books and pamphlets; tragedies; comedies; comic operas; farces, &c.; music, vocal and instrumental). Boston is given as the place of publication because this catalogue is very similar, both in layout and content, to the 1799 catalogues of Thomas and Andrews, David West, and John West. The implication is that Thomas and Andrews probably supplied the Hanover Bookstore with both its stock and its catalogue. This supposition is enhanced by the advertisement on p. [36] which states that 'the principal in this business is a Bookseller, in the Town of Boston.'

Bristol 10798; m.p. 48868; Stark 1269; *STE*, p. 337.

NN* (16.5×9.5 cm. — unbound), NhD.

[Israel, Samuel

Catalogue of the valuable library of an English gentleman, in excellent condition. To be sold by Samuel Israel, at his vendue store, Front Street, Philadelphia, July 20, 1799. Philadelphia, 1799.]

Advertised in the *Aurora General Advertiser*, July 19–20, 1799; title based on McKay entry. McKay 142J; Evans 36107; *STE*, p. 381.

[Lang, William

The remainder of a large catalogue of books; to which have since been added many worth attention, to be sold at auction by William Lang, at his office, Essex Street, Salem, Mass., Dec. 31, 1799. Salem, 1799.]

Advertised in the *Salem Gazette*, Dec. 31, 1799; title based on McKay entry. McKay 142M; Evans 36270; *STE*, p. 407.

265 LIBRARY COMPANY OF PHILADELPHIA

Fifth supplement to the catalogue of books, belonging to the Library Company of Philadelphia. Communiter bona profundere deorum est.—Philadelphia:—Printed by Zachariah Poulson, Junior, Librarian, no. 106, Chesnut-street. Nearly opposite to the Bank of America. July 31, 1799.

8°: [A]⁴B–D⁴; 16 leaves, pp. [1–3] 4–30 [31] 32. [1]: title; [2]: blank; [3]: catalogue of books added 'since the thirtieth of November, 1798'; [31]: catalogue of restricted books (as in the 1798 supplement, item 254 above).

Social library catalogue. Catalogue of books added: 325 full author entries, with place and date of publication, and, for donated books, name of donor; arranged by format and in full alphabetical order within format, and numbered with shelf/accession numbers. Catalogue of restricted books: 11 full author entries, as above.

Evans 36100; Sabin 61785; Cutter 38; *STE*, p. 676.

CtY* (2 copies: one separate, lacks pp. [31–32]; other bound with 1789 catalogue), NN* (21×13 cm. — bound), PPL*.

[Moses, Isaac, and Sons
Catalogue of an extensive and valuable collection of French books, to be sold at auction by Isaac Moses and Sons, at their auction room, 147 Pearl Street, New York, June 14, 1799. New York, 1799.]

Advertised in the *Commercial Advertiser*, June 13, 1799; title based on McKay entry. McKay 142I; Evans 35949; *STE*, p. 544.

266 NEWTON LIBRARY SOCIETY, Newton, Massachusetts
Constitution of the Newton Library Society. [Newton?, 1799?]

8°: A⁴; 4 leaves, pp. [1] 2–8. [1]: title (caption); on [1]: constitution; on 4: catalogue; 8: list of proprietors.

Social library catalogue: 110 short author entries, arranged alphabetically. Date: dated [1799?] by MiU-C and Bristol. The constitution bears no dates. The latest books listed in the catalogue are several first published in 1797. More helpful is the list of proprietors, which includes 'Mr. Wm. Wiswall's heirs'; according to *Vital Records of Newton, Massachusetts, to the year 1850* (Boston: New-England Historic Genealogical Society, 1905), p. 519, William Wiswall died Oct. 27, 1798. This makes the 1799 date quite likely. The latest the catalogue could be is 1804, the year another proprietor, Daniel Hyde, died (*Vital Records*, p. 465).
Bristol 10886; m.p. 48949; *STE*, p. 614.
MiU-C* (21.5×13.5 cm. — unbound).

267 NORRISTOWN LIBRARY COMPANY, Norristown, Pennsylvania
The act of incorporation, bye-laws, and catalogue of books, of the Norristown Library Company. Philadelphia: Printed by John Ormrod, no. 41, Chesnut-street. 1799.

8°: [A]⁴B–C⁴; 12 leaves, pp. [1–3] 4–11 [12] 13–22 [23–24]. [1]: title; [2]: blank; [3]: act of incorporation; on 7: list of members; on 8: bye-laws; [12]: catalogue; [23]: blank.

Social library catalogue: 160 medium and full author entries, numbered with shelf/accession numbers, and arranged by subject and by format within subjects. Subject headings: history, biography, geography, voyages and travels; natural philosophy, metaphysics, laws and politics; moral philosophy, religion, and elocution; poetry and dramatic works; agriculture and gardening; physic and farriery; novels and romances; miscellanies.

Evans 35982; *STE*, p. 616.

PHi* (23 × 14.5 cm. — unbound).

268 PAWLET LIBRARY, Pawlet, Vermont
     Constitution, and catalogue, of Pawlet Library. Bennington: Printed by Anthony Haswell. MDCCXCIX.

12°: [A]⁶; 6 leaves, pp. [1–12]. [1]: title; [2]: blank; [3]: constitution; on [6]: catalogue; [9]: list of proprietors; [11]: blank.

Social library catalogue: 50 short author entries, arranged by subject. Subject headings: divinity; ecclesiastical history; prophane history; miscellanies.

Evans 36046; Sabin 59260; McCorison 536; *STE*, p. 641.

MWA* (16.5 × 10.5 cm. — bound), Vt.

[Rutgers, Harmon G., and Company
Catalogue of a large consignment of valuable books, per the Fair American, from London. To be sold by H. G. Rutgers and Co. at their auction room, New York, April 26, 1799. New York, 1799. Broadside?]

Advertised in the *Commercial Advertiser*, Apr. 22–24, 1799; title based on McKay entry. McKay 142F; Evans 35947; *STE*, p. 753.

269 RUTGERS, HARMON G., AND COMPANY
     Catalogue of books, for sale by H. G. Rutgers & Co. no. 145, Pearl-Street, on Saturday evening, January 12th, at 6 o'clock. [New York: Printed by Isaac Collins, 1799.]

Broadside. 40 × 26 cm. 3 cols.

Auction catalogue: 200 short title and author entries, some available in multiple copies, arranged in no apparent order. Attribution of printer by analogy with Rutgers's 1798 catalogue, item 257 above. Date: according to McKay, Rutgers was an auctioneer in New York in 1798 and 1799; only in 1799 did January 12 fall on a Saturday.

Evans 35946; McKay 142; *STE*, p. 753.

NN*.

[Rutgers, Harmon G., and Company

A large catalogue of books, comprising a general assortment, handsomely bound. To be sold at auction by H. G. Rutgers and Co., Feb. 9, 1799. New York, 1799.]

Advertised in the *Commercial Advertiser*, Feb. 8–9, 1799; title based on McKay entry. McKay 142B; Evans 35948; *STE*, p. 753.

[Shaw, Robert G.

Catalogue of a large, valuable and well chosen assortment of books, intirely new, in the several branches of useful and polite literature, to be sold by R. G. Shaw, at his office, Boston, Sept. 19, 1799. Boston, 1799.]

Advertised in the *Columbian Centinel*, Sept. 14, 18, 1799; title based on McKay entry. McKay 142K; Evans 36299; *STE*, p. 774.

270 THOMAS, ISAIAH, 1749–1831, AND EBENEZER TURRELL ANDREWS, 1766–1851

Catalogue of books, (American editions) for sale at the bookstore of Thomas & Andrews, Faust's Statue, no. 45, Newbury-Street, Boston. Where may also be had, an assortment of European editions of books. Printed at Boston, for Thomas and Andrews. Feb. 1799.

12°: A–C⁶; 18 leaves, pp. [1–3] 4–36. [1]: title; [2]: note explaining how volume 'size' (format) is indicated in the catalogue; [3]: catalogue.

Bookseller's catalogue: 650 short to full author entries, American editions, most of them in one alphabetical list, with several brief subject lists at the end (plays; farces; sacred vocal music; small books; pamphlets). See also the 1799 catalogues of David West and John West, items 272 and 273 below, and the Hanover Bookstore, item 264 above.

Evans 36416; *STE*, p. 830.

MSaE, MWA* (17×10 cm. — unbound).

271 WARREN LIBRARY SOCIETY, Warren,
Rhode Island

The charter and by-laws for the regulation of the Warren Library Society in the town of Warren, and state of Rhode-Island. [motto and seal of R.I.] Warren (R.I.): Printed by Nathaniel Phillips, M,DCC,XCIX.

8°: [A]⁴B⁴[C–D]⁴; 16 leaves, pp. [1–3] 4–7 [8] 9–13 [14] 15–25 [26] 27–31 [32]. [1]: title; [2]: blank; [3]: charter; [8]: by-laws; [14]: catalogue; [26]: list of proprietors; [32]: blank.

Social library catalogue: 150 short author entries, arranged alphabetically.

Evans 36668; Sabin 101495; Thompson, p. 258; Alden 1649; STE, p. 961.

MWA* (17.5×10.5 cm. — bound), NHi*, RHi* (lacks pp. 17–[32]), RPB, RPJCB*.

272 WEST, DAVID, 1765–1810

Catalogue of books, printed and published in America, and for sale at the bookstore of David West, no. 56, Cornhill, Boston: where may also be had a general assortment of European editions of books, in the various branches of literature. Printed at Boston, for David West, no. 56, Cornhill. 1799.

12°: A–C⁶; 18 leaves, pp. [1–3] 4–36. [1]: title; [2]: note on the sizes of books; [3]: catalogue; on 35: advertisement for West's edition of Rowson's *Reuben and Rachel*, 'A New Novel, and a Cheap one. This Day Published,' with a copy of the book's preface.

Bookseller's catalogue: 650 short to full author entries, American editions, most of them in one alphabetical list, with several brief subject lists at the end (tragedies; comedies; comic operas; farces; small books and pamphlets). This catalogue is very similar to Thomas and Andrews's 1799 catalogue, item 270 above, and to John West's 1799 catalogue, the next item. Rollo G. Silver offers other evidence of a business connection between David West and Thomas and Andrews. He notes that 'the Company Bookstore, nearly opposite the Custom House, State St., was evidently a joint undertaking of Thomas & Andrews, D. West, and E. Larkin.' ('The Boston Book Trade, 1790–1799,' in *Essays Honoring Lawrence C. Wroth* [Portland, Me.: Anthoensen Press, 1951], p. 285).

Evans 36701; STE, p. 987.

MSaE, MWA* (19×12 cm. — unbound).

273 WEST, JOHN, 1770–1827

Catalogue of books, printed and published in America, and for sale at the bookstore of John West, no. 75, Cornhill, Boston: where may also be had a general assortment of European editions of books, in the various branches of literature. Printed at Boston, for John West, no. 75, Cornhill. 1799.

12°: A–C⁶; 18 leaves, pp. [1–3] 4–36. [1]: title; [2]: note on the sizes of books; [3]: catalogue; on 34: list of 40 European editions, a sample of those for sale at West's; on 36: stationery.

Bookseller's catalogue: 650 entries, as in the previous item. This catalogue is very similar to David West's 1799 catalogue, the previous item, and to Thomas and Andrews's 1799 catalogue, item 270 above. This item is not reproduced in *EAI* because the record copy (MHi) could not then be located; the suggestion there and in *STE* that Evans 36702 might be a ghost of 33205, John West's 1797 catalogue, is incorrect.

Evans 36702; Sabin 102735; *STE*, p. 987.

MHi* (15.5×10 cm. — unbound), RPJCB*.

See also McKay 142A (Clark), 142C (Clap), 142E (Clark), 142G (Clark), 142H (Clark), 142L (Clark)

——————————— 1800 ———————————

[Bentalou and Dorsey, auctioneers, Baltimore
Catalogue of scarce and valuable books to be sold at auction, Thursday evening, May 15, 1800, at David Fulton's tavern, Congress hall. Baltimore?, 1800.]

Advertised in the *Telegraphe and Daily Advertiser*, May 14, 1800. Minick 559; Evans 36883; *STE*, p. 75.

274 BLAKE, WILLIAM PYNSON, 1769–1820, AND LEMUEL, 1775–1861

Catalogue of W. P. & L. Blake's Circulating Library, at the Boston Book-Store, no. 1, Cornhill. A general assortment of books and stationary for sale at the above store. Catalogues gratis. Boston: Printed for William P. and Lemuel Blake. 1800.

12°: A–D⁶; 24 leaves, pp. [1–3] 4–41 [42] 43–45 [46] 47–48. [1]: title; [2]: conditions; [3]: catalogue; [42]: advertisement (additions to library are constantly making); 43: advertisement (noting that the books are for sale also and that catalogues of the books for sale 'may be had separate'); 44: list of 100 tragedies, comedies, and farces for sale, short title entries; 46: stationery.

Circulating library and bookseller's catalogue: 1000 short to full author and title entries, arranged in full alphabetical order. The majority of the entries are novels.

Evans 37000; *STE*, p. 96.

MBAt* (17.5 × 10.5 cm. — bound).

275 BOSTON LIBRARY SOCIETY
Catalogue of books in the Boston Library. March 1, 1800. [Boston, 1800.]

12°: π1 A–B⁶χ1(π1 and χ1 conjunct=printed blue paper wrapper); 14 leaves, pp. [i–ii], [1] 2–21 [22] 23–24 [25–26]. [i]: half-title: 'Catalogue of books in the Boston Library'; [ii]: blank; [1]: title (caption); on [1]: catalogue; [22]: rules and regulations; [25]: blank.

Social library catalogue: 700 short author entries, arranged in full alphabetical order.

Evans 37001; *STE*, p. 106.

MWA* (20 × 12 cm. — unbound), NcD, RPJCB*.

276 BYBERRY LIBRARY COMPANY, Byberry, Pennsylvania
Constitution, by-laws and catalogue of books belonging to Byberry Library Company instituted the 29th of 12th month 1794. Philadelphia, Printed by John Ormrod, no. 41. Chesnut-street. 1800.

12°: A⁶; 6 leaves, pp. [i], [1–2] 3–4, 6–9 [10–12]. [i]: title; [1]: blank; [2]: constitution; 6: list of members; on 6: duties of librarian; on 6: rules and regulations; on 7: by-laws; 8: catalogue; [10]: blank.

Social library catalogue: 150 short and medium author entries, with, for donated books, name of donor; arranged in no apparent order.

Evans 37073; Thompson, p. 254; *STE*, p. 127.

MnU, RPJCB* (19.5 × 11.5 cm. — bound).

[Catalogue of a choice collection of well bound new books to be sold at auction Friday evening, May 23, 1800, at Mr. David Fulton's, Congress hall. Baltimore: Printed by Thomas Dobbin?, 1800.]

Advertised in the *Telegraphe and Daily Advertiser*, May 23, 1800. Minick 564; Bristol 11008; m.p. 49044; *STE*, p. 138. Evans 36882 and *STE*, p. 75, also list this catalogue under Bentalou and Dorsey.

[Clap, Samuel, 1745–1809
Catalogue of a large collection of books, on almost every subject, by the most celebrated authors. . . . Several hundred volumes have been in a circulating library, and belonged to a person, who has quited the bookselling business. To be sold at auction by Samuel Clap, April 8, 1800. Boston, 1800.]

Advertised in the *Columbian Centinel*, Mar. 22, 29, Apr. 5, 1800; title based on McKay entry. McKay 143B; Evans 37016; *STE*, p. 152.

[Clap, Samuel, 1745–1809
Catalogue of a valuable collection of books, belonging to the estates of two gentlemen, late deceased. To be sold at auction by Samuel Clap, Oct. 21, 1800. Boston, 1800.]

Advertised in the *Columbian Centinel*, Oct. 18, 1800; title based on McKay entry. McKay 143J; Evans 37017; *STE*, p. 152.

277 CLAP, WILLIAM TILESTON, 1770–1818
Catalogue of books, &c. for sale, by William T. Clap, at his book-store, Fish-Street, corner Proctor's Lane, Boston. [Boston, 1800?]

Broadside. 56×44 cm. 4 cols.

Bookseller's catalogue: 300 short author entries, arranged alphabetically, plus a list of stationery and other articles. Date: dated [1800?] by MB and Bristol; could be 1799 or earlier since Clap advertised in the *Columbian Centinel*, May 8, 1799, that he is selling his stock because he intends to quit his bookselling business (Silver, 'Boston Book Trade,' p. 285).

Bristol 11013.

MB*.

[Clark, Thomas

Catalogue of a large, valuable and extensive collection of books, the whole of which are new, in handsome bindings. To be sold at auction by Thomas Clark, at his office, Boston, Feb. 6, 1800. Boston, 1800.]

Advertised in the *Columbian Centinel*, Jan. 29, Feb. 1, 5, 12, 1800; title based on McKay entry. McKay 142N; Evans 37019; *STE*, p. 153.

278 CUSHING, HENRY, 1770–1860

Catalogue of Henry Cushing's Circulating Library: at the sign of the Bible and Anchor, Providence: consisting of the most approved modern authors in history, voyages, travels, novels, miscellanies, biography, philosophy, divinity, geography, magazines, poetry, plays, &c. &c. Providence: Printed by B. Wheeler, 1800.

Small 8°: [A]⁴B–E⁴; 20 leaves, pp. [1–3] 4–39 [40]. [1]: title; [2]: blank; [3]: catalogue; 38: advertisements (mentions, without listing, magazines, tragedies, comedies, operas, farces, charts, books on navigation, 'The Child's Library,' classical and school books, and stationery); [40]: blank.

Circulating library catalogue: 950 short author and title entries, arranged alphabetically.

Evans 38341; Alden 1666; *STE*, p. 198.

RHi* (16 × 10 cm. — bound).

[Dutch, John

Catalogue of books. . . . To be sold at auction by John Dutch, at his office, Feb. 17, 1800. Salem, Mass., 1800.]

Advertised in the *Salem Gazette*, Feb. 14, 1800. McKay 143; Evans 38456; *STE*, p. 235.

[Eustis, William

Catalogue of a new and valuable assortment of books, entirely new, in the various departments of literature, uniting amusement with instruction, and suited to the different tastes of different readers. To be sold at auction by William Eustis, at his office, Boston, May 8, 1800. Boston, 1800.]

Advertised in the *Columbian Centinel*, May 3, 7, 1800; title based on McKay entry. McKay 143E; Evans 37022; *STE*, p. 254.

279 FENNO, JOHN WARD, 1778–1802

Supplementary catalogue, consisting of books, imported from London, per the latest arrivals. By J. W. Fenno, no. 141, Hanover-Square. October, 1800. New-York: Printed by John Furman, op. the Fed. Hall. [1800.]

12°: [A]⁶B–C⁶; 18 leaves, pp. [1–3] 4–33 [34] 35 [36]. [1]: title; [2]: blank; [3]: catalogue; [34]: advertisement (books recently published in America); [36]: blank.

Bookseller's catalogue; 325 short to full author (mostly) and title entries, mostly 'fine' editions, illustrated, bound, and gilt, with prices, most of them in one alphabetical list, with one subject list (architecture) at the beginning; some entries are followed by laudatory comments.

Evans 38098; Brigham, p. 63; STE, p. 265.

MWA* (19.5×12.5 cm. — bound).

[Hoppin, Benjamin, 1747–1809, and Company

Catalogue of a sale to be held at B. Hoppin and Company's auction room, Thursday, September 4, 1800. Providence, 1800.]

Advertised in the *Providence Gazette*, Aug. 23, 1800, and in the *Providence Journal*, Aug. 27, 1800. Alden 1675; Evans 38340; STE, p. 367.

[Israel, Samuel

15 boxes and trunks of new books, just imported. . . . To be sold at auction by Samuel Israel, at his auction room, Philadelphia, May 7, 1800. Philadelphia, 1800.]

Advertised in the *Philadelphia Aurora*, May 6–7, 1800. McKay 143D; Evans 38254; STE, p. 381.

280 LIVINGSTON, ROBERT R., 1746–1813

Catalogue of books, in the library of the hon. Robert R. Livingston, of Clermont. February, 1800. Poughkeepsie, State of New-York—Printed by John Woods.——1800.

4°: [A]²B–I²; 18 leaves, pp. [1–3] 4–7 [8] 9–22 [23] 24–34 [35–36]. [1]: title; [2]: blank; [3]: catalogue ([8] and [23] blank); [35]: blank.

Private library catalogue: 750 short and medium author entries, most of them arranged by format and alphabetically within format, with several brief non-English language lists at the end (French books; Latin books). This item is the only printed catalogue of a private library up to 1800 that is not an auction or sale catalogue, but the reason for its publication is not known.

Evans 37839; *STE*, p. 428.

MWA* (21.5×15 cm. — bound), NHi* (lacks pp. [35–36]).

281 NEW YORK SOCIETY LIBRARY

A supplementary catalogue of the books belonging to the New-York Society Library, which have been added since the year 1793. New-York: Printed by T. & J. Swords, no. 99 Pearl-street. 1800.

8°: [A]⁴B–F⁴; 24 leaves, pp. [1–5] 6–36 [37] 38–45 [46–48] (45 misnumbered '46'). [1]: title; [2]: blank; [3]: advertisement (reasons for putting off a complete new catalogue of the collection); [4]: blank; [5]: catalogue; [46]: blank; [47]: additional bye-laws and list of trustees; [48]: blank.

Social library catalogue: 425 medium and full author and title entries, with place and date of publication, and, for donated books, name of donor; most of them in one alphabetical list, arranged by format within each letter, with a special list (pp. [37]–45) for 'Novels, Adventures, &c.', title entries, in alphabetical order.

Evans 38099; *STE*, p. 610.

MH* (lacks pp. [47–48]), MWA* (23.5×13.5 cm. — unbound), NN*, NNS, NjP.

282 PEIRCE, CHARLES, 1770–1851

Valuable medicines, just received from Lee and Co's. Patent and Family Medicine Store, Baltimore, and for sale by Charles Peirce, at the Columbian Book-store, no. 5, Daniel-street, Portsmouth, New-Hampshire. [Portsmouth, 1800.]

Broadside. 49×30.5 cm. 5 cols.

Medicine and book catalogue: 4½ columns list and describe medicines; the last half column has a subheading: 'Stationary & Books. Charles Peirce, Has lately received per late arrivals from London, and from the first Book-stores in Boston, a very extensive assortment of Books, Stationary, &c.' Mentions pocketbooks, Bibles, testaments, classical books, seamen's books without listing individual titles, and then lists 35 short title entries, more or less by subject (religion, law, history, travel, though without headings), plus a list of stationery. Date: a notice in the fifth column, specifying that Peirce has the approbation of an experienced physician and is the only one in Portsmouth who sells these medicines, is dated 'Oct. 11, 1800.'

Evans 38310; *STE*, p. 643.

MHi*.

283 POTTER LIBRARY COMPANY, Bristol, Rhode Island

The by-laws and catalogue of the Potter Library Company, in the town of Bristol, and state of Rhode-Island. Warren (R.I.) [:] Printed by Nathaniel Phillips. M,DCCC.

8°: [A]⁴B–C⁴; 12 leaves, pp. [i–iii] iv [5] 6–13 [14] 15–18 23–24 19–22 [=24]. [i]: title; [ii]: blank; [iii]: introduction; [5]: rules; [14]: catalogue.

Social library catalogue: 225 short author entries, arranged in full alphabetical order. Pages in corrected order on Microprint.

Evans 37049; Alden 1660; *STE*, p. 114 (under Bristol).

NHi* (17.5×10.5 cm. — unbound).

284 ROSS, JOSEPH, AND GEORGE DOUGLAS

A catalogue of books, &c. now selling by Ross & Douglas, booksellers and stationers, Petersburgh. N.B.—As they expect fresh supplies of books and stationary from both Europe and Philadelphia, new or additional catalogues will be published occasionally. [4-line quotation encouraging reading.] Petersburgh [Va.], Jan. 1800.

12°: π²[=C5–6?] A–B⁶C⁶(–C5–6); 18 leaves, pp. [i–iv], [1] 2–31 [32]. [i]: title; [ii]: advertisement for stationery, medicines, prints; [iii]: advertisement for a spelling book; [iv]: advertisement for Douglas's printing office, and lists of spelling books, grammars, arithmetics, and mention of a variety of plays; [1]: catalogue; [32]: advertisement for an almanac.

Bookseller's catalogue: 825 short and medium author and title entries (listing perhaps 700 separate books), arranged alphabetically and by format within each letter.

Evans 38237; *STE*, p. 747.

NcU (18×12 cm. — unbound).

[Shannon and Poalk

Catalogue of a quantity of books, French and English, in good preservation. To be sold at auction by Shannon and Poalk, at their store, 177 Market street, Philadelphia, May 12, 1800. Philadelphia, 1800.]

Advertised in the *Philadelphia Aurora*, May 8, 10, 12, 1800; title based on McKay entry. McKay 143F; Evans 38257; *STE*, p. 773.

[Shannon and Poalk
Catalogue of scarce and valuable books, in good preservation. To be sold at auction by Shannon and Poalk, at their store, 177 Market street, Philadelphia, Aug. 27, 1800. Philadelphia, 1800.]

Advertised in the *Philadelphia Aurora*, Aug. 27, 1800; title based on McKay entry. McKay 143I; Evans 38258; *STE*, p. 773.

[Shannon and Poalk
Catalogue of very select and valuable books, to be sold at auction by Shannon & Poalk, at their vendue store, Market Street, Philadelphia, April 21, 1800. Philadelphia, 1800.]

Advertised in the *Philadelphia Aurora*, Apr. 18–19, 21, 1800; title based on McKay entry. McKay 143C; Evans 38256; *STE*, p. 773.

[Shaw, Robert G., and Company
Catalogue of a stock of new books (belonging to William Spotswood), to be sold at auction by R. G. Shaw and Company, 22 Marlboro' Street, Boston, December 9, 1800. Boston, 1800.]

Advertised in the *Columbian Centinel*, Nov. 29, Dec. 6, 1800; title based on McKay entry. McKay 143M; Evans 37012; *STE*, p. 774.

[Shaw, Robert G., and Company
Catalogue of a very valuable collection of books, to be sold at auction by R. G. Shaw and Company, at their office, Boston, February 27, 1800. Boston, 1800.]

Advertised in the *Columbian Centinel*, Feb. 22, 26, 1800; title based on McKay entry. McKay 143A; Evans 37014; *STE*, p. 774.

[Shaw, Robert G., and Company
Catalogue of valuable books to be sold at auction by R. G. Shaw and Company, at their office, Boston, December 24, 1800. Boston, 1800.]

Advertised in the *Columbian Centinel*, Dec. 24, 1800; title based on McKay entry. McKay 143N; Evans 37013; *STE*, p. 774.

Troy Library, Troy, New York

Laws and catalogue . . . Troy: Moffitt, [1805?]

This item is dated [1800] by Evans, Sabin, *STE*, and MBAt, but it could have been published no earlier than 1805 because an 'Ordinance' on p. 13 is dated: 'Passed 14th January, 1805.' Though outside the scope of this checklist, it is mentioned here to correct the misdating.

Evans 38674; Sabin 97074; *STE*, p. 849.

MBAt (could not be located, 1974).

285 WHITE, JAMES, 1755?–1824

For sale, by James White, at Franklin's Head, opposite the prison, Court-street, Boston, a large collection of books. . . . [Boston: Printed by James White, ca. 1800?]

Bristol states that this item is a broadside (39.5 × 31.5 cm.), that it was dated by John Alden, and that MH has two copies of it. However, neither I nor the editors of *STE* were able to find it at MH. Bristol 11186; m.p. 49192; *STE*, p. 993.

[Wild, Daniel

Catalogue of a large and general assortment of new and valuable books, to be sold at auction by Daniel Wild, at his office, Boston, Oct. 23, 1800. Boston, 1800.]

Advertised in the *Columbian Centinel*, Oct. 22, 1800; title based on McKay entry. McKay 143K; Evans 37004; *STE*, p. 1001.

[Wild, Daniel

Catalogue of a large and general assortment of valuable books, (all new), to be sold at auction by Daniel Wild, at his office, Boston, Nov. 15, 1800. Boston, 1800.]

Advertised in the *Columbian Centinel*, Nov. 15, 1800; title based on McKay entry. McKay 143L; Evans 37005; *STE*, p. 1001.

[Wild, Daniel

Catalogue of a large, and well assorted collection of books (all new, and in handsome bindings). To be sold at auction by Daniel Wild, at his office, Boston, May 29, 1800. Boston, 1800.]

Advertised in the *Columbian Centinel*, May 28, 1800; title based on McKay entry. McKay 143G; Evans 37006; *STE*, p. 1000.

[Wild, Daniel

Catalogue of a small, but very valuable collection of new books, in the various departments of the useful, necessary, and polite branches of literature. To be sold at auction by Daniel Wild, at his office, Boston, July 2, 1800. Boston, 1800.]

Advertised in the *Columbian Centinel*, June 28, July 2, 1800; title based on McKay entry. McKay 143H; Evans 37007; *STE*, p. 1000.

See also McKay, 'Additions,' p. 179 (Fennelly)

————————— ADDENDUM —————————

10a HANCOCK, THOMAS, 1703–1764

A catalogue of new and valuable books most of them lately imported from London, sold by T. Hancock, at the Bible and Three Crowns near the drawbridge Boston. [Boston,] 1730.

8°: A⁴B²; 6 leaves, pp. 1–12. 1: title (caption); on 1: catalogue. The only known copy may have originally had a title leaf and an extra final leaf, now lacking.

Bookseller's catalogue: 365 short title entries, most of them arranged by format, and then alphabetically within format, with separate lists of law books and physick books.

MH* (16×11 cm. — bound).

Chronological List of Catalogue Item Numbers

1	1693	**32–33**	1759	**97**	1781
2	1717	**34–41**	1760	**98**	1782
3–4	1718	**42–43**	1761	**99–100**	1783
5	1719	**44–45**	1762	**101–104**	1784
6	1720	**46–48**	1763	**105–108**	1785
7–8	1723	**49–50**	1764	**109–112**	1786
9–10	1725	**51–55**	1765	**113–121**	1787
10a	1730	**56–60**	1766	**122–126**	1788
11	1733	**61–63**	1767	**127–135**	1789
12	1734	**64–66**	1768	**136–145**	1790
13–14	1735	**67–70**	1769	**146–152**	1791
15	1741	**71**	177?	**153–166**	1792
16	1743	**72–74**	1770	**167–182**	1793
17	1744	**75–76**	1771	**183–195**	1794
18–19	1746	**77–81**	1772	**196–209**	1795
20	1750	**82–90**	1773	**210–230**	1796
21–24	1754	**91–92**	1774	**231–247**	1797
25–27	1755	**93**	1775	**248–259**	1798
28	1756	**94**	1777	**260–273**	1799
29	1757	**95**	1778	**274–285**	1800
30–31	1758	**96**	1779		

INDEX

The following index to this checklist is one alphabetical listing into which several kinds of entries have been integrated. First, it is an author index, listing the book-sellers, book auctioneers, publishers, and libraries of several kinds that were the 'authors' of catalogues. Titles of catalogues are indexed only for those with no known author. Generally, the titles of catalogues are too similar to be of much use in an index. The printers of the catalogues, both individually and under any firm or partnership names, are also indexed.

The name of a city in the index, by itself, without any qualifying names or phrases, is followed by a list of the catalogues published there. In a few cases, a catalogue was published in a city other than the one where the individual or institution issuing it was located; in these cases the latter location is also indexed.

For auction catalogues, the owners of the books sold at auction are indexed (identified by the phrase, 'books sold'), as well as the author (auctioneer) and printer, making this a more complete index to the eighteenth-century entries in George McKay's *American Book Auction Catalogues* than its own index, which lists only the owners of the books. In references to items in that earlier checklist, McKay has been abbreviated 'McK.' These references are given in parentheses following the year in which they were supposedly issued and under which they are listed in this checklist (see p. xvii above for an explanation of this system of reference).

Also indexed are the subject headings from those catalogues with a subject organization. Of course, the catalogues listed in the index under any given sub-ject heading are not the only ones including books on that subject. But since catalogues with subject organizations provide such a convenient way to get at material in the different subject areas, it seemed useful to index them, even though the index listing does not account for the occurrence of books on these subjects in catalogues with other types of organization. Compound subject head-ings (i.e., history and biography) have been listed under each of their compo-nents.

Three different kinds of reference numbers are used in the index. Lower-case roman numerals refer to page numbers in the Introduction. Boldface numbers refer to the item numbers of located catalogues. Unlocated catalogues are indexed under the year of publication. When, as in the case of a printer, the name indexed differs from the name under which the catalogue is listed in the checklist, the latter name (in parentheses) follows the year.

The designation of role following a name (bookseller, printer, etc.) relates only to the roles in which these people appear in this checklist. Different roles for the same person are separated within the entry for that person. The dates in parentheses following the role designation refer only to the dates of the relevant catalogues in this checklist (birth and death dates of the authors of catalogues are given in the main entries of the checklist itself). The city following the date gives the location of the person or institution, which usually, though not always, is also the place of publication for the catalogues listed.

Preceding the Index is a 'Chronological List of Catalogue Item Numbers' to facilitate the quick identification of the date of publication for any item number.

A

C

Carter, John, bookseller (1783–96 Providence), **100**, **199**, 1796; printer, **100**, **180**, **199**, 1796 (Carter), **215**

Carter and Wilkinson, booksellers (1795–96 Providence), **199**, 1796; printers, **199**, 1796 (Carter), **215**

Catalogue of a choice and valuable collection of modern works . . . (Baltimore), 1790

Catalogue of a choice collection of . . . books . . . (Baltimore), 1800

Catalogue of a collection of books . . . (Philadelphia), 1779

Catalogue of a curious and valuable collection of books . . . (Philadelphia), 1782

Catalogue of a great variety of valuable books . . . (Baltimore), 1793

Catalogue of about two thousand volumes . . . (Baltimore), 1792

Catalogue of books . . . auction . . . City Vendue-Store (1769 Philadelphia), **68**

Catalogue of books to be sold at auction (Philadelphia), 1744/45

Catalogue of curious and valuable books . . . (Philadelphia), 1750/51

Catalogue of jewels and diamonds . . . (Philadelphia), 1786

catalogi (subject heading), **138**

Chandler, Jane Emott, seller of husband's books (1790 Elizabethtown, N.J.), **137**

Chandler, Rev. Thomas Bradbury, books sold (1790 Elizabethtown, N.J.), **137**

chapmen's books (*see also* children's books), xiii, **34**, **76**, **100**, **114**, **116**, **121**, **127**, **136**, **147**, **160**, **165**, **183**, **184**, **189**, **193**, **198**, **214**, **217**, **220**, **226**, **228**, **229**, **234**, **246**, **247**, **248**, **249**, **252**, **264**, **270**, **272**, **273**

Charleston, S.C., xx, **73**, **77**, **78**, 1786 (2: Roberts, Wright), 1790 (Charleston), 1795 (Muirhead), **210**, 1796 (Young)

Charleston Library Society (1750–90 Charleston, S.C.), **20**, **73**, **77**, **78**, 1790

Charles-Town, S.C., *see* Charleston, S.C.

charts (*see also* seamen's books), **117**, **134**, **183**, **184**, **193**, **208**, **212**, **213**, **247**, **248**, **249**, **252**

Chattin, James, bookseller (Philadelphia), 1757; printer, **24**, 1757 (Chattin)

chemistry, **40**, **94**, **101**, **103**, **109**, **114**, **127**, **131**, **138**, **144**, **146**, **147**, **153**, **154**, **155**, **156**, **157**, **158**, **162**, **165**, **170**, **171**, **176**, **177**, **181**, **182**, **183**, **184**, **185**, **208**, **209**, **212**, **213**, **214**, **229**, **234**, **240**, **247**, **249**, **261**

children's books (*see also* chapmen's books, Newbery books), xiii, **48**, **59**, **64**, **79**, **100**, **109**, **114**, **117**, **121**, **123**, **144**, **145**, **148**, **161**, **165**, **229**, **244**

Childs, Francis, and Co., bookseller (1793 New York), **171**; printer, 1785 (Campbell), 1786 (Campbell), **171**

Childs, Nathan, printer (Charleston, S.C.), 1786 (Roberts), 1786 (Wright)

Childs and Swaine, printers (1793 New York), **171**

Childs, Haswell and M'Iver, printers (Charleston, S.C.), 1786 (Roberts)

Childs, M'Iver and Co., printers (Charleston, S.C.), 1786 (Wright)

chronology, **16**, **27**, **40**, **131**, **138**, **144**, **162**, **165**, **177**, **229**, **239**, **253**

Church, Benjamin, auctioneer (Boston), 1743/44 (McK 37), 1744 (2: McK 39, 40), 1748 (McK 48A)

chyrurgery (*see also* medicine, surgery), **16**, **27**, **110**

circulating library catalogues, vii, x (n. 8), xviii–xix, xxv, **54**, 1769 (Bradford), **82**, 1778 (Bell), 1783 (Prichard), 1784 (Murphy), **110**, **111**, **118**, **124**, **129**, **149**, 1793 (Baltimore), **168**, **186**, **188**, **189**, **211**, 1796 (Carter), **217**, **222**, 1796 (Rainbow), 1797 (Todd), **248**, **251**, 1799 (Baltimore), **260**, **261**, **274**, 1800 (Clap), **278**

Cist, Charles, printer (1784–85 Philadelphia), **103**, 1784 (Boinod), **106**

Clap, Samuel, auctioneer (1781–1800 Boston), 1781 (McK 104D, 105B), **125**, **164**, 1797 (McK 139E), 1798 (McK 140B), 1799 (McK 142C), 1800 (2)

D

E

H

I

J

K

U

V

W

Y

Z